GROWING EXECUTIVE FUNCTION

EMPOWERING SECONDARY STUDENTS WITH SKILLS FOR LIFELONG SUCCESS

SARAH KESTY

Solution Tree | Press
a division of Solution Tree

555 North Morton Street
Bloomington, IN 47404
800.733.6786 (toll free) / 812.336.7700
FAX: 812.336.7790

email: info@SolutionTree.com
SolutionTree.com

Visit **go.SolutionTree.com/lifeskills** to download the free reproducibles in this book.

FSC
www.fsc.org
FSC® C012681
The mark of responsible forestry

Printed in the United States of America
Library of Congress Cataloging-in-Publication Data
Names: Kesty, Sarah author
Title: Growing executive function : empowering secondary students with skills for lifelong success / Sarah Kesty.
Description: Bloomington, IN : Solution Tree Press, [2026] | Includes bibliographical references and index.
Identifiers: LCCN 2025008117 (print) | LCCN 2025008118 (ebook) | ISBN 9798893740035 paperback | ISBN 9798893740042 ebook
Subjects: LCSH: Academic achievement | Educability | Learning, Psychology of | High school students--Psychology
Classification: LCC LB1062.6 .K47 2026 (print) | LCC LB1062.6 (ebook) | DDC 370.15--dc23/eng/20250708
LC record available at https://lccn.loc.gov/2025008117
LC ebook record available at https://lccn.loc.gov/2025008118

Solution Tree
Cameron L. Rains, CEO
Edmund M. Ackerman, President

Solution Tree Press
Publisher: Kendra Slayton
Associate Publisher: Todd Brakke
Acquisitions Director: Hilary Goff
Editorial Director: Laurel Hecker
Art Director: Rian Anderson
Managing Editor: Sarah Ludwig
Copy Chief: Jessi Finn
Senior Production Editor: Sarah Foster
Copy Editor: Mark Hain
Proofreader: Elijah Oates
Text and Cover Designer: Rian Anderson
Content Development Specialist: Amy Rubenstein
Associate Editor: Elijah Oates
Editorial Assistant: Madison Chartier

For all of my students, past, present, and
future: You inspire and teach me every day.
It is your faces I see when I push through
challenges and stretch myself to create
solutions. It is for you that I wrote this book.

Acknowledgments

My heart fills with gratitude when I think of the team of people to whom I owe thanks for their support, guidance, and inspiration in creating this book. This book is the culmination of years of learning from the wonderful people I call family, friends, and colleagues. Without you, this book would not have been possible.

First, I thank Monica Diamond, my professor and friend. You saw the educator and innovator in me before I ever did, and it changed the course of my life.

I feel so much gratitude for my teams at California Teachers Summit, California Department of Education Working Group, Children and Adults with ADHD, Edutopia, my "Neuro Nerds" group, and the creative staffs at districts across the globe, including the Sacramento County Office of Education, Mendocino County Office of Education, Roseville City School District, Twin Rivers School District, Landers Schools, South Bay Union School District, Sweetwater Union High School District, Renfrew County District School Board, Autism Tree, CAPTAIN (California Autism Professional Training and Information Network) and Rise Up Belize. I give deep thanks to my coteachers and colleagues throughout the years: I learn so much from each of you and admire your drive to better our classrooms and our world.

I have grown due to my personal mentors, coaches, teachers, guides, and friends, including Jennifer York, Reyna Beckler, Trish Rebello, Angela Barnett, Nancy Cunha, Nancy Balcom, Nancy Maelo (three of you in a row!), Debra Doman, Jackie Box, Tracy Butts, Laurel Hill-Ward, Sydney Thomas, Sara Colborn, Taryn Blizman, Rachel Babre, Rebecca Rabe, Kris Jennings, Kim Hughes, Terry Dawn, Laura Kirby, Mead Ploszay, Sharlene Harness, Mike Laharty, Seth Perler, Mitch Weathers, Patty Schetter, Terry Davis, Danielle Hylton-Kopshinsky, Ava Lennon, Melissa Winegar, Jeanette York, Vanessa Lujan, Laura Kirby, Peter Paccone, and so many more. I have endless gratitude for my amazing humans: Myron, Dana, Maya, Onyx, Ava, Maisey, Aidric, Kian, Mattie, Becca, Mushi, Ryin, Lindsey, Henry, Zach, Elena, Ben, Wendy, Lauren, Adelle, Ethan, Everett, Bodie, Ryan, Brayden, Mason, Evelyn, Hunter, Kye, Piper, Dylan, Caryn, Sonya, Vi, Arden, Espy, MJ, Tennie, Sadie, Liam, Bennett, Mel, Reese, Nicole, Kelly, Zeah, Bekah, Michael, Maelee, Kara, Charlotte, Hudson, Ian, Magen, Phillip, Isaac, Nick, Savannah, Imogen, Alexa, Kira, Josh, Lyra, Blake, Andrew, Kamora, Walker, Colin, Arlo, Felicia, Brody, Zack, Sara, Jordan, Jessica, Jen, Rose, Louis, Will, Nathan, Grace, Toph, Lilah, and Emy: You are each a gift to me.

I was so lucky to have my Solution Tree team, including Hilary Goff, Kendra Slayton, Sarah Foster, Rian Anderson, and the many creative humans who dedicate their lives to helping students.

I have so much love for my sister, Amy, who bought me a video bird feeder to celebrate the book. It's a visual reminder of our unwavering sister connection. I am grateful for my mom, Diane, who sent me funny memes when the writing process got tricky. Your humor kept me going. And, I'm thankful for my dad, Dave, who reads everything I publish and often boasts about it online. Family, your support means the world to me.

Finally, a true, enormous thanks to my husband, Adam, whose support, encouragement, creativity, and joy are mixed into every word of this book. You are an idea factory, holding a vision of a better world for teachers and students and celebrating the beauty of all brains. I love you.

Solution Tree Press would like to thank the following reviewers:

Nathalie Fournier
French Immersion Teacher
Prairie South School Division #210
Gravelbourg, Saskatchewan, Canada

Caitlin Fox
Chair and Instructor, Bachelor of Education
Red Deer Polytechnic
Red Deer, Alberta, Canada

Kelli Fuller
Assistant Principal
Howard Perrin Elementary School
Benton, Arkansas

Kelly Hilliard
Gifted and Talented Mathematics Educator
Darrel Swope Middle School
Reno, Nevada

Johanna Josaphat
Educator and Founder
The Urban Assembly Unison
Brooklyn, New York

Amy Kochensparger
Biology Teacher and Science Department Chair
Eaton High School
Eaton, Ohio

Josh Kunnath
11th Grade English Teacher and Department Chair
Highland High School
Bakersfield, California

Table of Contents

Reproducibles are in italics.

Chapter 6

Appendix A

About the Author

Sarah Kesty is an executive function, autism, and attention deficit hyperactivity disorder (ADHD) coach, author, speaker, and host of *The Executive Function Podcast.* Kesty began her career in education as a classroom aide in Northern California, quickly discovering the positive impact of empowering students with executive function skills. Her educational roles saw her developing mentor and after school enrichment programs at Oakdale K–8 School, a socioeconomically disadvantaged campus in Sacramento, California. She served as an instructional coach for teachers in Imperial Beach, California, captaining the development of inclusive learning center models to serve struggling students. Kesty is proud to have piloted social communication classes at Castle Park Middle School in Chula Vista, California, where she also began to develop executive function lessons for students in her study skills classes. For several years, Kesty presented best practices for students with autism with the California Autism Professional Training and Information Network.

Kesty is a member of Children and Adults with ADHD (CHADD), and in 2013 and 2024 she received the Innovative Program Award for her executive function methodologies with students. She is an educational adviser with Red Rover and an advisory board member of the Charcot Marie Tooth Association. A four-time teacher of the year, Kesty was recognized as Classrooms of the Future Innovative Teacher of the Year in 2021 and Outstanding Special Educator of the Year with the National Association of Special Educators in 2019.

Kesty regularly writes and presents for education groups and publications, including *Psychology Today*, Edutopia, and KQED public media in San Franciso. Her international speaking engagements empower school teams and parents with tools to grow executive function. In 2008, Kesty created and delivered a three-day professional development on classroom management to hundreds of teachers in Belize.

Kesty graduated summa cum laude from California State University, Chico, before continuing to earn her master's degree in special education at California State University, Sacramento.

To learn more about Sarah's work, follow her on YouTube at youtube.com /@SarahKesty, Instagram at instagram.com/braintoolscoaching, Facebook at facebook.com/executivefunctionpodcast, or Psychology Today at psychologytoday.com/us /contributors/sarah-kesty.

To book Sarah Kesty for professional development, contact pd@SolutionTree.com.

Introduction

Myron sits across from me in the booth, his pancakes mostly untouched, his face smirking in reflection on his seventh-grade self. "I was such a mess back then," he laughs. "I can't believe you put up with me." Myron's in town to collaborate with fellow rental managers, called on to share his strategies for connecting tenants with community resources. His employer and the communities he serves celebrate his impact.

Seventh-grade Myron, however, was a different story. Devastated by a family death and struggling with undiagnosed attention deficit hyperactivity disorder (ADHD), Myron was *that student* on campus: the one all teachers knew but few had reached. His inner struggles were highly visible in his actions, words, and conflicts. When we met, he had, mostly accidentally, stepped on my foot on his way off the school bus, which was the same foot that had seventeen surgeries. It was a painful start to what would be an incredible journey together.

"Did you see my Facebook post a few days ago?" he asks while we eat breakfast. He hands me his phone and tears well up in my eyes at the photo of us: me in my favorite first-day-of-school dress and him with his backpack looking heavier than him. "It all started with a binder party," his post begins, "and it was the first time I learned that I could learn how to learn and do school."

Myron's post celebrated a turning point that, at the time, felt like just another Thursday when we organized his backpack together. I got him a snack, he chose some music, and we dumped the contents of his backpack onto a table. While we explored his understanding of organization, we tested out systems that might work for his brain. We talked about school, home, and the waves of self-doubt that left him feeling defensive.

"What do you think was important about that time?" I ask him.

He ponders for a moment. "I don't think I realized that there were options for me, that I could learn ways to do things that were hard for me. I thought everyone else was good at school, and I never would be. Everyone told me to try harder, but you taught me *how* to do the things. Sometimes, it was like we could hack school together."

"Hacking" school began when Myron learned about and grew his *executive function skills*, which are the broad spectrum of mental actions people take to reach goals. When we empower students to grow their executive function, their school experience changes tremendously. Students slowly emerge from the fixed mindset of school being hard for them and begin to realize their potential for academic and executive function success.

Whether diagnosed with a learning difference or just growing up as an adolescent, inside each student is a Myron, who may feel lost, defeated, or confused about how to do well in school. While school requires layers of specific skills, such as organizing and planning, our busy schedules may not allow time to teach these requisite skills or, better yet, teach students how to identify their own needs and find resources to grow their skills. We may lament that students turn in their work late or don't seem to focus in class, and yet we may also feel lost about how to address these challenges. It's not like we can hit pause and teach How to Be a Student 101. How would we even teach these executive function skills?

Developing students' executive function skills will take time (albeit not a lot of prep or sweeping changes to your teaching). It will require you to think about your own brain, learning, and the systems you use to facilitate your life. It will feel overwhelming at times. Yet, it may prove to be one of the most important shifts of your teaching experience.

As with many of the challenging journeys we undertake, developing students' executive function skills is rewarding. It's a positive snowball, a shot of espresso, an alive time in your classroom that begins as a hum and ends as a roar. The small environmental, teaching, and intervention changes in this book will infuse your perspective and pedagogy, leading to lasting student impact.

Executive function skills stretch beyond your classroom walls. Investing in teaching students to self-regulate, plan, prioritize, and know and adjust for their brains' needs will spill into their home, college, and work lives. You won't see the blooms that come from the seeds you're planting, but you may, like I did over breakfast with Myron, catch a whiff of the blossoms your students have grown because of their awareness of executive function. Our journey in these pages together will teach you how to recognize, support, teach, and coach your students' executive function.

Students will become aware of their executive functions and the strategies that work for them. Further, they will develop a framework for continuing their growth beyond the classroom walls, knowing how to explore, test, and hone their executive function strategies.

Why Executive Function Matters

Executive function isn't new. It's not a pendulum swing, a fad, or something research may later contraindicate. We've been there with fads, and it's not fun. Executive function is here to stay, and for a good reason: It provides the base on which all classrooms are built and all students succeed. Executive function is present whether we recognize it or not.

Executive function describes the broad set of skills we use to manage our lives and facilitate our futures. In school, it's the skill set we use as teachers to plan lessons, organize materials, manage time, and so much more. Executive function is also the skill set our students use to calendar their homework, manage their attention, and even determine the approaches they use to study.

In 2020, when students and teachers began to conduct school from home because of the COVID-19 pandemic, executive function skills were drivers of the experience. Students who were able to reconstruct their student skill set from home flexed their executive function muscles to get to online class on time, manage attention on their own, and keep track of time and energy without the external cues of school adults. Unfortunately, students who struggled likely lacked executive function skills and needed the built-in executive function support that teachers and the classroom environment provided. Student learning during 2020 and 2021 created a new appreciation and understanding of executive function, helping educators see the disparities and needs that may have been less apparent in our usual classrooms.

While we're no longer primarily teaching and learning online, executive function is still essential, and many teachers share that students' executive function skills are lagging in the return to in-person school, potentially driving disengagement and other behavioral concerns. In fact, it is my belief that addressing executive function deficits is an impactful way to decrease student behavior challenges. When students can engage, participate, and succeed, their need to protest or avoid work decreases, and their academic success increases (Jacob & Parkinson, 2015). When students can anticipate and meet their self-regulation and attention needs, they are less likely to disrupt the learning environment (Duckworth, Taxer, Eskreis-Winkler, Galla, & Gross, 2019). Empowering a classroom with executive function tools is indeed a powerful answer to the urgent teacher question, "How do we reach and support today's students?"

Zooming out from the individual classroom, executive function skills are also important for social mobility as well as supporting students with special needs or neurodivergent brains (those with autism spectrum disorder, ADHD, dyslexia, or other brain differences). While a growth mindset builds students' vision, executive function is what paves the way, allowing them to identify and complete the small steps toward their futures. Socioeconomic status impacts executive function development, meaning we have an opportunity to provide students with tools and skills that life circumstances made more difficult for them (Davis et al., 2014). Additionally, students with neurodivergent brains often have lagging executive function skills, and this book seeks to support them in their general and special education experiences. Research indicates that early recognition and support for executive function needs can prevent future school failure, reduce job loss, and draw attention to psychological issues (Morrison, 2016).

By teaching students to recognize their executive function needs, to find and test out tools, and to own their learning processes, we also help students develop resilience within the context of today's pressures. Executive function skills can help students manage their attention, distractions, and emotions, and having sturdy student skills means less overwhelm and anxiety around school. Students who have strong executive function are independent students, allowing teachers to step back a bit and, hopefully, feel less stretched over time. With well-developed executive function skills, students are more engaged and successful with academic pursuits, which positively translates to improved behavior and social-emotional states.

This book teaches educators how to teach students to be students. It honors the range of developmental readiness levels for students with disabilities and empowers teachers with small but impactful strategies that work. Its open tone and easy-to-implement ideas make it a prime resource for teachers like us, who want positive change and better student behavior without investing huge amounts of time.

Our Assumptions and Agreements

Human brains are beautiful, complex, and ever changing. They are also susceptible to taking cognitive shortcuts and creating biases, which are possible coping mechanisms for managing the vast amounts of information coming into our brains at once (Ruhl, 2023). It's likely that you have some beliefs about students' (or even your own) executive function; I certainly know that I do. In support of our shared commitment to student growth and to establish a shared understanding of assumptions moving forward, I invite you to consider the following assumptions and agreements.

Executive Function and Intelligence Are Not the Same Thing

It's likely most teachers have experienced a confusing observation of a student who scores incredibly high on assessments but loses papers daily or a student who continues to need reminders or support for repeating classroom tasks but can write a stellar, engaging essay. While initially counterintuitive, the truth is a student can be highly intelligent and still have a hard time taking student actions (executive functions). It is possible for someone to be capable of complex cognitive tasks and, at the same time, struggle with meeting deadlines or forget to turn in completed work; this is because intelligence and executive function are entirely separate things.

There are many reasons a student might be bright, enjoy learning, and yet struggle with executive function. Disorders like ADHD, autism spectrum disorder, and many learning disabilities do not indicate impaired intelligence, but they are associated with executive dysfunction. ADHD, for example, results from smaller, less developed, or less active areas of the brain associated with executive function (Cleveland Clinic, n.d.).

What's more, executive function development can be associated with brain development. A foundational study published in *Nature* in 2006 reveals a connection between how quickly the thickness of a brain's cortex (the gray, wrinkled, outermost area of nerve tissue in the brain) develops and that individual's intelligence and executive function (Shaw et al., 2006). Interestingly, the research reveals that when a child's cortex is thinner for a longer period of childhood, they likely have more neuroplasticity (the brain's ability to change and improve) and a more rapid learning ability. In other words, slower development of cortical thickness is related to higher IQ (Kircher-Morris, 2021). The flipside is that cortical thickening is necessary for executive function to develop. These findings mean that many of our gifted, highly intelligent students may also have delayed executive function skills; their brains are waiting for the cortex to thicken up so that the prefrontal cortex and its executive function come on board (Shaw et al., 2006).

When we separate intelligence from executive function, we can help students preserve their self-esteem and dignity, shining light on a new perspective: Even very smart people still need to grow executive function skills. In my experience, when students no longer feel the threat of feeling "stupid" for lacking skills, they become much more open to developing the skills, no longer needing the protective armor of apathy or fierce (false) independence. When a former student of mine learned that executive function and intelligence aren't connected, she sighed with relief and celebrated, saying, "If that's true, and I'm not stupid, then just teach me how to do the student things."

Performance Reflects Missing Skills, Not Lacking Effort

We live in a world that celebrates performance. Our efforts as teachers are measured and acknowledged largely based on the results we create, such as test scores, well-managed classrooms, and well-facilitated school events. Our students earn awards for their academic and athletic achievements, for earning high grades or attending every school day without fail.

What most people don't recognize are the underground components that make these achievements possible: going through trials and errors, overcoming self-doubt, shedding tears, and developing skills to perform in the visible ways we do. It makes sense in our performance-celebrating world that we tend to conflate performance with effort. Much of the rhetoric around student (and teacher) experiences reflects an assumption that lack of performance means lack of effort or that one's intelligence or drive will always show up as high performance. This book challenges some of these commonly held beliefs about behavior, offering new perspectives and opportunities to adjust your own beliefs.

Educational researcher Ross Greene (2010) says, "Kids do well if they can." This book assumes that a student's observed shortcoming is the outward manifestation of a lack of skills. Students who do not perform—study, meet deadlines, or take good notes—do not yet fully know how to do so. This book argues that, given the right amount of time, practice, and adjustments, all students can grow their executive function skills and, therefore, perform better in our classrooms.

Executive Function Is Not a Reflection of Morality

You may have heard of the much-admired five a.m. club, whose virtuous members can claim epic amounts of productivity from starting their workday very early. Contrast that with a student who doesn't turn in their work. The assumption is a lack of effort caused the missing assignment. The word often used is *lazy*. Many of our cultural narratives conflate morality with executive function. We tend to think virtuous people have impeccable executive function, so we assume those who struggle with time management, forget to turn things in, or consistently interrupt conversations must be lazy, not trying, or of poor moral character.

Let's bust this myth. Executive function is a set of mental skills impacted by myriad factors, many of which our students cannot control. As you'll soon learn, executive function skills are the last to develop, as our brains mature back to front, and our executive function is most associated with our prefrontal cortex (behind our foreheads; Shaw et al., 2006). Factors like home environment, sleep, nutrition, mental health, disabilities, and age can impact executive function, making it slower or more difficult to develop and engage. While executive function skills impact performance, they do not reflect a lack of effort or poor character. Instead, our struggles reflect needs for understanding, learning, skills, and strategies.

We occupy a hopeful space when we can detangle executive function from morality. We and our students are no longer "bad" for being late or for having a moment of emotional dysregulation. Instead, we have the opportunity to regroup, reflect, and recommit to learning the missing executive function skills. It is safe to explore and discuss the vulnerabilities of underdeveloped skills when we don't see them as character flaws but, instead, as natural outputs of a system that's still developing.

Assume a Lens of Curiosity Instead of Judgment

Deanna Singh (2022), author of *Actions Speak Louder*, describes one of her favorite memories of her dad. On my podcast (Kesty, 2022a), Singh shared with me that her father, as a Sikh man, wore a turban. When she walked the streets of their Midwest town with her dad as a child, Singh watched an amazing moment on repeat (D. Singh, *The Executive Function Podcast*, July 18, 2022). When children would point to or comment on his turban, their caretakers would swoop in to hush them. "It's not polite to ask," they'd scold, or they'd quietly pull their children away, apologizing to her dad with their words or eyes. Singh's father would lower himself near the child, praising their curiosity, and sharing information about his turban. He gently told the parents that it's good to ask and be curious because we can connect by exploring the things we notice in one another. As an adult, Singh glows in realizing how right her father had been that when we are open and willing to talk about possibly uncomfortable things, we grow and connect.

The opposite is also true. When we pull away, avoid, assume morality, or maintain a similar fixed mindset, we become stuck. Our brains learn to avoid the uncomfortable or confusing parts of ourselves and life and, instead, begin to think we cannot change anything. It's possible you or your students have some "stuck spots" in executive function. Students who have been judged or shamed about their executive function skills may come to believe they are "just bad at" whatever skill they've been told they lack. Phrases like, "You just need to try harder," "Everyone else can do it," or "You're just being lazy," may have formed a protective layer that we need to remove.

Curiosity is our tool to peel away the protective layers of self-doubt and self-limitations. Replacing a stance of judgment, curiosity employs gentle reflection and open questions of executive function coaching (tools you'll learn in chapter 4, page 85) to explore a student's executive function skills. And, dear teacher, this applies to you too. When a lesson flops, when you lose the class a bit, when you stay up late grading (because maybe you also procrastinated a tiny bit), you're invited to treat yourself to a curious perspective. Instead of judging or shaming yourself, this book encourages you to zoom out one level and observe, asking yourself the same kinds of reflective questions that help your students grow. This book asks you to be on your own team, growing your executive function skills as you empower your students.

How to Use This Book

This book empowers you, a sixth- through twelfth-grade teacher, with the perspective and tools needed to grow students' executive function. Think of it as coaching from a friend who has been there, tested out the research, and can give you proven strategies.

Each chapter will deepen your understanding of executive function and give you specific tools to implement right away, often with low or no prep. After reading the first two chapters to create your understanding of executive function, you can choose your next chapter based on your needs. For example, if you work with students with disabilities, chapters 5 and 6 (pages 115 and 139) for executive function deficits and supports may be the best place to proceed. Or, if you're ready to start directly teaching executive function skills, move on to chapter 3 (page 73), which explores how to teach executive function

To make the invisible visible, when you design your path through the book, you're using your executive function skills of planning, prioritizing, and likely scheduling. Much of your experience will be like that; you'll be noticing and possibly growing your own executive function as you learn how to enhance executive function in your students. To help this process, many chapters offer short prompts or activities to reflect on and hone your skill set. The idea is that everyone's executive function is in constant development. There is always room to smooth out our approach to life and create strategies to support our movement toward our goals.

Like any growth, growing executive function skills can feel uncomfortable. You may notice your brain offering self-criticism, possibly reflecting the societal narrative that executive function skills just *should* be strong and that if you're not performing an executive function skill well, then you're broken or lazy. This book guides you to show yourself compassion and patience along the journey. Noticing, understanding, and improving your and your students' executive function will be clunky at first, and that's entirely OK. You will have wins, lessons will flop, and you'll feel stuck between knowing and doing. And yet, you will love the ride. Embracing executive function in your classroom is a game changer. You have the power to solve classroom challenges that have impacted your students for years, the opportunity to expose them to a new way of thinking that will unfold new paths in their lives, and the chance to reach the Myron inside of each of them, who desperately wants to do well, if only they knew how.

Write in this book (unless it's a library copy). Talk back to me. Ask questions. Take photos of what resonates and email them to yourself. Leave the book somewhere prominent so you're not likely to forget it. The ultimate goal is for this book to help and change you. Feel free to read, digest, and use the learning in the way that works best for your brain. And spoiler alert: You'll be learning so much about what works for your brain that, chances are, you'll have some new methods for managing your learning process!

What to Expect Moving Forward

Our journey together starts with a strong shared base of knowledge: what executive function is and how you can start supporting it in your students right away. We'll take a broad view to explore classroom environmental and pedagogical approaches proven to grow students' executive function. We'll then move into direct ways to teach and coach executive function skills before narrowing our focus to interventions and tools for special populations. We will close with notes of hope. The following list details what to expect in each chapter.

- **Starting with executive function 101:** Expanding on the introduction, chapter 1 establishes a working definition of executive function and provides examples of executive function in action for students and for teachers. This chapter is your chance to explore your assumptions, understandings, and personal experiences with executive function, setting a solid base to grow on. You will learn how taking executive function—empowering actions—will change your classrooms, along with methods for explaining executive function to students.
- **Creating the executive function–empowered classroom:** In chapter 2, practical application is the name of the game. Where are the easy wins for infusing executive function into what you already do? Where are the small changes that yield big results, and how do you both find those opportunities and make those changes stick in your practices? This chapter holds easy-to-implement tools and adjustments to everyday classroom practices, filling your teacher toolbox with executive function builders.
- **Teaching executive function skills:** Chapter 3 empowers you to write your own lessons to explicitly teach specific executive function skills. You will learn the rationale and how-to for each of the lesson components, with examples to serve as models for your lessons. Written to be student friendly and designed for a gradual release of responsibility, the included example lessons are low- and no-prep options for teachers who are ready to act. With adaptations for differing student developmental ages and needs, the

lessons broadly address common executive function skills such as planning, prioritizing, self-regulating, managing focus, studying, and note-taking. It also teaches you the rationale and how-to for each lesson component, as well as steps for teachers to write their own executive function lessons.

- **Understanding executive function coaching:** Chapter 4 celebrates a simple and profound shift in student-teacher interactions, positioning you as an executive function consultant rather than a manager. It supports you in developing your executive function coaching abilities, particularly the art of asking questions that challenge students to become self-aware and co-creators of strategies. The chapter explores question stems, examples, and common pitfalls.
- **Exploring executive function deficits:** Chapter 5 offers a deeper dive into both brain science and the manifestations of lagging executive function. Although this chapter includes discussion of special populations, it is written for *all* students and *all* teachers. You'll gain perspective on what drives some of the behaviors associated with lagging executive function and explore the surprising ways and situations that lagging executive function skills show up (for example, social interactions, testing, avoidance, and apathy).
- **Planning executive function supports:** Picking up momentum from the executive function deficits chapter, chapter 6's topic of planning for executive function supports offers perspectives for designing interventions for executive function needs. Empowering teachers to use their own executive function skills to prioritize, plan, and reflect, this chapter offers templates and task breakdowns for individuals and teams ready to systematize their approach to growing students' executive function skills. Special populations and their associated plans (gifted, 504, and individualized education plans [IEPs]) are addressed as well. The chapter also addresses accommodations to support executive function needs.
- **Using executive function lessons:** Ready-made, specific lessons and reproducibles for directly teaching executive function are in appendix A. Written to be student friendly and designed for a gradual release of responsibility, the included lessons are low- and no-prep options for teachers who are ready to act. With adaptations for differing student developmental ages and needs, the lessons broadly address common executive function skills such as planning, prioritizing, self-regulating, managing focus, studying, and note-taking.

- **Understanding formal executive function diagnostic tools:** Appendix B explores the formal assessment tools your school psychologist or a student's medical professional may use to gauge how well executive function works for a student.

By the end of this book, you will be able to describe and identify executive function in yourself and your students. You will notice executive function opportunities and demands in your classroom and have a bank of approaches, lessons, coaching tools, and intervention ideas from which to draw. You most likely will share some space on the executive function soapbox with me, telling your colleagues about its impact and celebrating the powerful potential unlocked in your students.

Each chapter includes learning and action steps, both for behind the scenes and direct materials for students. Reproducibles for student use, implementation checklists, examples, and more will take your learning from theory to practice. Each chapter concludes with a chapter summary, potential action steps, and reflection questions designed to be compatible with individuals or learning groups like staff book studies or collaborative teams within professional learning communities (PLCs).

To help solidify the presence of executive function in your own mind, you will notice periodic moments to reflect on your thinking processes as you implement strategies. Not only are these great opportunities to celebrate and hone your executive function, but they also provide a chance to take what I call an "empathy walk" in your students' shoes, where you imagine what it feels like to be a skills learner.

If you stick with the gentle shifts and easy classroom tools, by the end of the book you will have created a new teaching and learning experience. Your students will be more independent, freeing up the time you once used to manage students' academic actions. The changes you make are designed to be easy and small, but don't underestimate their impact. Author James Clear (n.d.a) offers a terrific perspective on the positive impact of very small adjustments. Working out the mathematics of exponential growth, he writes, "If you get one percent better each day for one year, you'll end up thirty-seven times better by the time you're done" (p 16). Ready for our executive function adventure? Let's do this!

Key Points

The key points from the introduction include the following.

- This book assumes that executive function is separate from and not a reflection of intelligence, performance, or morality.
- This book employs a lens of curiosity and encourages you to do so also.

- The first two chapters provide a base for learning. After that, you can choose how you proceed through the chapters.

Potential Actions

After reading the introduction, consider taking these potential actions.

- Add times to your calendar (and set reminders) for when you will read this book.
- If discussing this book within a collaborative team, consider starting a shared document for questions, reflections, and next steps as a team.

Journal or Discussion Questions

After reading the introduction, answer these questions in your journal or within a book discussion group.

- When you were a student, which skills seemed easy for others but hard for you?
- What, if anything, do you remember about learning how to study, take notes, organize, or plan a project?
- What tools do you use now, as a teacher, that may also help your students?
- What do you hope you can teach students to do for themselves?

CHAPTER 1
STARTING WITH EXECUTIVE FUNCTION 101

When I was ten years old, I was passively practicing my spelling list by rewriting the word *communicate* with little thought. My brain woke up when I realized *communicate* no longer had meaning. Did I ever know what *communicate* meant? It was as if hearing and seeing it too much dissolved its presence in my mind.

Executive function may be like that for you. Sure, you've probably heard the term mentioned in a few TED Talks or professional development sessions, but after a while, its meaning dilutes, creating a vague sense of being yet another education buzzword. I'm here to show you that executive function is neither a buzzword nor a passing fad; it is a fact of being a living human being. This book serves to both illuminate executive function's presence as well as empower you to propel it within your students' lives.

This chapter will help you understand executive function, learn that you're using executive function right now, understand that executive function skills can be taught, explain executive function to students, and recognize executive function in the classroom.

CHAPTER SNEAK PEEK

By the end of this chapter, you will understand the following.

- **Executive function and its implications for you and your students**
- **How to recognize executive function in your life**
- **Ways to teach students about executive function**
- **How to imagine a day in the life of executive function in your classroom**

Understanding Executive Function

In its simplest definition, *executive function* is the set of skills we use to facilitate success and move toward our goals (Baggetta & Alexander, 2016). Many analogies describe executive function: the conductor who leads the orchestra, the office manager who makes everything run smoothly, or the air traffic controller who directs planes (Center on the Developing Child, n.d.; Zeigler Dendy & Hughes, n.d.). While these analogies highlight the *role* of our executive functions, they leave room for confusion. After all, most of us aren't overseeing musicians, employees, or pilots; an expanded definition of executive function helps us identify the function and the associated skills. The two following sections will help you better understand executive function by using a visual of the executive function tree.

Use the Executive Function Tree

We're going to explore executive function using the image of a tree to anchor a broader understanding of the skills involved in executive function as well as provide a visual for conceptualizing what can otherwise feel overwhelmingly complex. See figure 1.1.

I organize executive function into the following three main components, or main branches.

1. **Future skills:** Things we do now to serve our future selves
2. **Emotions and attention:** Self-regulation, emotional regulation, and attention management
3. **Learning and memory:** Strategies to capture, retain, and recall information

As you can see, related skills sprout from these three main branches. For example, *future skills* encompass anything we do mentally to prepare for the immediate, near, or distant future, such as planning, organizing, scheduling, and prioritizing. Table 1.1 (page 16) provides more examples of the future skills main branch. Table 1.2 (page 16) shows examples of the skills in the emotions and attention branch. Table 1.3 (page 17) includes examples of the skills in the learning and memory branch.

Beyond the basic skill branches, we can envision strategies and behaviors that support these skills as leaves. For example, consider the leaf *mental flexibility*, which is a vital executive function for all of us, and growing the image of your own executive function tree will require it (Dajani & Uddin, 2015). *Mental flexibility* (sometimes called *cognitive flexibility*) is the ability to adjust your thoughts and actions to a changing environment. It involves curiously being aware of your brain, monitoring

Figure 1.1: The executive function tree.

the environment around you, and adjusting your mental and physical approach as you see fit. It's a cycle where you tweak the recipe of your moment, adding a dash of this and that while the temperature of your stove and the availability of ingredients change.

You may be tempted to agonize over where a skill goes on the executive function tree or whether a skill deficit stems from future skills or maybe learning and memory. Although these mental explorations are worthwhile for uncovering your own and students' thinking and behaviors, they don't lead to the destination of being right. There is no right way to build the *perfect* conceptualization of an executive function tree because such a conceptualization doesn't exist.

Let's explore the messiness of placing a skill on the executive function tree (figure 1.2, page 18). Let's say you're observing a student who's not starting her worksheet. You may interpret her behavior as avoiding the work due to missing academic

Table 1.1: Future Skills Main Branch

Skill Set	Teacher Example	Student Example
Planning	Writing lesson plans	Planning homework time after school
Organizing (physical)	Arranging classrooms for student use	Using binders and folders
Organizing (digital)	Using an email management system	Using folders in digital form
Organizing (mental)	Rehearsing the flow of a lesson or conversation	Testing out word order to develop a strong thesis

Table 1.2: Emotions and Attention Main Branch

Skill Set	Teacher Example	Student Example
Managing energy levels	Taking deep breaths after a tough conversation to bring your heart rate back down	Asking for and taking a break to re-energize for class
Processing a big emotion	Allowing time to rest or decompress when feeling overwhelmed	Identifying and sharing a feeling that's getting in the way of learning
Communicating body or emotional needs	Communicating your need for movement during staff meetings and agreeing with your principal on what your movement can look like	Asking for support or a break when emotions feel big
Avoiding distractions	Changing your phone to silent mode or turning it off during a meeting	Closing distracting tabs when working on a device

Table 1.3: Learning and Memory Main Branch

Skill Set	Teacher Example	Student Example
Being mentally flexible	Pivoting a lesson when students are lost and need more support	Trying several different approaches to a mathematics problem
Learning actively	Taking notes when learning something new; reviewing them later	Interacting with text by taking notes or annotating while reading
Memorizing deliberately	Repeating the names of new people to help you remember them	Using flash cards or other quizzing methods to practice recall
Managing multiple steps	Creating a list of steps for reference in your phone	Taking photos of steps to have a visual reference for later

skills. Therefore, you may assume the learning and memory branch will work best, and so you give her a memory aid, such as a multiplication chart. However, another teacher may see her behavior as a form of protest due to dysregulation. Therefore, this teacher may offer to talk about emotions or offer a rest break. Yet a third teacher may hypothesize that the student isn't working because she doesn't know how to start. Therefore, this teacher may offer the student a way to chunk the directions or otherwise manage the task of working.

All the teachers' predictions and strategies have merit. Each embodies a detective perspective of supporting rather than judging and providing tools rather than punishing. But this is where the tree analogy falls short; the goal is to anchor understanding in the tree but not to rely on it for diagnosing a student's need. We can appreciate the complexity and nuance of executive function skills by visualizing the tree, but we cannot accurately place a student's lagging skill without investigation. We must talk with our students to understand. As we use the table of contents to find a section of a book, exploring with a student guides you to the right strategy leaves. And, not to worry—the upcoming chapters will fill your brain with strategies and interventions to support your students' executive function.

You can download a blank version of the tree in figure 1.2 (page 18) at **go.SolutionTree.com/lifeskills**, which you can use to explore and develop your conceptualization of executive function. Even experts who spend their lives in the executive function world evolve their understanding as they learn from others and from experience.

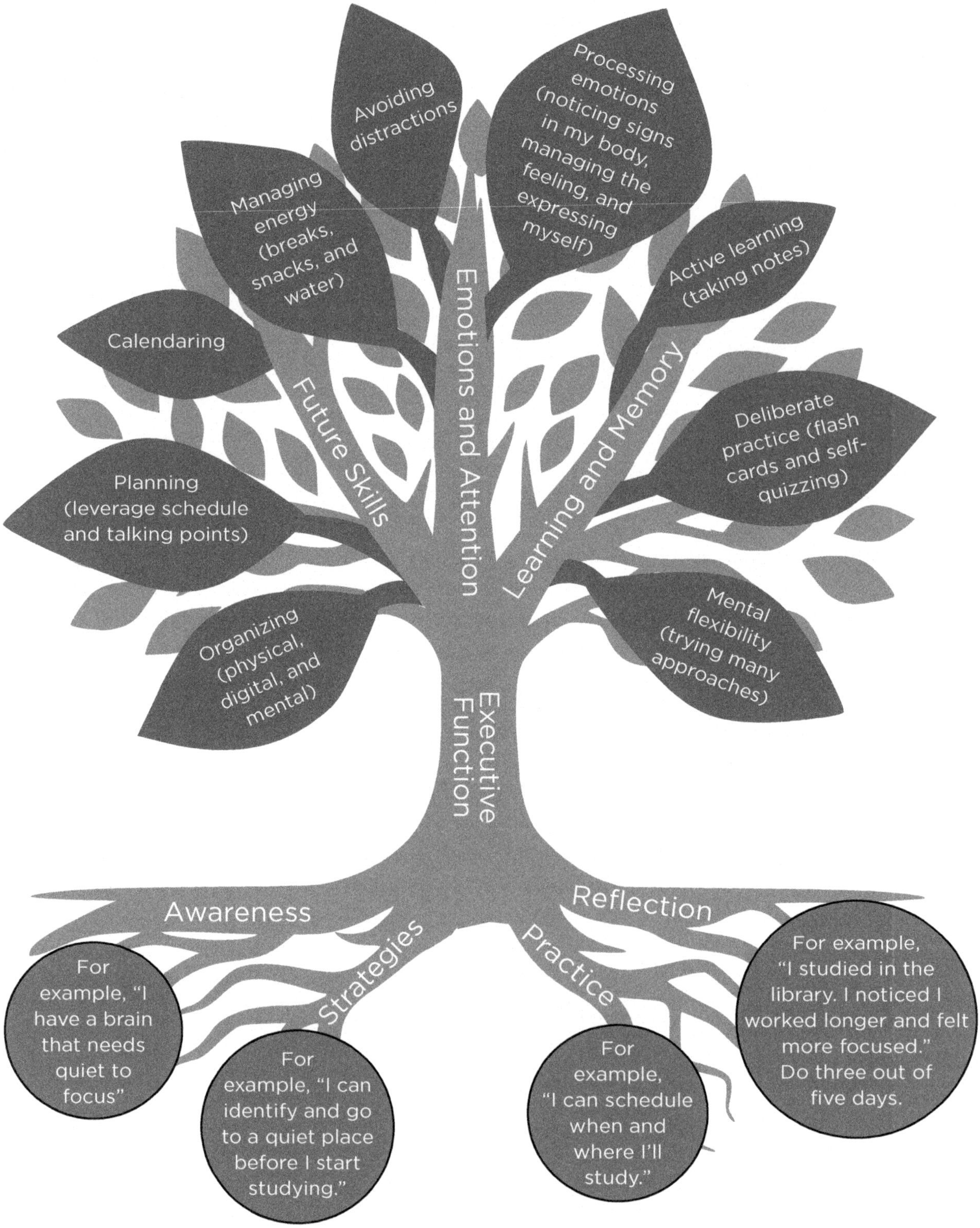

Figure 1.2: The executive function tree with branches, roots, and leaves.

*Visit **go.SolutionTree.com/lifeskills** for a free reproducible version of this figure.*

Add Roots to the Executive Function Tree

Your initial interactions with the executive function tree (figure 1.2) will parallel those of your students when they begin learning about executive function—it's all about awareness and starting to recognize the presence and impact of executive function. The upcoming chapters will help you bridge knowing and doing, taking your new learning into real-life application.

About that bridge between knowing and doing: It can be a little tricky to cross (more on that soon). Adding roots to our executive function tree helps visualize the process we and our students will take to incorporate and use new skills. I divide the aspects of applying executive function into four main roots: (1) awareness, (2) strategies, (3) practice, and (4) reflection, each of which I explain in the following sections.

1. **Awareness:** This is the root of executive function you're currently developing by reading this book. You're learning about it, starting to see it (possibly everywhere), and asking questions about what's next. You may have some *cognitive dissonance*, which is the discomfort in your brain when old ideas are shaken up by new learning. The awareness root feels exciting and sometimes overwhelming for teachers and students. When developing the awareness root of executive function, it's important to engage students in recognizing their own needs and affinity for different types of strategies.

   For our students, the awareness root has three components: (1) awareness of executive function, (2) awareness of strategies to support it, and (3) self-awareness of their own executive function strengths and struggles. Just like you, students will continually develop their self-awareness of their executive function needs and toolbox, and the forthcoming chapters have resources to support and extend this process.
2. **Strategies:** The strategies root of the executive function tree involves matching actions with information gleaned in the awareness stage. You're choosing and trying different tactics for building and supporting executive function skills. This may feel exciting, or it may feel clunky. Strategies will sometimes feel like magic transformations and, sometimes, like deflated parade balloons. This process is messy, and it takes time to settle into the chaos of classroom changes.
3. **Practice:** After you have identified and tested a few strategies, you'll head into practice mode, where students begin to own the strategies and adapt them to their personal needs (based on the awareness they've built into the first stage). Practice can extend for long periods of time and overlap with both strategy launches and reflection. The key components of the

practice root are opportunity and time. You and your students need time to implement and adjust your tools.

4. **Reflection:** An oft-skipped root, reflection is an essential element for developing executive function. It allows the opportunity to tease out what went right and what still needs support. It helps students close the feedback loop by directly connecting their choices and tools with results and empowering independence and self-efficacy. Chapter 4 (page 85) will give you loads of ways to make reflection an easy and impactful part of your day.

Learning That You're Using Executive Function Right Now

As a teacher, you are an executive function machine. Indeed, your executive function skill set supports your teaching, planning, and even reading this book. Let's celebrate the incredible executive function you're currently using.

- **Planning and time management:** You've done the get-ready work to be here now. You've developed and honed a routine that serves you, allowing you enough time to complete a series of actions to prepare for this moment. For example, you've set an alarm (or several) to wake up in time to get ready for the day, which involves estimating time and backward planning.
- **Prioritizing and inhibiting behaviors:** You've acted and resisted other actions to serve your future self and meet your short- and long-term goals. For example, you inhibited the impulse to engage in more instantly gratifying tasks, like sleeping in or browsing the internet, by using self-talk or limiting your access to tempting options (usually accomplished through planning).
- **Monitoring your needs and attention:** As you read, you're engaging with concepts, putting them in your working memory, and connecting them to concepts you already know, which moves them to your short-term memory. You're noticing when your brain or your gaze strays from the page, and you're gently bringing your attention back to this book. When you notice that your body and brain have an unmet need, you attend to it using a variety of tools, including taking a break, eating a snack, or adjusting your physical experience.

Executive function skills, as ADHD experts Chris A. Zeigler Dendy and Ruth Hughes (n.d.) argue, may be more important than IQ in predicting positive life outcomes! Researchers have found that executive function skills are correlated with adaptable behavior and are better indicators of academic success than IQ (Gravråkmo et al., 2023). Such skills are also the foundation of successful employment. For example, the list of top reasons an employee is fired includes executive function skills such as poor time management (chronic lateness) and difficulty with multistep directions (poor work performance; Asbill Law Group, 2020). In short, these skills matter a lot.

You may be making lists of executive function skills without realizing it. When you notice yourself thinking or saying, "I wish my students would . . . ," "Why don't they just . . . ," and "You're in ___________ grade, you should know how to . . . ," remember that these frustrating moments are goldmines for executive function exploration, learning, and teaching opportunities. Your brain is identifying the many ways that executive function needs emerge in your world. In fact, let's employ an executive function strategy to grow your own executive function awareness by making a physical or digital space where you can capture your list of missing skills as you illuminate them for your students or yourself. Chapter 3 (page 73) shows how to use this skills list as fodder for teaching!

As you increase your executive function awareness, the world around you may change. What used to seem like a behavioral choice may appear a bit more like a skill deficit; what was once annoying ("Click that pen one more time!") can now feel like an invitation to explore ("I wonder if his body needs movement or if he's self-aware enough to recognize that sound is bothering others"). Of course, lagging executive function doesn't mean that students avoid consequences of their actions. A student who's still learning impulse control, for example, will experience the consequence of acting on the impulse to use a permanent marker on his desk. What changes is *your* approach to the consequence.

Executive function awareness allows us to see the desk graffiti in a new light. Previously, we might have made assumptions about the student's character, motivation, or personal nature of the offense. We might have presumed any student who writes in permanent marker on a desk is a naughty student who doesn't care about school and probably wants to upset us, and we could support these assumptions with our outward observations. However, taking a slight twist to review the behavior provides potential new meanings and opportunities to explore both our thinking and the student's skill set.

> **Oh, you've written on your desk. Was this one of those moments when your body took over before your brain kicked in? Let's talk about it while you clean it up.**
>
> **That looks like permanent marker. How do you plan to clean it up? Where can you write next time so you're not missing your personal time to clean up?**

> **Seems like you had an impulse to write on your desk. I imagine you're pretty tired of getting in trouble for your impulses. Do you want to explore some ideas to help your brain while you clean?**

Before becoming executive function aware, many teachers are reactive and disempowered, feeling like they are reacting at the end of a behavior cycle and subconsciously hoping students will just get their executive function skills squared away through osmosis or good luck. When we don't yet see executive function as a developing (and teachable) skill set, we're prone to thinking in binary, limited ways. Students either have executive function or they don't.

With executive function awareness comes a brand-new perspective. We start to see the many implications of executive function strengths and challenges and appreciate our role in developing them. We notice our own patterns of executive function skills and treat ourselves with more compassion as we also learn new tools. We become detectives, wondering what skills to teach or interviewing students to explore their understandings. The patterns of challenge emerge as puzzles to solve rather than poor behaviors that we endure. Executive function awareness helps us recognize our valuable role in supporting students' skill development instead of painfully waiting for students to "just do it." Before we know about executive function skills, we may have a more fixed mindset about student struggles, as if the behaviors we observe are reflections of character flaws or lack of effort and permanently fixed. Once we embrace what Carol S. Dweck (2016) describes as a growth mindset for student executive function skills, believing students (and adults) can develop any skill over time, we're able to step into the space where executive function is taught, nurtured, and honed.

Understanding That Executive Function Skills Can Be Taught

Teaching executive function skills represents what's next after helping students (and ourselves) develop growth mindsets and self-awareness. Research on neuroplasticity indicates that not only can these skills be learned, but they also can be practiced to automaticity, freeing up students' working memory to consider the content instead of using purposeful effort on their executive functioning (Voss, Thomas, Cisneros-Franco, & de Villers-Sidani, 2017).

Researchers Christina Barrasso-Catanzaro and Paul J. Eslinger (2016) identify social modeling and schooling as two of the four main influences on children's executive function development, giving a profound context for our work: Teachers and parents can help children develop the mental actions and resources they need to grow their executive function. Through modeling, direct instruction, and executive function–nurturing environments, they change children's brains (Center on the Developing Child, n.d.).

Zooming out to see executive function as its most basic components reveals a hopeful simplicity. Yes, executive function represents a long list of skills. But, *skills* can be learned. Therefore, even wildly lagging executive function skills are enveloped in potential because students can grow how they think, what they do, and the resources they employ, one skill at a time.

While you may focus on one set of executive function skills and choose to wait to address others, consider exploring ways to externalize some of the executive functions. You may want to mindfully augment lagging executive function skills with technology, classroom setup, and routines. Chapter 2 (page 35) has quick and easy changes to your lessons and environment that can empower easier executive function for your students as their skills build.

For example, a student who is not yet independently organizing his belongings and has final exams in two weeks may need to focus first on his study strategies, prioritizing based on the most pressing need. His disorganization represents a skill set not yet learned, but it is best not to address it at the expense of the more urgent skill of studying efficiently. In this case, you may choose to externalize organization systems for him (temporarily) until you're both ready to tackle organizing. Externalized organization could look like having labeled places for items, prompts and time in class to organize items, and reminders through his devices. These augmentations can support him through the student process while allowing him to focus on the prioritized executive function skills. This support does not mean you're taking over for him or disempowering him by doing too much. As you move along in your executive function teaching experience, the nuance will become clearer. You will be able to see when it's time to absorb some executive function leadership to empower focused executive function skill growth.

Explaining Executive Function to Students

We can all probably imagine our students' faces if we launched into a lesson to teach them all about executive function! However enthusiastic our approach, we'd lose our students pretty quickly. On the surface, executive function isn't really engaging. But, because it's everywhere, because it impacts students' school, home, and social lives, and because it's very hackable, we can package executive function in ways that capture and empower students. The following are some considerations for explaining executive function to students.

Lean In to Students Wanting (and Already Using) Hacks or Strategies

Human brains are constantly experimenting, noticing results, and using new learning to plan (strategize) the future. Therefore, pitching executive function skills to students can begin with celebrating and possibly laughing about how they already strategize. For example, ask them about the video games they play. When they keep losing a level or struggling with a spot in a game, they adjust and keep trying until they're able to break through. These adjust-and-try-again cycles count as strategizing!

Students tend to laugh a bit when you bring up strategizing to get what they want. They know how to negotiate with their parents, just as we teachers know how to engage or push our students. Students can share about how they get later bedtimes, permission to go somewhere, or other wins from their parents. Every approach that they share is a strategy! Illuminating that strategies are everywhere can set the stage for upcoming executive function strategy lessons.

Helping students become aware of their brains' awesome strategy cycles helps open the door for new executive function strategies. They'll see that these new tools are just like those they already use, and that connection to previous learning will increase both their understanding and their memory of the lesson (Willingham, 2009).

Additionally, laying the groundwork of strategy prevalence and impact reduces student pushback in the future; they're open because their brains are already "sold" on the idea. (I provide more information on how to extend this approach, through executive function lessons in chapter 3, page 73 and appendix A, page 167.)

Provide Executive Function Tools to Give Context and Relevance to Adolescent Self-Discovery

A middle schooler explained being an adolescent as "wanting to be totally unique and different but also wanting no one to look at me." Truer words have never been spoken! From about third and fourth grades, when students' brains start to develop deeper perspective taking and empathy, to their late twenties, students discover who they are and how they fit in with others (Ferguson, Brunsdon, & Bradford, 2021).

Executive function awareness and tools can help students feel empowered during this process and may even be welcomed by those who are starting to notice—but do not know what to do with—some struggles in their lives. For example, as you teach about emotional-regulation tools, you can connect with what students are experiencing, such as, "You know how when you're really upset, it's hard to think?" or "You know how sometimes you get in a bad mood and feel like you can't shake it?"

If students are still developing self-awareness (we know some brains impacted by autism spectrum disorder or those with learning differences may need more time to be able to see themselves), encourage them to relate the tools to what they've observed in others. "You know how when your coach gets really excited, he sometimes doesn't make sense?" or "Think about a time you've seen a friend get upset and stay upset all day, even when things got better."

Start With an Easy Win Even if It Isn't in Academics

The power of executive function is its prevalence. Close your eyes and point to an area of your life, and there's executive function in action! To capture students' investment, you may consider addressing executive function with less immediate academic applications. Planning school events, navigating social or self-advocacy needs, or learning calendaring systems within the context of fun events can help open the door for future executive function lessons. Just as you open the school year by teaching the systems and protocols of your classroom in nonacademic ways, you can also introduce executive function gently.

Wait to Use the Term *Executive Function Skills*

You don't have to label executive function skills to grow them in students. You know your class. If they seem to need a few wins or examples before going big picture, it's OK to delay the full explanation of what executive function encompasses. When teaching reading, for example, most teachers don't label phonemic awareness before they teach it. Explore when and why the label could help your students. Rest assured that the skills will benefit your students with or without an official term. After a few lessons or strategies, you can provide the mental folder where students can store their new understandings: *executive function skills*.

Explain Executive Function as Brain Tools or Life Hacks

Executive function facilitates our futures, helping us smooth out the bumps in the road to achieve our goals—and enjoy the ride. Executive function can often be understood by its utility first. Statements like, "You know how sometimes it helps to . . ." or "Have you noticed that your brain seems to need . . ." can provide a relatable experience for exploring executive function. The broader introductory statement may sound like, "You know how you have brain tools that help you get things done and make life go smoothly? That's your executive function." In my experience, students also tend to lean in when we contextualize executive function skills as life hacks. "Want an easier way to get your work done? Let's explore some life hacks!"

Draw the Executive Function Tree

Use a visual representation of executive function to allow your students to interact with their learning in a multitude of ways over several weeks. You can use the tree from figure 1.2 (page 18) to anchor or introduce lessons and as a reference when coaching students to tap into strategies from previous lessons.

Recognizing Executive Function in the Classroom

Everyone's brain has different executive function strengths and struggles, which are dynamic characteristics that change in the short term based on factors such as fatigue or hydration (Aubrey, 2018) and in the long term by setting, context, strategies, and accommodations. It's not uncommon to have what appears to be splintered executive function skills. For example, some students have high levels of competence in one area of executive function and great needs in another (Barrasso-Catanzaro & Eslinger, 2016). In fact, students identified as *twice exceptional* are those with high IQs and a learning challenge like autism or ADHD. The high-IQ brain develops asynchronously, its learning capacity staying open longer than typical, but at the cost of the development of the prefrontal cortex, the main executive function area of the brain (Brown, Reichel, & Quinlan, 2009; Kircher-Morris, 2021). Think about a student you know who can write an incredible paper, using mental organization and synthesizing learning, but does so at the very last minute, demonstrating some time and attention-management needs.

As a teacher, you may be aware of some of your own executive function strengths and struggles, and it may be tempting to batter yourself with *should*: "You're a teacher, you *should* be able to . . ." Just as we explored in the introduction, there are a variety of reasons why our executive function skills appear at different rates and to different levels of utility. What is certain within all this variability are two things: (1) impaired executive function skills don't reflect a lack of effort or a character flaw, and (2) executive function skills can be taught, learned, enhanced, and augmented (Jacob & Parkinson, 2015).

In some cases, a student's executive function needs may indicate a need for support outside of the classroom. Parents may explore student coaching, courses, or parent training to help them navigate the needs associated with underdeveloped executive function. While you help students become aware of their brains and their needs, you may consider sharing about executive function with parents, extending the opportunity for wraparound support at home and at school.

Acknowledging the reality that no student (or teacher) will have perfect executive function skills, let's explore some of the common classroom activities and the executive function skills they rely on by recognizing where executive function happens before school, at the beginning of class, and during class.

Recognize Executive Function Before School

One of the most executive function–heavy parts of a student's day happens before school. Creating and managing a morning routine takes planning, prioritizing, time and attention management, and more skills. Here's an example of when the routine goes well with the skills that ensure success. A student wakes up with an alarm that is set at the right time to allow enough sleep and time to get ready (planning, prioritizing sleep, resisting impulses to stay up, estimating time for morning tasks, and managing attention so that tasks take the allotted time). The student engages in her morning prep routine, staying on track with time and attention, leaning into her tools to pick out clothes, pack her bag, attend to hygiene, and take care of chores (self-regulation for emotions and attention, organization skills, and short-term memory). She leaves for the day with a parent, talking as they commute and arriving at school in time to visit with friends, go to her locker, and get to class on time (emotional regulation, communication, routines for daily habits, time management, and self-awareness).

This ideal student morning is likely smoother than any we adults experience, so it follows that any skill deficit impairing the morning routine may result in rushed mornings, friction with caretakers, and high levels of emotions before the school day starts. And, while it's tempting to pass the onus to the family to "just figure it out," we can't ignore that the "sixteen-hour curriculum" of home lives impacts our students at school. In fact, and thankfully, when we work on executive function skills at school, it can also transfer to better executive function at home. Throughout the book, I will illustrate methods of ensuring generalization of executive function skills so that students' progress with you improves their lives at home, in sports, in other classes, and in social settings.

Recognize Executive Function at the Beginning of Class

Any transition, whether a shift in activity or space, is going to take some executive function effort. When students begin class, they're asking their brains to transition from movement to sitting, from talking to listening, and from high stimulation to lower stimulation, even in the most engaging of settings (managing attention). This asks their brains to regulate and shift their energy and attention. These shifts demand both self-awareness and self-regulation. Students need to assess where their energy is, what the environment demands, and adjust if they find a mismatch.

Once regulated, students must often move into item and digital space organization mode, gathering their homework, collecting the tools they will need, and organizing their space to be functional for learning. This can also be a time to self-advocate, particularly if they need a different space in which to focus better, more time to complete an assignment, or help to locate something required for the day.

Many class-opening routines ask students to copy from the board or otherwise engage in independent learning, orienting them to the lesson while teachers finish quick clerical tasks. This independent time requires students to be both self-aware and have tools to inhibit impulses. Our brains likely want the fun, quick dopamine reward of socializing, and our executive function skills kick in to remind us that our priority is using class time for academics.

Recognize Executive Function During Class

During the lesson, students' executive function demands continue. They are self-regulating so their energy matches the demands of the activity, finding ways to increase alertness when they feel like they're slumping or decrease high energy when they need to be still and quiet. Taking notes is a full orchestra of executive function: listening and prioritizing what to write down, capturing the essence of the lesson in written form (which includes managing spelling, organizing thoughts on paper, and adding personal touches to communicate importance on the notes page), tracking the discussion while also writing, and ignoring distractions or at least coming back from them quickly.

Closing a class period is a final sprint for our students' executive function, which may have waned a bit, exhausted from the previous demands (this explains the paper-shoving-into-backpacks behavior we see and explains why students don't write down the assignment, thinking they will remember). As students prepare to shift back into transition mode, moving to another class, they're going to need to first tap into some attention management, allowing them enough time to capture their to-do items in a system that works for them. They need to visualize and use their organization systems to pack up in a way that serves them well in the next class and at home, potentially stopping by a locker to swap necessary tools. They will check in with their needs, prioritizing self-care over socializing during their break between classes.

Recognizing the omnipresence of executive function skills in your classroom can be a game changer. What used to feel baffling, personal, or hopeless can transform into an opportunity to build skills. Where frustration once prevailed, a new sense of steeled focus takes its place; you begin to illuminate the skill prerequisites and, from there, can help students fill in their skill gaps. This awareness also allows you to appreciate the full scope of your incredible influence. You're teaching academic content while empowering students with skills for life. Please see the "Executive Function Skills Checklist" reproducible at the end of this chapter (page 31) for an expanded list of student executive function skills.

In the upcoming chapters, you will find tools and strategies to saturate your pedagogy and students' experiences with executive function–supporting and executive function–building components. The upcoming chapters will gently guide you through identifying small adjustments for big impact as well as using direct teaching and intervention for students with significant executive dysfunction. Welcome to the executive function team, teacher. We've got this.

Key Points

The key points from the chapter include the following.

- Executive function is the set of skills we use to facilitate success and move toward our goals.
- Executive function skills can be developed and are ever-present in academic life.
- There are many ways to introduce and explain executive function to students.
- Becoming aware of executive function can profoundly change your teaching approach, and knowing the executive function demands in your classroom can help illuminate opportunities for skill development.

Potential Actions

After reading the chapter, consider taking these potential actions.

- Walk through your typical day and list some of the executive function demands on you and on your students.
- Draw the executive function tree and explain it to a loved one, allowing your brain another chance to interact with your learning.
- Start a list describing shoulds, justs, or other moments when you are uncovering missing skills. This will be a treasure chest of ideas and lessons, when you're ready to use them.
- Schedule a time when you'll read the next section of this book and set a reminder.

Journal or Discussion Questions

After reading the chapter, answer these questions in your journal or within a book discussion group.

- How would you describe executive function skills to someone who is wondering about them?
- What are your personal executive function strengths and struggles? How do they show up in your classroom?
- What did you notice yourself doing, thinking, or wondering while you read?
- How do your new awareness and understanding change your perspective? How do they change your motivation?
- What are you eager to explore in your pedagogy or with your students?

Executive Function Skills List

When students have strong executive function skills, we observe the following abilities in them. Please keep in mind that these skills represent some of the observable behaviors, but this list is not exhaustive.

Future Skills

- Plan tasks, free time, and self-care at hour, day, week, month, and year scales.
- Use a calendaring system.
- Use time organizers like clocks, watches, and timers.
- Organize their physical space.
- Organize their digital space.
- Break tasks into steps or chunks, assigning due dates to each step.
- Use strategies to initiate tasks, even when they're dreaded or boring.
- Use a work management system to capture their tasks, schedule their completion, and remind themselves in the future.
- Use the backward plan technique to create short-term deadlines from a due date.
- Prioritize actions based on urgency or importance.
- Develop routines for common tasks (making food, getting ready, completing homework, and so on).
- Develop to-do lists as well as master lists of important tasks and due dates for future tasks.
- Write an email and reply to a colleague, peer, or teacher.
- Ask for help in specific, productive ways
- Set short-term goals, including working on skills, and monitor them
- Manage independent time (in class and at home) to complete tasks.
- Charge devices and bring chargers as necessary.
- Estimate the time a task will take within five to ten minutes of reality.
- Process through directions with a plan and in order.
- Write due dates at the top of assignments and in their calendar system.
- Organize workspace, removing distractions and gathering necessary materials.
- Schedule and use regular time to organize and clean spaces (physical, digital)

Page 1 of 3

Emotions and Attention

- Recognize distractions.
- Avoid distractions (as possible).
- Plan workspaces and approaches that support focus.
- Regain focus after a distraction.
- Use methods for increasing focus.
- Use methods for increasing mental or physical energy.
- Manage breaks and rest for refocusing and reregulating.
- Self-monitor during work time.
- Express and receive attention and emotional needs to and from others.
- Recognize signs of stress and overwhelm.
- Use tools to manage stress and overwhelm.
- Communicate needs proactively to others.
- Use tools to regulate emotions when upset.
- Understand their sensory needs and limitations.
- Recognize when technology is helping versus hurting their focus.
- Self-advocate for what they need.
- Work in a group effectively (meet deadlines, communicate with group, and so on).
- Know and use their accommodations (as applicable).
- Know and use campus resources.
- Anticipate impulses and temptations, planning strategies to avoid taking unproductive actions.
- Use self-talk to manage emotions and attention.
- Raise hand instead of impulsively shouting out.
- Move on flexibly from a topic (even one of choice or of emotional significance).
- Transition between work and play or between activities and tools for maintaining focus and energy with ease.
- Tolerate schedule changes.
- Use tools to get back on task when distracted or engaged in off-task activities.
- Use reminders and notifications.

Learning and Memory

- Use systems to manage learning.
    - Review or rewrite notes.
    - Study in an active way.
- Maintain awareness of short-term memory and its limitations.
- Use systems of offloading working memory (writing things down, using references).
- Develop shorthand techniques for notes.
- Use strategies for note-taking, including personal ways to capture and organize ideas.
- Use assistive technology for academic tasks.
- Know their brain's strengths and struggles with academic tasks.
- Use strategies for reading and understanding large amounts of text.
- Use teacher feedback and assessment scores to recognize growth areas.
- Create strategies to develop in recognized areas.
- Evaluate their understanding of a topic, using this evaluation to organize studying efforts.
- Check grades periodically and adjust academic approach as necessary.
- Use a syllabus or online resources to manage approach to class.
- Create visuals and references for multistep processes.
- Process through an academic task in sequence, beginning to end.
- Organize research for easy use.
- Use writing tools (like outlines) or oral rehearsal, matched with their need.
- Solve problems flexibly.
- Adjust mental approaches when schedule or situation changes.
- Take perspective of characters, peers, or teachers.
- Organize their thoughts for speaking and writing.
- Annotate directions or prompts to make a list of steps.

References

Baggetta, P., & Alexander, P. A. (2016). Conceptualization and operationalization of executive function. *Mind, Brain, and Education*, *10*(1), 10–33.

Barkley, R. A. (2012). *Executive functions: What they are, how they work, and why they evolved.* Guilford.

CHAPTER 2
CREATING THE EXECUTIVE FUNCTION–EMPOWERED CLASSROOM

Retailers know that the new school year often finds teachers, students, and parents creating shopping lists inspired by the feeling that a fresh start needs fresh materials. We may fill our carts with sticky notes, planners, folders, markers, and more, with a vision of using each new item to create a streamlined, easy school experience. A few weeks later, reality reveals that some of the materials may not have been useful (or are potentially already forgotten) or that we've used them in ways we didn't predict. There's a brain-based difference between the excitement of planning something and actualizing those plans.

After reading this far, it's possible your brain is experiencing something akin to what our students also experience—new information feels exciting, invigorating, and enticing! Then comes the application and you experience the feeling of, "So now what?"

In our brains, this makes sense because dopamine, a feel-good chemical, is released when we are presented with novel stimuli like learning and planning (Lieberman & Long, 2018). When we shift to *using* our learning, dopamine fades away, no longer available as a reaction to novelty, with its job of seeking

CHAPTER SNEAK PEEK

By the end of this chapter, you will understand the following.

- Several ways to identify and prioritize the executive function skills you want to teach
- Easy adjustments to your classroom environment that support executive function
- Strategies for embedding executive function support and development in your everyday lessons

complete. In short, when we get the thing dopamine propelled us to get, it diminishes in our brains since it fulfilled its role of motivating us to act (Lieberman & Long, 2018). The drop-off from this feeling can drive us to seek again or avoid applying new learning, since dopamine-filled new learning feels exciting and energetic, while using the learning can feel overwhelming, especially given that dopamine is no longer driving us.

For students and teachers, this may be where we see some procrastination, such as long get-ready rituals, smaller tasks intruding on the real work to be done, or diving into more and more preparation (research or asking about the work with peers) in an effort to delay the inevitable start of using our new information. It's also where our executive functions are impacted; the complicated inner workings of our neurochemistry influence the activation of the prefrontal cortex. In other words, we need to use some executive function to get through a wandering dopamine executive function slump!

Using new learning demands executive function skills. Students and teachers must prioritize which components of the new learning to enact and plan when to enact them, inhibit distractions, self-regulate to engage in the new task, and manage learning and memory of the new information (which is a cognitive elephant to lift again and again). This is where executive function awareness meets executive function actualization.

This chapter empowers you with the small steps and easy ways to put your learning to good use, crossing what I like to call the knowing-to-doing bridge. Instead of remaining in the learning-only phase, we will use brain-friendly ways to easily implement strategies, allowing you to ease through the transition from learning to doing and showing your brain just how rewarding teaching executive function can be. To move from knowing to doing, this chapter will help you recognize executive function–building moments, support your own teacher executive function needs, embed executive function for effective implementation, consider classroom physical environments and routines, and explore teaching approaches to support executive function.

Recognizing Executive Function–Building Moments

Challenge your brain to consider our students' two jobs: learning and studenting. *Learning* is growing knowledge or gaining skills. Learning happens throughout life, in all environments, and may or may not be reflected in one's grades. Students may love to learn and be highly skilled in soaking up content and ideas, but if they are unable to complete work or study for assessments, their grades may not reflect their learning.

In contrast, I define *studenting* as the tasks and skills of being a student, the results of which impact classroom experiences and grades. Studenting encompasses the invisible requisite skills for performing in class and earning grades, such as studying, class and homework management, communicating about academics, calendar usage, and other academic executive function skills.

The distinction here is subtle but can help form a new appreciation of our students' experiences. Students are doing double duty by learning how to be a student while also learning the content. When we can see these two components at play, we can use the perspective to adjust our approach. If it seems students are struggling with content, we can reteach or allow more practice; if they are struggling with initiating the task, we can scaffold the executive function demands or teach the missing executive function skills.

> Making the invisible visible for this section is an exercise in both metacognition and prioritization. It's empowering your brain to zoom out and take an observer's view of your thoughts and actions, with the thinking job of considering, "What inspiration do my observations give me for my teaching practice?" Taking time to reflect allows you to pause and gather data to make decisions about your priorities.

A common first bridge between being aware of executive function and using that awareness is determining which skills you'd like to boost. After looking at the executive function tree (figure 1.1, page 15) and possibly sketching your own, it's likely you're realizing just how wide the executive function tree spreads its reach. It's ripe with possibility and a bit overwhelming. How do you know where to start? Following are some strategies for determining which executive function skills you want to prioritize or schedule.

Attune to Your Words and Thoughts

As you learned in chapter 1 (page 13), one of the most reliable ways to uncover executive function deficits is to attune to your own narrative. Your thoughts and words often highlight executive function needs when they lament classroom challenges. For example, if you find yourself frustrated by a lack of student preparedness, you're also revealing a need for students to develop preparation skills like planning and organizing.

Almost anything that completes the following sentences likely represents a missing executive function skill—or several missing skills.

You're in xth grade, so you should know or be able to . . .

I wish my students would just . . .

I don't understand why you don't just . . .

> ***My students really should . . .***
> ***You should have . . .***
> ***Why can't you just . . . ?***

Consider keeping a list, making a parking space for sticky-note ideas, or asking a colleague to help you stay aware of your *should* and *just* statements. You may even challenge yourself to listen for them at faculty meetings! As you become a curious observer of your words and thoughts, you'll begin to see that you've already begun to both identify and prioritize the executive function deficits and challenges in your classroom.

Monitor Your Behavior

Another hidden treasure chest of executive function–skill ideas is in your interactions with students. Are you holding their pencils or devices and doing things for them? Are you assuming the role of secretary or embodying their work management system? Are you opening the grade book and checking their grades more often than they are? While it's possible that these supports are currently necessary for your students to get through, they are also demonstrative of students' missing executive function skills.

Reflect on Class Trends and Student Interest

You know *that* small group or class period? Do you dread *that* time of year or schoolwide event? When you notice a pattern that doesn't match your expectations of grade-level or age-appropriate abilities, you've identified an area of low executive function skills. It's possible that your students' executive function struggles are impeding their learning or behavior, and the trends you notice reveal an opportunity to explore the need behind the challenges. If behavior is the primary concern, it's likely self-control or self-regulation are in a high-need zone.

Students may also be a great source of data and inspiration. In coaching conversations, students may reveal feeling less able to perform certain executive functions or may ask you directly how to use a strategy. There are also moments that make more sense to students to practice and learn certain executive function skills. Before an important test, for example, students will be more likely to apply study strategies to their work than when learning without context or urgency.

Use the Calendar

Just like the pulse of the school year evolves throughout the months, so too do the executive function demands change. You can use the calendar to prioritize teaching executive function skills before they're in high demand. For example, a few weeks before exams are a wonderful time to teach students how to study, while a project introduction opens the door for teaching students how to develop their own work management systems. When you give students a preview a few weeks ahead of what they will need to be able to do, the executive function lessons of today become easier to identify. Table 2.1 (page 40) shows the executive function skills students need most at different times of the school year, based on common occurrences during those times.

Go to Your Executive Function Tree

Some teachers love to use the visual of the executive function tree to prompt their brains to consider executive function needs or moments. Exploring a visual representation can allow your working memory more space to, well, work. Using the tree illustration circumvents the cognitive act of remembering the executive function skills because they're concrete and right in front of you. Freed up by the visual, your brain may be able to play with deeper ideas and considerations for your students.

Supporting Your Own Teacher Executive Function Needs

You've probably heard that being a teacher is the hardest job you'll ever love. Some of the "hard" and some of the "love" come from executive function, as we teachers need the same executive functions we hope to grow in our students. Planning lessons, managing time, and prioritizing tasks are the daily mental heavy-lifting tasks that are necessary but are not necessarily taught in credentialing programs.

Teacher brains need executive function support. Every brain has executive function strengths and struggles, manifestations of both your neurology and the skills you learned and grew throughout your life. In addition, stressful times will make accessing your executive function skills trickier. When your limbic system engages in an emotional or stressful response, it is more difficult to use your prefrontal cortex, where executive function reigns (Pedersen, 2021). If you're a teacher with ADHD, autism, or a number of other neurodivergent conditions, your executive function is also likely in need of some support! (Don't worry, many of the upcoming strategies for designing executive function–friendly spaces or even teaching executive function skills will also apply to your life!)

As I discussed in the introduction (page 1), some cultures tangle executive function with morality and character. That person who is late? Well, he must not care about your time. The person who loses her keys every day? Hmm, she's probably just not trying hard enough. You may find yourself in a school culture where your own

Table 2.1: Student Executive Function Needs and the Related Skills to Teach Based on Time of Year

Time of Year	Common Student Needs at That Time of Year	Potential Executive Function Skills and Topics to Teach Students
August or September (first month)	• Transitioning to the school year and needing to learn routines and expectations • Learning a new schedule and transitioning between classes • Possibly higher energy at the start of the school term	• Classroom and school routines and expectations • How to meet expectations • How to set up physical organization systems • How to create and use reminders and systems to automate daily transitions
September and October	• Dealing with fading engagement and fatigue • Possibly falling behind in work • Waning use of the systems students set up earlier to stay organized or manage work • Working on essays and projects	• How and when to use self-regulation strategies • Where and how to work for better focus; different ways to get started on work • How to adjust physical organization systems, now that students have had time to use their systems • How to re-engage and personalize systems for organization and approaching work • How to create work management systems for handling many assignments and due dates • How to chunk tasks into small steps
November and December	• Increasing distractions with the holidays • Decreasing exercise due to time change • Final exams • Project deadlines	• How to use attention-management tools • How to apply self-care awareness and strategies • How to study most effectively • How to manage test anxiety • How to reflect on and adjust work management systems

January and February	• Increasing social executive function skills (Valentine's Day and spring dances) • Waning or lacking use of organization strategies in physical and digital spaces • Possibly reviving energy after a break	• How to communicate with peers and teachers • How to use problem-solving approaches • How to expand and test out options for digital and physical organization • How to use reminders to revisit organization and work management systems periodically
March and April	• Increasing demands may cause work pile-ups (missing or late assignments) • Fluctuating energy and momentum • Increasing project management needs with many long-term assignments • Preparing for state or other standardized tests (ACT, SAT, and so on)	• How to recognize values and set goals • How to increase energy by modifying environment or approach • How to expand methods to chunk assignments, use backward planning, and schedule work time • How to extend skills already learned • How to take care of physical needs, like sleep and exercise
May and June	• Potentially increasing levels of stress and overwhelm • Upcoming transitions to new grades or phases of life • Studying for finals • End of term social events	• How to use brain dump and self-soothing strategies • How to use longer-term planning • How to connect with resources and support • How to hone effective studying approaches and handle test anxiety

executive function challenges are judged as moral shortcomings, and in this space, it's hard to make lasting change. However, being aware that executive function skills are separate from morality is the first step to freeing yourself from this trap. When you notice your thoughts or words reflect judgment of your or others' executive function skills, ask yourself to pause. Is it true that someone who is late is uncaring, defiant, or rude? Is it possible that the behavior you're observing is related to an invisible struggle, a need for strategies? It's one thing to *cognitively* recognize that executive function skills are not character flaws and an entirely different thing to embody that truth in your self-talk and actions. You may have some embarrassment or shame about struggles with planning, classroom management, or time management. You know what you want to improve, and it may feel overwhelming and frightening to get started. The truth is, those feelings may be residents in your brain throughout this process, sometimes living in the background and sometimes prominently announcing themselves as self-doubt or criticism.

What if this experience, as unpleasant as it is, is actually an empathy walk with your students? An ugly, painful gift of understanding what the students in your care go through? By walking a parallel path, you become both a guide and a model, navigating the twists and bumps and showing students that with perseverance, tools, and time, you arrive on the other side.

As you become aware of your own executive function challenges, you can approach them with a similar framework that you might use with your students. Ask yourself the following questions.

- "What's causing me the biggest pain, or what's easiest to address right away?" This question will help you prioritize where to start.
- "Do I have the bandwidth and resources to create new strategies and systems for this need?" If yes, it's time to find and test out some strategies! If no, determine how to augment your bandwidth by finding tools or enlisting supporters to help you take on the challenge.
- "How will I keep future me supported and accountable?" This question will help you design the systems and rewards to keep your momentum throughout the messy process of change.

Examples of teacher executive function appear throughout these chapters. I encourage you to reflect, take action, and explore the moments when these pages speak to your experience.

Embedding Executive Function for Effective Implementation

Your executive function skills are always under construction, as are those of your students. Therefore, infusing executive function–skill building into what you already do can help improve your students' executive function skills and not add to your already full plate. Two means of embedding executive function include finding easy wins and making small changes for big impact, discussed in the following sections.

Find Easy Wins for Embedding Executive Function Support

You will learn more about routines, classroom environment, and instructional strategies in the following pages. However, let's start with the easy wins. Routines, environment, repeating challenges, and daily chores are areas where adjustments are fairly obvious and often easy to make, smoothing out our daily classroom experiences. The following are some questions you can ask to help find the easy wins.

- **Where are the routines in your day that are on autopilot?** For these routines, you can make small shifts in your approach to pass some of the cognitive load to your students. Can students initiate or manage the process more independently? Can you routinize or make the steps visual so students are not managing so much information in their working memories? Examples of routines you can empower students to manage include organizing materials for the day, collecting papers, and completing warm-up activities.
- **What structures of your classroom environment help or hinder your students' executive function?** Examining the role of the classroom environment can provide a chance to support or extend students' executive function skills, with minimal effort on the frontend. Are there distractions you could address? Do the visuals and references serve your current students' needs? Are there environmental options for spaces to take a break or deeply focus?
- **What is the most frustrating or confusing part of the day or week?** Our most bumpy moments often reflect a need for clarity and structure, both of which are empowered by executive function. Are there moments that you (or students) dread? What skills or learning could improve student performance in these moments? What visuals could help them navigate on their own?
- **What's a daily chore that students could take over?** Where are you assuming the role of students' executive function and doing their task to save time? The reflection in figure 2.1 (page 44) can help you discover opportunities for student independence and reduction of your daily tasks.

My Easy Wins

What can students be responsible for in our routines? How can I add a reliable structure and visuals so students can easily flow through the routine on their own?

What structures of my classroom environment help or hinder my students' executive function? What adjustments could I make? How can the visuals and resources in the classroom support students' independence and executive function?

What is the most frustrating or confusing point of my day or week? What skills or understanding might my students be missing? How can I teach or augment these skills so students are engaged and successful?

What's a daily chore that students could take over? How will I teach and remind them?

Figure 2.1: My easy wins reflection.
Visit ***go.SolutionTree.com/lifeskills*** *for a free reproducible version of this figure.*

Make Small Changes for Big Impact

The following explorations offer great starting points for making your classroom more executive function friendly. In this section, we continue our easy-wins idea and look for opportunities where small changes to daily activities can result in executive function growth for your students. Many of these ideas will fall into what I refer to as the "heavy hitters" categories, which have big impacts. The three main heavy hitters for building executive function are (1) working memory, (2) classroom environment, and (3) emotional regulation. Each will be discussed throughout the book.

The Opportunity of Directions

There's a gift of opportunity in the teacher tasks that are on autopilot for you. Giving directions is one such task. Making a small shift to some of your daily, probably repeated, directions passes the cognitive load to students. Teachers often use imperative phrases like, "Please do this . . ." Instead, we can shift our language to ask students to think, using questions and declarative sentences. When we do so, student engagement increases, with their brains having a problem-solving job instead of passively listening (Willingham, 2023). It also allows students to begin owning the tasks that drive their success. They're learning how to *student* rather than waiting to be told what to do.

The following are some examples of changing imperative phrases to using questions.

- "Please take out your book" becomes "What do you need to be ready for reading?"
- "Get ready for math" becomes "What do you picture on your desk during this time?"
- "Stop clicking your pen" becomes "Sounds like your brain wants some activity. How could you get movement without making a distracting sound?" (Student taps leg instead.)

Another great way to adjust how we give directions is to use declarative statements, which state an observation, helping students notice the cues in the environment but not telling them what to do (Murphy, 2010). These moments are not sarcastic but allow students the chance to pause and observe, often resulting in discoveries that shift their thinking. Because declarative language is not demanding or implying a right or wrong response, it allows students to become curious and active problem solvers (Flynn, 2023).

> Declarative sentences factually state an observation, allowing students an opportunity to pause, notice, and adjust their behavior. This offers students the chance to both recognize a problem and solve it instead of only complying with a teacher's command without much thought.

The following are some comparisons using declarative sentences.

- "What do you need to be ready for reading?" Add, "I see that some students have *X* on their desks." (Or, "I notice there is a list on the board.")
- Instead of the direction, "Please pick up your pencil," we can say, "There's a pencil on the ground," helping the student both notice and think about how to address the problem on their own.

Anchor Charts and Visuals

Look around your classroom. Chances are your walls have visual content and models of student work. These references are important for students as they allow learners to access necessary information quickly, without much disruption to their work process.

Adding visual references for executive function works in the same way by allowing students to remain focused on their work rather than having to pause and divert their attention to processing the executive function demands. For example, if your science students are writing a short response, a visual to support the process of scientific writing would scaffold their journey, freeing up more of their working memory for considering the science content and response rather than juggling the concurrent task of figuring out how to write their ideas.

Another reference to consider is student examples on the wall. You or your students may try annotating the invisible thinking, the executive function strategies, or the "what went right" on student work, providing a visual of what both finished work and the process can include. For example, you could display a final student project that includes multiple steps, along with a mock-up schedule of how the student broke the project into pieces.

Interactive student bulletin boards are an additional option that infuses executive function strategies into the physical environment. To set them up, consider executive function areas that your students need strategies to support. Skill sets like time management or organization that are broad enough to include a few different subcategories work well for a more permanent board setup. You can modify the bulletin boards by adding teaching points from your executive function lessons or updating reflection questions throughout the year. Invite your students to contribute to the interactive board. When a student shares or tries out a strategy, encourage them to add their ideas on a sticky note, which goes onto the board. The interactive student bulletin board then becomes a model and a reference for students, a place where you can send them for ideas when they are stumped, allowing agency in choosing strategies that work for their brains, as figure 2.2 shows. If your school limits the amount of paper allowed on wall space, consider dedicating whiteboard space, with the option for students to contribute by adding small sticky notes or writing in whiteboard markers.

The following are some signs that an executive function visual would help your students.

- If it's a routine for which steps can be listed
- If you repeat it all the time
- If it's a resource that's only ever verbal
- If it's a process that repeats in class
- If it answers a *should* ("My students should do *X* on their own . . .")
- If it's buried digitally (it takes several steps to find a digital resource)

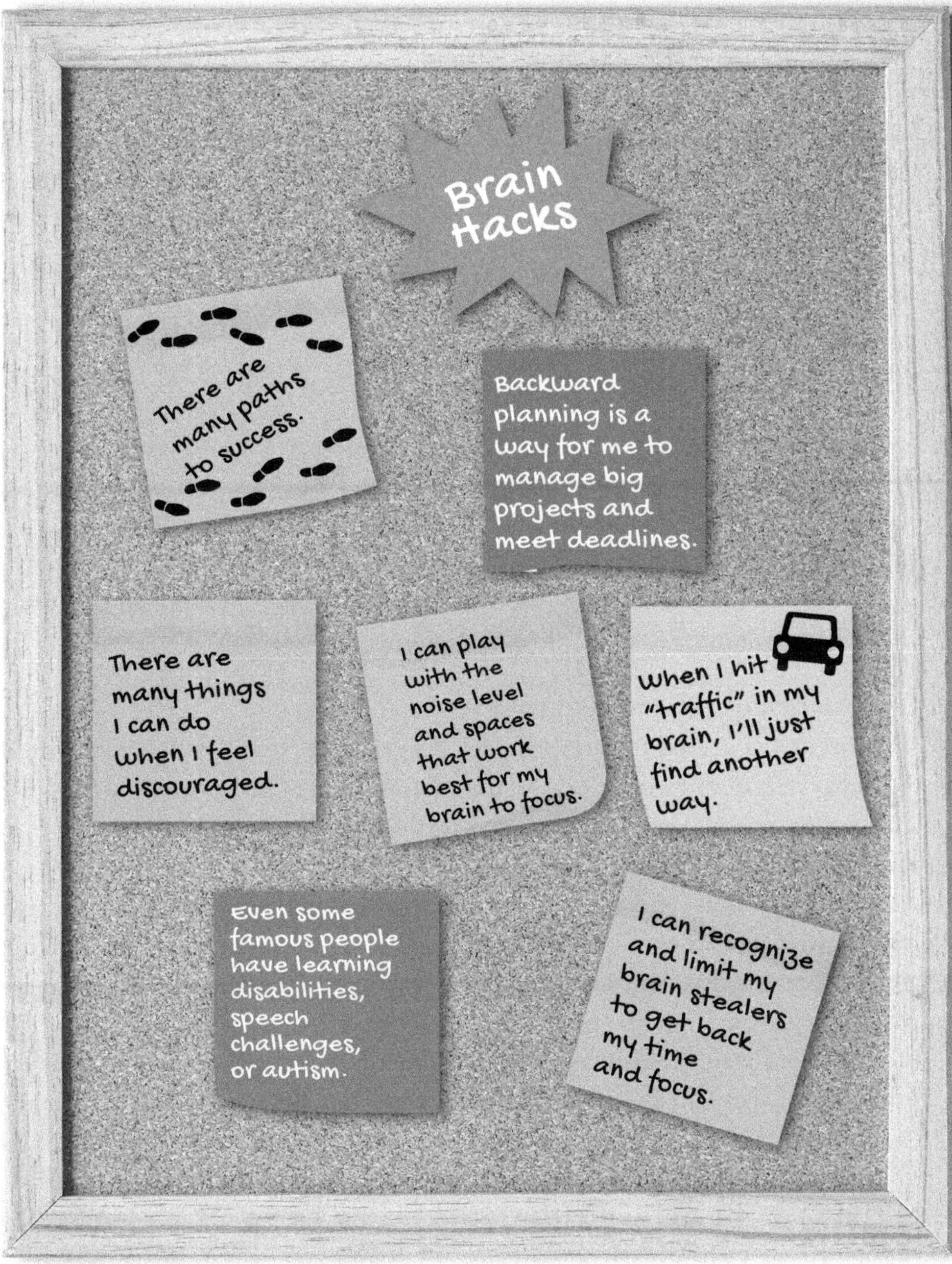

Figure 2.2: An interactive bulletin board where students add strategies to support one another.

Projects and Essays

The layers of executive function required for projects and essays provide a paradox. They are the reason projects and essays are incredibly tricky for some students and, at the same time, are prime cognitive real estate for developing executive function! When you assign anything in class, you have the chance to model, support, and develop executive function skills for your students. And, as with most executive function approaches, there is no right or wrong way to do so. Figure 2.3 explores some potential approaches.

Direction Deconstruction

When assigning something with multiple steps or a long prompt, consider demonstrating how to annotate the directions to make them brain friendly. This can look like underlining the actions (verbs), making a comic strip or having the student make a mental movie to show what the steps may be, or denoting the steps in a list in the margin of the page. The lessons in appendix A (page 167) walk you through a few ways to expand this process. Figure 2.3 provides an example of an annotated assignment with directions deconstructed.

Backward Planning

Projects that extend over several class periods or weeks may prove challenging for students with developing executive function skills. The dopamine of a new project is fickle, and when it departs, it can take with it any memory of the assigned project. Students experiencing the excited-then-forgetting cycle may need support to keep the project front of mind and in manageable bits. In these instances, it is helpful to chunk projects or essays into smaller components and assign checkpoints throughout the project timeline. You can do this through a process called *backward planning*, in which you determine the due date and look backward through the calendar to today. To backward plan, you collaborate with students to calendar the small chunks of the project from the due date backward to today. The concrete visuals and clarity that backward planning provides can anchor students with a map for project completion and serves as a tool for accountability along the way, making sure students aren't waiting until something is late to receive feedback. Figure 2.4 (page 50) depicts a backward plan with executive function annotations to help students navigate multiple steps and meet internal deadlines.

Supporting the Executive Function Load

Pace and demands are real considerations when planning for executive function support and instruction. Not all situations will allow the time to teach complicated executive function skills along with completing a project. In these instances, it may be wise to offload some of the executive function demands on your students so their

Name: ______________________

Of Mice and Men Assignment

Chunk Assignments

Required

Design an excitement map. Choose eight to ten key events from the novel. Summarize them in order, writing a paragraph for each. Then draw and color a sketch for each, and finally, rank them according to their level of excitement on a scale of 1 to 10. Use large, unlined paper for the final draft.

[Wed.]

- 8–10 events
- Paragraph for each event
- Sketch and color
- Rank excitement (1–10)

Choose one of the following options.

1. Write one long poem (at least thirty lines) or at least three short poems (totaling at least thirty lines) in the form of your choosing about the story or one or more of the characters. The poem can be from your own perspective, or it can be from the perspective of one of the characters. For example, Lennie is writing the poem, or George, or another character. (I don't want elementary school rhyming like "roses are red / violets are blue / Lennie is sweet / and George is too." I want thought and insight.)

Pick a character or theme.

2. Create a mobile or collage (at least 11 × 14) that captures one important aspect of the story. It can be about one of the characters, one of the novel's themes, or some other aspect of the novel. (When making a collage, the poster board should be filled.) Write an explanation for each item you chose to include. Explain why you included it and what it represents.

Pick and cut out 10 to 15 things that go with step 1.

Say why: essay about each collage element.

Note: You will have some class time to work on these projects, but you will need to complete most of your project at home. Your final project will be due Friday, March 6.

Backward Plan

Mon	Tues	Wed	Thursday	Fri
Day off make excitement map	Sketches	Essay about collage. Check work against rubric.	Final drafts	

Figure 2.3: An example of annotations to chunk and backward plan an assignment.

Element T-Shirt Project

Due Date: April 7th

Purpose: To design a T-shirt representative of the element you are assigned

Materials needed:

1. One T-shirt (any color). You can even use an old one. Turn the shirt inside out if it has printing on it already.
2. Fine-point permanent markers, puff paint, fabric pens, or other marking tools
3. Glitter, ribbon, buttons, or anything else you want to use to decorate your shirt!

Required Information:

- Name, symbol, atomic number, and atomic mass of the element
- Melting point and boiling point in Celsius and Kelvin
- Density
- Composition: metal, nonmetal, or metalloid
- Store at room temperature (25°C). Is it a solid, liquid, or gas?
- Chief uses of the element (at least 2)
- At least two pictures to highlight important element information (these can be pictures of its uses or of facts)
- Atom diagram of the element including protons, neutrons, and electrons
- Name of the person who discovered the element and time it was discovered

How will I be graded? 90 Points Total

1. Name, symbol, atomic number, and atomic mass of the element = 8 points
2. Melting point and boiling point = 8 points
3. Density = 2 points
4. Solid, liquid, or gas? = 2 points
5. Uses for the elements = 8 points
6. Interesting facts = 8 points
7. Atom diagram = 20 points
8. Discoverer and year element discovered = 5 points
9. Composition: metal, nonmetal, or metalloid = 2 points
10. Spelling = 10 points
11. Creativity = 5 points
12. Neatness = 7 points
13. Pictures = 5 points

Tues: 7 Research ≈ 10 min.
Wed: 1, 2, 5, 6
Thursday: 3, 4, 8, 9 *Double check
Fri: @ Lunch: look-over due

Figure 2.4: Backward plan with executive function annotations. Note that the elements worth the most points were prioritized first in the plan for the week.

working memory and focus are available for the project's tasks. In the Exploring Teaching Approaches to Support Executive Function section (page 58), you will find many ways that you can support students' executive function needs so they can focus on the content and academic skills needed in the moment.

Opening and Closing Routines

The bookends of your classes, the opening and closing routines, are prime real estate for adding executive function–skills development lessons. The first actions and expectations of class often set students up for learning and are opportunities to practice skills such as organizing physical space, self-regulating for focus, and initiating tasks. Author Mitch Weathers (2024) suggests using a written template for opening and closing routines where students respond to reliable prompts asking them to reflect on content, prepare for the day, and reflect on it.

Closing routines can be more rushed for time but are also an excellent chance to support students in calendar skills, planning, prioritizing, and communicating about missing work or needed follow-up. To help support your own executive function challenges and the fast pace of the end of a period, consider having students co-lead your routines. Table or row captains can check that students have written down their homework, returned items, and finished work, for example.

Considering Classroom Physical Environments and Routines

As stated earlier, classroom spaces can help support students' executive function. Your classroom setup, navigation systems, wall spaces, and organization provide opportunities to empower students to be more independent and less hindered in completing daily tasks. Here, we explore perspectives and adaptations to make your classroom space executive function friendly.

I've written this book in a variety of environments. I've written it at home, on a planned "writing day" where I eliminated distractions and cleared my schedule. I've also written it outside of the house, in the library or a coffee shop, and even on the go, when a potentially great idea struck, adding a thought to my phone's notes app. In each location, my ability to focus, to be creative, and to process deep thought varied, in great part influenced by the environment around me. Science backs this up. In an article in *Scientific American*, writer Emily Anthes (2009) indicates how factors like light, greenery, and even ceiling height influence human brains. And while we can't adjust our classroom ceilings, we can adjust other aspects of our classroom spaces to significantly support our students' executive function.

In general, the more predictable and clear our classroom environments are, the better our students are able to function. When we automate routines and eliminate any guesswork for daily needs, like supplying materials and easy movement through the classroom, our students' working memories are more available to manage learning rather than the business of getting ready to learn (Simms, 2024). For example, if the method for returning work varies day to day, students may be spending mental energy and time figuring out how to get their work returned, a tax they're paying before engaging with the day's content (Pham & Archibald, 2020). The following sections explore key considerations for classroom physical environments and routines, including making distractions harder to access, using anchors and visuals, avoiding clutter, systematizing and scheduling organization, considering sensory clutter, using parking spaces, and considering a launch pad.

Make Distractions Harder to Access

Many apps, devices, and other technologies are designed to capture and keep our attention. Experts are paid handsomely to translate brain research into technological development, speaking directly to our brains' wiring to keep us engaged. While we teachers can borrow from some of the brain awareness, we also must plan to protect our students (and ourselves) from the vulnerabilities and distractions. Luckily, research has our backs. In a 2017 study, college students' working memory and fluid intelligence were measured and compared to their physical proximity to their cell phones (Custer, 2019). You probably guessed the results: The farther away the phone, the better the mental performance. Another article describes how students' phones divide their attention, making focus and encoding new learning particularly challenging (Edutopia, 2019).

One could argue that managing attention in the presence of a phone is a skill to learn. However, for students whose inhibitory control is still developing (which is all K–12 students), the challenge is not yet appropriate (Petersen, Hoyniak, McQuillan, Bates, & Staples, 2016). You can blame the research if students complain, because for best attention and learning, cell phones must be inaccessible, parked far away from students, and powered off. Many schools and districts are adopting policies that limit and even prohibit cell phones in the classroom, as of this book's publication (Tabachnick, 2024).

In his book *Atomic Habits*, Clear (2018) makes the case that for new habits to stick, we must make undesirable (and possibly more tempting) habits harder to access. In the case of phones in the classroom, this means developing schoolwide policies that disallow phones in the classroom. It also can mean teaching students how to manage their phones outside of class, having them explore ways that they can make it harder to grab their phones on impulse.

Some approaches to consider include the following.

- Make phones a pain to access by zipping them into pockets in a backpack that requires walking over to it.
- Make phone apps a pain to access by hiding apps in a folder inside a second folder and requiring a sign-in each time. On student devices, this can mean blocking websites and apps, as well as having students identify the distractors that steal their brains. Students can then partner with you to monitor and adjust the moments that the "brain stealers" take them from their learning.

These strategies help students avoid the distraction of their phones by creating barriers, time, and space between their impulse and their actions. Adding levels of difficulty impedes accessing the identified distraction, decreasing engagement with the distraction. Additionally, imposing a momentary pause between the impulse and action also allows students' brains the chance to pause and reflect; if an impulse doesn't result in immediate action (and reward), students have a chance to ask themselves whether they want to take that action.

Use Anchor Charts and Visuals

While anchor charts and interactive bulletin boards provide specific references for executive function tools and classroom assignments, we can also consider the general visual navigation and routine support we provide in our physical environments. Most of our instruction is verbal. Therefore, our most mobile tools are our voices! For students with attention or auditory processing challenges, receiving instruction and directions in a solely verbal way can be challenging, as their brains are managing the cognitive demands of listening, comprehending, and acting on the heard and understood information. Students with specific learning disabilities identified as difficulties with "the basic psychological processes involved in understanding or using spoken or written language" represent about one-third of students with special needs (National Center for Education Statistics, 2024). Another 8 to 11 percent of students are likely identified as having ADHD, with their primary challenges manifesting as difficulty attending (Li et al., 2023). In short, up to 40 percent of our students with learning challenges will struggle with processing language or attending to our teaching.

In brains for which listening, processing language, or attending is effortful, students are splitting their attention, coaching themselves to "listen" or "pay attention," which uses some of their bandwidth to manage their focus. To ease some of the demands of effortful listening, consider creating a classroom with clear labels and visuals that do not need verbal clarification. Envision a space students can navigate based on signs and visual indicators where you do not need to verbally instruct for repeated or routine actions.

Since some students may take months to memorize the steps for classroom routines, having the steps laid out where they can access them provides a navigation tool. This tool helps students manage the usual get-ready activities, decreasing the chance that they will become distracted or discouraged before they've even begun the lesson (CAST, 2024d).

The following five-minute fixes can enhance the concrete visuals of your classroom.

- **Charts and lists with visuals:** For classroom routines requiring more than three steps, consider creating a chart or list with visual examples of each step. Focus on the verbs, stating the steps in only a few words. Hang these visuals in the location of the actions; for example, if the instructions are on how to return physical work, hang it where students return the work.
- **Calendar:** The calendar for the month is an excellent anchor for students. Providing a visual that includes both class and schoolwide activities allows students to see time, which for students with challenges like ADHD is a construct that can feel untethered in their brains and may be a significant struggle. The calendar will also serve as a reference for future executive function tools, like backward planning.
- **Schedule:** A daily schedule provides structure and predictability for students. While you don't have to include the exact times for each activity, consider listing the general blocks of time so students know roughly how long or short an activity will last. Seeing the schedule empowers students to independently navigate their time in class, using the urgency of time to motivate themselves through a task.
- **Labels:** Using labels solves the challenge of hunting for the same items every day, since students can see where things are located. There's no need to buy a label maker or label every item. Instead, consider labeling areas where items are stored or actions take place. For example, making a label reading *Student Tools* for scissors, glue, and so on covers a broad category while still providing navigational support.

Avoid Clutter

Our tolerance for disorganization varies from person to person. What one person considers organized may be another person's version of messy, and there may be times in life, say the welcoming of a new baby, when you actively decide to accept a bit more mess.

While we can honor that levels of organization will naturally vary, a physically organized classroom is a baseline support for executive function. Studies on the impact of clutter reveal that the stress hormone cortisol increases in cluttered spaces, and higher cortisol is associated with difficulty in problem solving, memory retrieval, and decision making (Murtagh, 2023). Additionally, students' working memory and attention may diminish in an environment where overwhelming amounts of items compete for attention (Brody, 2023). Students and classrooms supported by physical organization systems use less time hunting for materials, saving both time and mental energy for cognitive tasks.

Do not despair if you're not naturally driven to organize or if your own executive function challenges make organizing overwhelming or difficult. You can use strategies to augment and routinize organizing your classroom space to ensure staying organized is just part of how you teach!

The following are guidelines for implementing an organizational routine.

- Choose a consistent weekly day and time to organize (once a week, potentially during every period and to help students organize their personal things as well).
- Use visuals as guides. The small steps help students stay anchored in what can be a distracting process.
- Make it fun. Consider adding music or a timer to increase the engagement and urgency.
- Throughout the process, reflect on the dependency of the systems. Are students able to access resources and update their organization systems without you? Do the systems and maintenance require

To make the invisible visible, using strategies to support our own executive function weaknesses is a parallel process to what we do for students. When students recognize a need but may not yet have the executive function mental systems developed to directly address the need, they take a similar approach to what we would do: validate the need, create a system to meet it, and add strategies to ensure the system maintains itself with automaticity.

The following is a reflection from the parent of a student with autism. "My daughter benefited from knowing what to expect. At museums and other visited educational spaces, she always wanted to do a fast sweep of the entirety of the space first, seeming to establish a mental map of what was there before devoting herself to more in-depth exploration. Likewise, classroom experience was much more satisfying and gave greater benefit when the teacher was organized and had regular class structure, such as small homework assignments due every day and a quiz every Tuesday. Regularity, in part, was its own rationale: The task was part of a routine." (K. Radcliff, personal communication, September 16, 2024).

your leadership and prompting? (There's no right answer here. Your students' developmental levels and readiness will vary. The idea with these questions is to keep your brain on the lookout for opportunities to pass the responsibility over to your students, allowing them to internalize the processes you're teaching.)

Systematize and Schedule Organization

Just as you have routines and scheduled times to collect student work or complete assessments, you can add a five- to ten-minute organizational system to your week. Consider hosting cleaning parties, with a student DJ providing the soundtrack while students complete organizing tasks for their own and classroom items. You may also want to engage student leaders on events or different class periods on the same day and time each week. For clarity, you can list the steps of the process.

Feel free to adjust the suggested flow in figure 2.5 to meet your needs. I call it the pile, sort, purge, put back, photo, and plan (PSP4) organizing strategy.

Pile: Gather all the things related to the area or topic of your binder or backpack.	**Sort:** Create piles of Yes/Keep, No/Trash, and Maybe (ask a teacher or peer).	**Purge:** The No/Trash pile goes into the garbage *as you sort*.
Put back: Return the Yes/Keep items to their proper spaces, possibly adding or clarifying labels to make using the system easier moving forward.	**Photo:** Take a photo of what "organized" looks like as a reference for yourself.	**Plan:** After organizing, reflect on the process. What went right? What did you learn? How do you plan to use your organization system throughout the week? How will you remember to use it?

Figure 2.5: PSP4 organizing strategy.

Consider Sensory Clutter

In addition to physical items piling up, there may be auditory, olfactory, or physical sensation clutter distracting your students. Since human brains are wired to attune to new and novel stimuli, many of our students will lose focus, even if just for a moment, when a noise, movement, or other sensation presents itself (Wetzel, Widmann, & Scharf, 2021). As you'll learn later, working memory (what I call the whiteboard in our brains that holds information temporarily for immediate use) needs to be protected for our learners because its capacity for three to seven pieces of information at any given time is precious (Cowan, 2010). Distracting stimuli steal a place in working memory while they are considered, replacing academic content for a moment while the brain chooses to respond or ignore the stimulus.

While you cannot control or predict many of the sensory distractions your students may experience, there are two approaches you can take. First, consider the easy wins of your space. There may be noisy light fixtures or devices that you can have replaced or powered down, or certain chairs or desks seem distractingly uncomfortable or noisy, that you can request to replace.

Second, engage students in recognizing and owning their sensory distractions. Show students how to move workspaces when they recognize the need and provide options for decreasing stimuli, such as headphones to block sound or study areas that block visual distractions and movement. Consider creating low-sensory-distraction areas that allow students to meet their own needs. Common examples of these include having headphones or ear protectors available to block sound, private study areas (even makeshift spaces between bookshelves can do), and tri-fold boards that create visually protected spaces.

> Auditory input needs and preferences can vary widely for students. While some may need absolute silence to focus, others may be distracted by the lack of sound. Interestingly, many students with ADHD have shared with me that the predictable sounds of well-known songs can create a better space for focusing, offering a single, less stimulating soundtrack versus the external novel sounds that could interrupt their focus. As one student shared, "If I have a rerun show on, my brain stops scanning the background for new sounds, and I can focus." A 2013 study shows that music supports emotional regulation and relaxation (Schäfer, Sedlmeier, Städtler, & Huron 2013), while a 2021 study proposes that a stable rhythm can be calming (Blanchfield, 2024). The lesson "Make Space Your Ally to Get Things Done and Feel Better" in appendix A (page 182) will guide you and your students to examine the types, qualities, and volumes of sounds that impact different levels of focus.

Use Parking Spaces

As a time and frustration saver, a designated and marked "parking space" in your classroom for common items can ensure you and your students always have what you need. A tape outline or other visual demarcation can outline parking spaces where an item "parks" when not in use, with a note of what item belongs in that space. For students with developmental delays and striving readers, this may include a visual or a life-sized photo of the item to go in the parking space. Not only does a visual clarify where the item goes, it also provides a prompt (a natural visual cue to take an action) that a needed item might be missing—possibly before it's needed (Rollins, 2020). Common items with "reserved parking spaces" in the classroom include staplers, tape dispensers, chargers, pencil cups, and whiteboard or smartboard markers.

Consider a Launch Pad

A launch pad can serve as your classroom's executive function tool hub. This developed space can include reference items that students consistently need, such as calendars, project instructions, schedules, school references, upcoming events or tasks, and help resources. Bundling references helps decrease distractions for students hunting for materials and increases the reliability of them using the tools (Clear, 2018).

Exploring Teaching Approaches to Support Executive Function

While later chapters explore direct lessons, coaching methods, and interventions for significant executive function deficits, here we celebrate the variety of broad pedagogical approaches to teach and support executive function. Inspired by the Center for Applied Special Technology's (CAST) Universal Design for Learning (UDL) frameworks and employing the language of Benjamin S. Bloom's taxonomy (Anderson & Krathwohl, 2001), the teaching approaches discussed in this section are separated into two bigger categories. The first mindfully offloads some of Bloom's "lower order" skills (Anderson & Krathwohl, 2001) and executive function demands of simply being a student. The second empowers students to develop and use the higher-level thinking skills of executive function (Anderson & Krathwohl, 2001; CAST, 2024b).

An often-invisible struggle learners face is a concept I call "work-to-do work," the prerequisite mental and physical actions that come before engaging in the academic task. Examples include gathering materials to start a project, locating online assignments and resources, developing a study plan, setting oneself up in a brain-friendly study space, and getting into a mindset to initiate a task or study. Students who struggle with executive function may linger in the work-to-do-work space, looking fairly busy without initiating the assignment. From the outside, this can look like they are wasting time, but more often than not, it indicates a student's attempts to start work are ineffective due to unclear steps or missing skills.

When we acknowledge the multiple layers of setup for students, we're able to choose an approach. For example, we can take some of the setup off students' plates, do some of it with them so they learn to complete the tasks with automaticity, or give them strategies to make the setup tasks less cognitively exhausting. The following sections detail two approaches for supporting executive function: (1) automating and easing lower-level thinking and (2) scaffolding higher-level thinking.

Approach 1: Automate and Ease Lower-Level Thinking

The first approach empowers you to choose ways that you can ease the demands of studenting for your class by making the resources for lower-order skills like recalling readily available. This frees your students to engage with you in the second approach, where you directly teach them the executive function skills for higher-order thinking, enabling them to learn both the content *and* how to learn. The following sections describe three methods for automating and easing lower-level thinking: (1) considering emotional regulation as baseline, (2) teaching students to set up for academic tasks, and (3) easing up working memory for studenting.

Consider Emotional Regulation as Baseline

It may seem strange to start executive function support with emotional awareness, as the two might seem very different. However, to access and grow executive function, students must feel regulated because calm brains provide the setting where they can think, reflect, and use strategies.

We can also think of it in reverse: Emotionally dysregulated brains are less able to engage with the prefrontal cortex, where executive function prevails. Author and researcher Daniel Siegel (2017) describes a model of the brain using your hand. The wrist represents the spinal cord, the base of the skull, and the brainstem. The thumb, crossed over the palm of your hand, represents the limbic regions of the brain, which are associated with emotions and the well-known fight, flight, and freeze responses. The fingers, folded over the thumb, illustrate the prefrontal cortex, where our clear thinking and executive function happen.

The hand model helps illustrate a key understanding of all brains but especially brains that are still developing, such as those of our students. For example, intense emotions cause the fingers in the model to lift up, creating a space between the limbic region and the prefrontal cortex (Siegel, 2017). That space illustrates that when brains experience big emotions or have a fight, flight, or freeze response, the prefrontal cortex is less effective in its communication with the limbic system, unable to send clear thoughts or calming tools to the brain (Siegel, 2017). A brain in limbic activation will seek to calm itself, or escape or fight what it perceives as a threat. In short, students who are dysregulated cannot use their executive function skills well because they must have calm brains first (Siegel, 2017).

You don't have to be a yogi or deeply understand therapeutic approaches to provide students with emotional-regulation tools. When you are aware that regulation is key, you have an excellent place to start because you will approach students with understanding and allow space to calm as needed. As the CAST UDL guidelines state, an effective approach to supporting student emotional capacity "requires providing sufficient options to support variability among learners" (CAST, 2024b).

Approaches to encourage and make emotional regulation available include the following.

- **Offer self-regulation resources, including a physical space that allows for self-regulation:** As you and your students become aware of the signs of dysregulation, a natural progression is to explore what to do when feeling dysregulated. Sometimes we can adjust our thoughts or name the feeling and experience relief. Other times, we may need to use physical tools, move around, or take a break to feel calm and ready to learn. Consider making soothing sensory objects available and normal in your classroom. A basket of fidget toys or calming items, like glitter jars and sand trays, can provide students a moment to collect themselves and reregulate. If your classroom space allows, consider creating a dedicated space where students can go when they need a moment to regroup. In my classroom, I had a small area separated by a short bookcase where students could go for a few minutes when stress or big emotions took over. We called it Tahiti, and it seemed to be a true gift to the students who needed a space to feel safe and calm themselves.
- **Normalize mistakes and gamify learning:** In a TED Talk, Mark Rober (2018) argues that powerful learning taps into the "Super Mario Effect," where the failing involved with learning feels engaging and penalties for failing are low or nonexistent. His assertion that *gamifying* learning increases student motivation and retention of learning is backed by research; when it's safe—and even fun—to try new approaches, get fast feedback, adjust, and try again, students are eager to learn (Brown, Roediger, & McDaniel, 2014).

  Here's where you (and I) may feel the rub: Because of the time and planning required, gamifying all learning would be nearly impossible. And, if there are no or very low penalties to mistakes, how do we grade and assess students? The good news is that, just like with our executive function perspective shifts, changing our classrooms to embrace a bit more of the Super Mario Effect can be gentle and easy, small changes for big impact. The following are ways to gamify learning using five-minute swaps.

  - *Create a reusable game template*—Students may love helping you create a gameboard or materials that provide a reusable game for review. A game setup, like Headbands (www.headbands.app), provides a template for review games. The bands and rules remain consistent throughout the year while index cards with vocabulary can shift each unit. Teacher-created games, like Andrew Arevalo's Top Middle Bottom (www.tmbgame.com), are also inexpensive and reusable formats to keep students engaged and lower your prep requirements.

- *Hide bonus points or tasks*—The surprise or inconsistent reward, also known as *intermittent reinforcement*, causes our brains to crave the reward and act in ways to receive it again (Ferster & Skinner, 1957). Think of the rush of the social media reaction sound or the thrill of "maybe this time" when you play a game of chance. We can tap into this behavioral persistence by sneaking in fun rewards for participating, answering certain questions, or even for making a mistake while learning.
- *Lean into tech*—Review game apps and platforms abound (for example, Quizlet [https://quizlet.com] and Kahoot [https://kahoot.com]), and for good reason—they work! Not only are they engaging for students, but the repetition and mirroring of flash cards also speak to a research-based learning phenomenon. Quick feedback and the just-right level of challenge motivate our brains to pay attention (Willingham, 2009).

- **Make mistakes less punitive:** Lowering the pressure on grades can support students' emotional regulation; they may enjoy or engage in learning more freely if they are safe to make mistakes without decreasing their grades. To encourage mistakes as learning experiences, do the following.
    - *Adjust your response*—Your reaction to a student's incorrect answer is powerful. Not only will your words and tone send a message to the student about the safety and value of trying again, but they will also model the experience for students who observe. Consider hearing all responses, validating each participant, and responding to the correct answer by further engaging. "Tell me more" or "How did you get to that?" can help expand the right answer without connoting a morality to being right or wrong (RedRover, n.d.).

> Your personal experiences and challenges with executive function can serve as an empathy walk, where you mindfully think from a student's perspective as they live through a similar experience. Consider when you face a lot of work-to-do work, with many steps to complete before you start a task. For me, it was putting in grades. It took two log-ins, a few tabs, and a paper grade book to get ready before I could even start the task. That often led to my avoiding inputting grades, and that realization helped increase my empathy when students also face work-to-do work. Other experiences that you can reflect on and use to empathize with students include managing your focus when distractions abound, self-regulating when you're tired or wired, finding the things you need in disorganized spaces or when under pressure, and addressing dread (for tasks like grading or replying to emails).

- *Consider grading approaches*—Students often report they're afraid that their mistakes will lead to lower grades, and in a points-for-accuracy classroom economy, their fears are real (Terada, 2020). Approaches like standards-based learning, denoting student progress toward a standard based on multiple pieces of evidence, can open new thinking for how and what you grade (Vatterott, 2015). Such approaches can also require a lot of time and energy to implement. If you're pressed for time, easy adjustments to grading include grading some assignments for completeness or demonstrated mastery; allowing students to revise and resubmit; and choosing to grade some, but not all, student work (Terada, 2020). Adjusting the "missing" work value from a zero to a 50 percent, an approach called minimum grading, is also proven to increase student effort (Carifio & Carey, 2015). As Joe Feldman (2019) reminds us in *Grading for Equity*, we can make adjustments so that our grading practices "value knowledge, not environment or behavior" (p. 11).

Teach Students to Set Up for Academic Tasks

Transitioning into independent or group work requires a different set of executive function skills. Students who were listening to a lecture, which demands regulating attention to a speaker and their notes, will now need to independently use their executive function to initiate work, monitor their progress, and manage their time and attention, to name a few skills. There are several simple and effective approaches we can take to support students to prepare for and engage with their assignments.

- **Address the work-to-do work:** As mentioned earlier, students may lose steam or direction when completing the academic tasks to get ready to work. Teach students how to set up for work time; actions may include gathering materials, creating or choosing an ideal work location, and making a short plan for their work time. Students for whom task initiation is extra tricky may want to walk through the steps with your guidance, with the ultimate goal of internalizing the process for independence.
- **Teach students how to study:** A common reflection after a poor test may mention that a student "should have studied harder," a nod toward an unclear process for many students. Teaching students how to study can boost both their test scores and their self-awareness as learners. You can teach the study process in general, as well as show students specific methods that match the type of assessment. Lessons in appendix A (page 167) will teach students how to actively study as well as how to adjust their approach based on test results.

- **Clarify your online resources and space:** Our online spaces, just like our physical spaces, can support or frustrate students, depending on their awareness and use of the organization systems. Students who feel like they cannot easily access online materials or resources may skip those resources or even the assignment. Plan to show students where to find what they need and add guiding language to your online resources so they are searchable. Ensure that what you call assignments on a learning platform is consistent with what they are called in the gradebook. You can also consider making a how-to-find-things video at the beginning of the year and sharing it with families. (Some teachers even add a link to the video on their email signatures!)
- **Give options for offline resources:** Some students may want the opportunity to work entirely on paper or entirely on a device, since shifting between two modes can be fatiguing. Additionally, having offline options can support students who may be distracted by screens. Printing all materials may not be feasible, but setting up a system for students to print out at school or print out at home a few days before can add a layer of access and flexibility for you and your students.

Ease Up Working Memory for Studenting

I like to call working memory the whiteboard in our minds, where we temporarily hold information to manipulate it, much like we might solve a problem on a whiteboard. *Working memory* is the limited mental space where we recall things from short- and long-term memory, add our new learning, and hold the task or process at hand (Simms, 2024). Imagine you're managing all of that on your whiteboard while also actively avoiding distractions and using metacognition (thinking about thinking) to assess your understanding!

Many studies suggest working memory's capacity is anywhere from three to seven items at any given time (Cowan, 2010). Therefore, storage space will depend on the additional cognitive challenges we apply to the learning, as we can see:

> What "fits" in working memory though will vary depending on the storage and processing demands of the task. For example, it is easier to remember three words than eight words, but remembering three words becomes difficult when we add a processing task, such as thinking of a rhyming word. (Pham & Archibald, 2020)

Additionally, research indicates that training working memory is context specific; unless you develop strategies to offload or encode (chunk) some of the information from working memory, training working memory shows little impact (Cowan, 2010).

What's a teacher to do when working memory is a student's problem-solving mental space and has so many limitations? The following list proposes some solutions.

- **Make a personal cheat sheet:** Guide students to capture the important, repeated information they will need throughout the year, such as schedules, passwords, and log-in information, as figure 2.6 (page 66) shows. When the information is an easy-to-find visual, it won't take up space in students' working memory.
- **Minimize shifting:** When students' focus and attention need to shift from one thing to another during a lecture or independent work, for example, or from online research to written work, working memory must recalibrate the space and focus after each shift. Some students may find it helpful to have reduced shifts, have their digital work printed, or receive a printed copy of the class notes to annotate rather than to refocus from the board to their notes.
- **Provide tools for recall:** Allowing students to access reference materials for recalled information is a great way to free up working memory for higher-level thinking. Vocabulary lists, mathematics facts, example problems, and other tools make way for deeper thinking, as students' brains have less to pull from long-term memory and hold in working memory (Soederberg Miller, Cohen, & Wingfield, 2006).
- **Emphasize some rote memory:** Daniel T. Willingham's (2023) research reveals that automaticity of basic facts and vocabulary is essential for students to engage and understand. While one may argue that every answer is an online search away, the searcher would have to employ several memorized facts (sight words, spelling, and so on) to complete the search. Gamifying memorization, as well as giving students practice with recall and storage, will help empower them with necessary information that doesn't need working memory's heavy involvement.
- **Chunk information in lectures:** Working memory may be limited, but chunking information is one great workaround. *Chunking* information means to "present the content in digestible bites" (Marzano, 2017). When you chunk your lectures, you plan for pauses where students will have time to consider the learning and encode it into their memories. To take it a step further, consider using sound-bite chunks, where you summarize a part of the lecture with an economy of words. These "cognitive pauses" allow students to check in with themselves, process information, and form any clarifying questions. They also ensure students refresh some space in working memory!

- **Chunk information for memory's sake:** Chunking can also be a helpful tool for condensing learning into an unpackable unit so it takes only one space in your students' working memory. Mnemonics are a great example of chunking information. If you remember the initialism PEMDAS (parentheses, exponents, multiplication, division, addition, and subtraction), that's an example of a chunk. PEMDAS is an example of a mnemonic condensed into one acronym that can be unpacked by listing each component mentally or on paper. Think of trying to memorize those mathematics functions, in order, without a mnemonic!

Approach 2: Scaffold Higher-Level Thinking

After considering the rote and routine aspects of learning, we can extend our approach to address higher-level thinking, including problem solving, metacognition, and personal executive function strategies. The following ideas will likely be familiar and most often require a small adjustment to your teaching rather than an additional element to prepare. As you guide students in becoming more aware of their brains and executive functions, you may also find that they are empowered to manage their learning more independently. The following sections explain four strategies for scaffolding higher-level thinking: (1) making metacognition and self-awareness part of the classroom way, (2) conducting post-test replays, (3) implementing grade investigations, and (4) sharing project and essay executive function strategies.

Make Metacognition and Self-Awareness Part of the Classroom Way

Executive function is all about helping students learn to learn; when our students are aware of how they think and what they need, they're empowered to personalize their learning (Kesty & Ploszay, 2023). Rather than creating a separate lesson or adding another thing to your plate, developing a metacognition-rich classroom involves making small shifts to what you already do, such as the following.

- **Infuse assignments with metacognitive opportunities to reflect and annotate:** The work you already plan to assign is a perfect place to embed moments of metacognition. Encourage students to use the margins to write notes to themselves about the learning process. You can also have students denote moments on their worksheets or assignments where they will pause and reflect. For example, I know of one high school teacher who asks her students to add reflective questions to the middle of their class assignments. These questions focus on the studenting components of the assignment, like what's going right, what may need adjusting, how students feel they are focusing, and what help they might need. One great resource to explore is

My School Info

Name: ______________________________

Student ID: ________________________

Online Classroom
Location:
Where I receive and return work:
Username:
Password:

Other Log-ins and Passwords	Other Online Spaces
Location:	Location:
Username:	Username:
Password:	Password:
Location:	Location:
Username:	Username:
Password:	Password:

My Schedule

Name: ______________________ Student ID: ____________

Homeroom, Counselor, or Case Manager	**Period ___**
Name:	Teachers:
Email:	Email:
Phone:	Office hours:
Office hours:	Assignment patterns
Assignment patterns	

____

____

____

Period ___	**Period ___**
Teachers:	Teachers:
Email:	Email:
Office hours:	Office hours:
Assignment patterns	Assignment patterns

____

____

____

Figure 2.6: Example student cheat sheets for common memory needs.

Visit ***go.SolutionTree.com/lifeskills*** *for a free reproducible version of this figure.*

The Metacognitive Student: How to Teach Academic, Social, and Emotional Intelligence in Every Content Area (Cohen, Opatosky, Savage, Stevens, & Darrah, 2021). Its appendix has excellent resources for self-questioning.

- **Create a routine and space for students' personalized learning tools:** Your students will have powerful reflections and deeply engage with chosen strategies. Help them capture these insights, as they can become templates for future classes and beyond. Methods to help students keep track of their personal tools and growth include journals, space in the back of their planners, interactive notebooks, or online notes files. Schedule a couple moments a month to allow students time to add to their lists, possibly after reflecting on growth with the class.
- **Teach the scan-and-plan approach:** There's a powerful moment right after students receive an assignment that I call the "scan and plan" (Kesty, 2025). In this method, students look over an assignment (scan it) with an eye on perceived difficulty, areas they may need help, estimated time it will take, and any content not yet clear. This preview can help reduce student stress and provide an onramp for engagement. The plan comes next; students use tools like annotating directions, backward planning, and scheduling time outside of class (if needed). After a scan and plan, students are likely to feel less overwhelmed, knowing what is expected and having the steps to complete it concrete!

Conduct Post-Test Replays

After an assessment, students have the opportunity to expand their metacognition by using their test experience and results as insights into how they learn and what they may need to adjust (Kesty, 2022b). Either before or after returning the graded tests, plan ten to twenty minutes for a "replay" to guide students through reflecting on the test experience. Students can do the following.

- **Instant replay:** Shortly after an assessment, students reflect on the process of the assessment, considering how and how well they prepared, predicting how they performed (and correlating those results to their study approaches), noticing test format and content trends, and observing where they felt strong or had a struggle.
- **Slow-motion replay:** After students have gotten back their graded assessments, lead them in reflecting on their specific results. Consider asking students what the correct and incorrect answers reveal about their approaches. Challenge them to find the context clues or structural indicators of answers scattered throughout the test and explore approaches

available for certain tricky problems. Test corrections can follow this discussion but are not the primary objective. Instead, you're teaching students to become aware of their skills and struggles in preparing for and taking assessments.

- **Write new plays:** After exploring the students' needs and revelations, guide them through the process of determining one new shift. Will they adjust their study approach, their test-taking approach, or try a new way of learning in class? Appendix A (page 167) has additional lessons to teach students how to study, as well as how to fill in some of the executive function needs to make studying efficient.

Implement Grade Investigations

Grade investigations involve taking a curious look at grades at any point in the year. The idea is to zoom out and allow students to discover the patterns of their results.

During a grade investigation, teachers encourage students to self-reflect, although initial reflections may also be modeled with an example student. Using the phrase "I earned" instead of "My teacher gave me," students look over their posted grades, asking themselves the following.

- "What do I notice overall? What trends and patterns seem obvious?"
- "How do my grades change over time?"
- "Where do I lose points?"
- "What seems to be a strength?"
- "What do I want to change after looking at my grade patterns?"

Share Project and Essay Executive Function Strategies

You learned that assigning projects, including essays, research papers, and labs, provides an embedded method to explore executive function with your students. Here, we take it to the next level, learning how to support and grow students' executive function throughout the project's completion. Strategies in the following list are also excellent accommodations for students who can handle the grade-level material but whose executive function skills are lagging behind. Remember, some students with executive dysfunction may have as much as a three-year gap between their biological age and their executive function skill level!

- **Chunk the tasks and assign mini-deadlines with check-ins:** Longer projects can overwhelm students, often resulting in procrastination. To combat the overwhelm, with your students or ahead of time, chunk projects into segments and assign deadlines for each (Gonzalez-Pons, 2021). This concretizes the steps and the timeline for students, eliminating a hurdle and embedding executive function support.

- **Provide models:** Plan to share peer work models, photos, and examples that showcase the end product and its possible interactions throughout the process. A vision of the end result helps students clarify their project journey, while models of the first steps and steps along the way help validate the messy process of getting started and staying on course. Models can express what our instructions sometimes lack, such as how students will know when they're done, what a great end product looks like, and how many mistakes are normal along the way. Additionally, for students who feel paralyzed by perfectionism, models can remove some of the performance pressure.

Remember the first years of teaching and those summer days of classroom setup? Your executive function–empowered classroom makeover may start to feel the same way! The small changes, twists, and adjustments inspired by executive function awareness have the potential to be game changers for your teaching and students' learning experiences. And, while they are effortful on the front end, these new approaches will save struggles and time throughout the school year. As you would with a student's learning and growing, be kind to yourself throughout the process of making your classroom an executive function–empowered space. After reading this chapter, you will have lots of options for applying your learning. Similarly, you have options for the order in which you read the upcoming chapters, as they do not need to be read in order. Peek back at the table of contents and decide what seems the most logical and helpful next chapter for you and your students.

Key Points

The key points from the chapter include the following.

- There are several methods to identify and prioritize the executive function skills you want to teach.
- Embedding executive function instruction, rather than separately teaching it, enables impactful and applicable skill building without adding to your plate.
- Using a UDL framework, teachers can create classrooms rich with executive function support that is available to all students.

Potential Actions

After reading the chapter, consider taking these potential actions.

- Reflect on the easy wins using figure 2.1 (page 44) to help you discover opportunities for student independence and reduction of your daily tasks.
- Test out one method of identifying and prioritizing executive function skills you'd like to help students grow. Schedule yourself twenty to thirty minutes for this exercise.
- Consider the prime moments for embedding executive function skill building and make one small adjustment to your plans in the following few days, using the "Exploring Teaching Approaches to Support Executive Function" section in this chapter as a guide.

Journal or Discussion Questions

After reading the chapter, answer these questions in your journal or within a book discussion group.

- What common frustrations come to mind when you reflect on student challenges and patterns?
- What do you hope executive function skills will empower your students to do in life?
- Are there classroom challenges that are still hard to tie back to lagging executive function skills?
- What environmental or systemic changes would enable greater executive function skill development? (Think big here! Schedules, curriculum, groupings, and so on are some ideas to consider.)
- How can you involve your students in creating an executive function-empowering classroom?

CHAPTER 3 TEACHING EXECUTIVE FUNCTION SKILLS

I love to travel. New people, sights, experiences, and food fill up my brain and senses—mostly in pleasant ways! Every trip offers an opportunity to reflect on my values and ways of doing things, as I often find myself learning and reflecting on new examples from my travels. For instance, there are so many ways to make and enjoy coffee! From home roasting green coffee beans, which we love to do, to brewing coffee with a bit of cheese, as people do in Finland, there's a range of ways to experience this ubiquitous beverage.

As I am exposed to new ideas and ways of moving through the world, my brain starts to consider why I do what I do, and even how I know how to do things in my own way. Becoming aware of executive function may feel similar. As you contemplate what your students need, you may also start to realize that you have methods for so many of the executive function skills, like how you organize your papers or how you naturally backward plan your morning times. This new awareness can open the door to creating incredible lessons for your students, as you share your personal approaches as models for students to try.

CHAPTER SNEAK PEEK

By the end of this chapter, you will understand the following.

- The components of an executive function lesson:
    - Connect
    - Teaching point
    - Practice
    - Invitation
- How to write your own executive function lessons
- Many ideas for visuals and tools to increase the lessons' impact

One of the most common questions teachers ask me is *how* to teach executive function skills. Sometimes, they can see a student's needs, but the next steps are fuzzy. They ask, "Do I show the student a tool to use?" or "Do I just tell the student to figure it out?" Importantly, they may also ask, "How do I know how to explain an executive function skill that just sort of *happens* automatically inside my brain?"

The bridge from being executive function–aware to teaching executive function skills can be tricky to navigate. We want to avoid shaming or pressuring students, but time constraints and the urgent need to develop skills are real, creating the need for a delicate balance between making space for exploration and implementing imperatives to ensure growth.

Therefore, I want to remind you that you have options in your approach. If you recognize an individual student has a particular need, you may want to start with a coaching conversation and explore solutions in the safety of coaching. If you notice that a small group, or your whole class, needs an intervention, you may want to begin by using the resources in chapter 6 (page 139), which provide clarity and perspective for understanding and identifying targeted skills to develop. Once you are clear on what skills would most benefit students to gain, you can use or create lessons to directly teach the identified skills.

As you've noticed by now, working on one executive function skill uncovers more executive function skills—the interconnections, nuances, and opportunities for growth unfurl and continue into infinity. This process can be inspiring because you'll never run out of things to teach, enhance, and innovate. But it can be overwhelming, and you may wonder where to start or how to prioritize skills when they all seem to matter! While recognizing the vastness of executive function skills, a few baseline skills and perspectives exist from which many other skills grow. For example, we need to get students thinking about their thinking (metacognition) and developing systems to manage and use their studenting tools. From these sets of baseline skills, I have developed the teaching points and lessons in this chapter.

As you progress in your own executive function journey, you will feel the pull to teach beyond the provided lessons, noticing student needs that are better served with a different strategy. Terrific! This chapter will help you understand the structure of executive function lessons and how to make these lessons work for your classroom. It also empowers you to create your own innovative lessons catered to your students' needs.

Understanding the Structure of Executive Function Lessons

The lesson format you will learn here is made to be a base recipe, something you can modify to your taste and preference. While I have tested and curated an approach that works for me and my students, this isn't the only way to teach executive function skills. Because a component of each lesson is capturing your own reflections, you will inevitably end up with adjusted lessons, so resist the tendency to feel locked in, limited, or otherwise hesitant to teach a skill on the fly because it might not be the "right" way. In fact, you will teach skills on the fly in coaching conversations and by modeling your own executive function strategies. Empower yourself both to internalize this lesson structure *and* experiment with it. You will be amazed by your impact and innovation! In this section, we will explore how to connect and open the lesson, establish and explore your teaching point, and practice together. We also will discuss the importance of inviting students to use the skills and including visuals. To see how these lessons work in practice, I've prepared eighteen lessons that are included in appendix A (page 167), and I discuss them in detail in this chapter's "Making These Lessons Work for Your Classroom" section. For now, let's look at how these lessons are structured.

Connect and Open the Lesson

Begin an executive function lesson by establishing the need for the skill and encouraging student buy-in, which, fortunately, is a bit easier with executive function skills. Students can often see (and feel) the direct impact of executive function skills on their academic and personal lives, opening the door for us to "sell" them on those skills. These lessons are ways for students to learn to lower stress and smooth out their experiences, with ready applicability to their lives. This immediate application of skills means the feedback loop between an action and its result is short; students can see that a tool works or at least improves conditions fairly quickly, increasing the likelihood that they will use the tool. The ready applicability of the taught skills also encourages students to predict that future lessons will be worth their attention (NeuroLaunch, 2024).

You can choose to connect and open a lesson in a variety of ways. If you get stuck getting started, here are two categories of ideas as springboards: opening a lesson with sentence starters and encouraging student buy-in.

Open a Lesson With Sentence Starters

Use the following sentence starters to connect and open a lesson.

- **You know how . . . ?** ("You know how you get really overwhelmed when you have several papers due in one week?")
- **The other day, a student was . . .** ("The other day, a student was saying they just couldn't get going on their writing, but then they found a new hack that I want to share with you.")
- **I'm looking at our calendar and I notice . . .** ("I'm looking at our calendar and I notice that finals are only three weeks away. That made my brain wonder what we could do now to help you get ready.")

- **I've been hearing a lot of you share that . . .** ("I've been hearing a lot of you share that you've been having a hard time knowing what to prioritize when you have work after school.")

In addition to the preceding sentence starters, you might also consider the following.

- Show a video of someone teaching an executive function skill or a scene from a show or movie that depicts the skill—or a lack of the skill.
- Use a meme, something that is academic or teen-focused, to open discussion about a problem or solution.

Encourage Student Buy-In

Use the following sentences starters to encourage student buy-in when connecting and opening a lesson.

- **The skill or strategy we're going to learn helps you . . .** ("The skill we're going to learn helps you quickly create a plan for your homework.")
- **You know how it's really hard to . . . ?** ("You know how it's really hard to know how and how much to study? Today we're going to learn how to make a study plan that will make it feel so much easier.")
- **These strategies will make a task easier because . . .** ("These strategies we're learning today will make getting up the energy to work easier because your brain will know what works for you.")
- **A different class said using these strategies helped them to . . .** ("Third period said that once they started using time blocking, they got more work done but felt like it took less time.")

Establish and Explore the Teaching Point

When you teach an executive function lesson, the teaching point comes after opening the lesson and uses the structure, "Today, I'm going to teach you . . ." However, when writing the lessons, the teaching point is usually the first place to start. You must get clear on what you intend students to be able to do through your lesson and guided practice. It can be helpful to think of models of discrete and concrete skills, like arithmetic and phonics, and try to model a teaching point down to that level of specificity.

For example, "Today, I'm going to teach you how to organize your backpack" is broad and multilayered. You probably won't be able to teach all the ways and smaller skills needed to organize one's space. However, "Today, I'm going to show you a system for deciding what papers to keep" is a promise you can deliver. Sometimes, your lesson will be a group brainstorm of strategies to meet a specific executive function need, like how to handle email pileup or how to self-monitor. In these cases, your teaching point may sound like, "Today, I want to teach you that there are many ways to do this executive function task, and we will explore them together."

Sometimes, you will teach students to use a specific tool that is one of many that can serve an executive function need, such as an online calendar program. In these instances, it's important to indicate that your method is only one way to meet the executive function need. Students may recognize the purpose of what you are teaching and share their twists on the system or similar tools that work for them. Additionally, I have found that adolescent brains are a lot less likely to reject a tool when it's presented in an invitational, open way. Therefore, we invite students to recognize the executive function need, test out a tool we present, and adopt it in a way that best works for them.

When identifying a teaching point, there are several guidelines to consider. A teaching point must identify one skill, be simple and repeatable, be clear and direct, and is often stated in one sentence. Usually, your teaching points are something you add to a chart or visual for future reference; keep them short and sweet, which makes them easy to remember.

To write your own teaching points, you can start with the need. What do you wish students could do, and then how do you propose they do it? For example, I wish my students could better manage their overwhelm, and one way they can do it is by using a brain dump process, listing all of their tasks and activities and then prioritizing and scheduling them. Here, you've identified your teaching point: "Today, I want to teach you how to do a brain dump when you feel overwhelmed."

Finally, your school culture is ripe with teaching points. There are ways of being a student, expectations of tools to use, and online learning platforms used schoolwide. These hidden ways of being a student on your campus can also become teaching points, allowing students both to learn how to succeed on campus and learn the purpose of some of the tools available.

Practice Together

After establishing and exploring the teaching point, move into shared practice, which applies to a real academic or social need students are experiencing. Some examples are patterns of struggle, upcoming assignments, or upcoming social demands, all of which are great areas to apply new skills. Some applications will be easy to identify. For example, students' messy backpacks or disorganized digital spaces are the perfect "life laboratories" to apply learning strategies for organizing. Other applications may take some stretching. You may see the need to teach students to self-advocate, for example, but struggle to find a unified, concrete application for your students. In this case, consider taking some creative license and invite students to problem solve for a real or imaginary fellow student, help you solve a real or imaginary problem in your life, or apply their learning to theoretically solve a problem outside of school.

When I was moving houses and had more to do than a full day allowed, I asked my students to help me prioritize my to-do list. While I technically already had a plan, the model allowed students to explore their thinking, hear others' thoughts, and witness the development of a few days of planning based on identified priorities. Their brainstorming allowed practice of the new skill before I asked them to test it out on their own to-do lists.

It's likely you will start with a model together before encouraging students to use the new skill on their own, with your supervision. For example, if you're learning to backward plan (put things in the calendar in small milestones, backward from the due date), you may all start together by listing the steps to complete a new project. You might take a few of those chunks and calendar them together, providing a visual model for students. Toward the end of the process, you will likely release students to complete the process, adding the final few milestones into their personal calendars, with your feedback. This process will be fluid and adjustable as you progress. Your lesson will allow for shared and guided independent practice, but the timing may differ from what you predict when you write the lesson. Students who really grasp the concept may be ready to practice on their own earlier than you predicted. Or, you may return to shared practice as a whole group if students flounder in their independent practice. The lesson format asks that you annotate and reflect on the lesson when you're done so you'll be able to capture what you learn and what you changed when teaching the lesson.

During shared practice, consider planning to share "starts" with the group. Often, for students with executive function deficits, task initiation is a formidable challenge. Allow students a few minutes to get started, then ask everyone to pause. Ask for students to share what—and especially how—they've started as a model for the class. You can project a student's start example or have them describe their thoughts and actions when they began their practice. Often, students who have been stuck struggling with task initiation will be able to progress after seeing a few examples of ways to start.

A final consideration when writing your shared practice section of the lesson is that of extended practice. Students with executive dysfunction will likely need many interactions with the skill before internalizing it. You may want to note in your lesson or planning system that you will follow the lesson up in small groups or with individual students after a period of time. I often use initials and bullet points as prompts for myself to check on certain students' progress with new strategies. The following are sentence starters and statements for transitioning into practicing the new skill.

- Let's see how it goes when we . . .
- Let's try it out.
- All right, ready to give it a shot?
- Let's use this new skill to . . .

Invite Students to Use the Skill

When skills are new, it can be hard to know when to use them. Students will likely need support in identifying the circumstances and signs they may need to use a learned strategy. In this section of your lesson, you mindfully call out the applications of the new skill and invite students to commit to how and when they will use it. This is typically a short conversation to explore applications of the new skill, in which students identify the indications that the new skill or strategy is needed. Since executive function applies outside of school, often the strategies will too. Consider exploring the skill or strategy's use in life outside of school, as well as the signs a strategy may be in order.

Following this discussion, plan to take actions to ensure follow-up. Consider introducing a visual, like an interactive board or anchor chart (more ideas to come). You may also want to have students create a reminder for themselves by setting a notification, emailing their parents to share their new strategy (and encourage follow-up at home), or creating a visual reminder in their personal space, such as a sticky note on their laptop or a digital icon to prompt them to use the strategy later. Questions to invite and remind students to use the skill include the following.

- When can you see yourself using this strategy?
- How will you know when you need to use this new skill?
- What are the signs it's a great time to use this new skill?
- How will you remember to try this new strategy?
- What do you see yourself doing when you use this new strategy?
- What does future you need so this new strategy works for you?

Include a Visual

This section of your lesson plan will likely be a bulleted list or a sketch of a visual. It captures your plan to anchor the strategy or skill into the classroom environment so students have a reminder of and reference to the skill after the lesson.

Ideas for visuals include the following.

- Create an anchor chart (general reference) that outlines the steps of the strategy for future reference.
- Add the strategy to an established list of strategies in a related category (for example, an organization hacks list).
- Create an interactive bulletin board where you and students can add strategies by category, possibly on sticky notes. Or, if paper on your walls is limited by fire code, consider creating a dedicated whiteboard for strategies with thought bubbles or bullet points. You can also create a digital space using an app like Padlet (https://padlet.com).
- Ask a student to draw a comic of the strategy or make a poster about it.
- Add a sticky note with a small summary or prompt to the calendar or launch pad area of your classroom.
- Have students create a visual for themselves and add it to a collection of strategies.

Making These Lessons Work for Your Classroom

Appendix A (page 167) includes eighteen lessons for you to share with individual students, small groups, or the whole class. You can use them in any order, based on identified student needs, to teach a study skills class or for a resource specialist program, or in anticipation of executive function demands, such as final exams. The following list shows the eighteen lessons.

- **Metacognition:** These lessons support students in developing awareness of their learning, executive function, and unique needs.
    - Practice On Purpose Will Help You Grow Any Skill (page 169)
    - Collect and use brain tools to make learning easier (page 172)
    - Think of your working memory like a whiteboard (page 175)
- **Self-regulation:** These lessons help students recognize and manage their energy, focus, and emotions.

    - Remember that stressed brains struggle with thinking (page 179)
    - Make space your ally to get things done and feel better (page 182)
- **Organization:** These lessons help students develop systems to manage their physical, digital, and temporal spaces.
    - Use differentiation to visually organize physical and digital spaces (page 186)
    - Use the pile, sort, purge, put back, photo, plan (PSP4) organizing strategy (page 189)
- **Time (Attention) Management:** These lessons develop students' awareness and effective use of time.
    - Plan work time with warm-ups and cooldowns (page 193)
    - Recognize your brain stealers to earn back your time and focus (page 196)
    - Use backward planning to meet deadlines (page 199)
- **Studying and Grades:** These lessons teach students to study, improve grades, and initiate work.
    - Perform a test replay to earn a better grade next time (page 202)
    - Find points vampires to give your grades a quick boost (page 207)
    - Use active studying to score better on assessments (page 210)
- **Planning and Prioritizing:** These lessons teach students to manage workload by prioritizing and planning their actions.
    - Motivate by making the task clear, social or fun, or urgent (page 213)
    - Use capture, schedule, and remind (CSR) systems to manage your work (page 216)
    - Use brain dumps to decrease overwhelm and help create a plan (page 219)
- **Social and Collaboration:** These lessons teach students to communicate and collaborate effectively.
    - Use the nice-ask-nice formula for easy emails (page 223)
    - Hack group projects (page 226)

These lessons have built-in assumptions of abilities and knowledge and could, if delivered exactly as written, accidentally leave someone out. As written, these lessons assume academic English proficiency, physical, visual, and auditory capabilities, and processing abilities of typical sixth to twelfth-grade students. These assumptions are not intended to exclude any classroom or learner. If, at first read, it seems like your students might struggle with a lesson, reread it with a detective's eye. How can you phrase or demonstrate the teaching point to be more accessible for your students? What ways of interacting with ideas are usually successful for your students? Can you turn up the volume of input by adding visuals or using captions as you present? I trust you know your class and have a variety of ways you can adapt these lessons to best fit your students.

At the top of each lesson, there's a quick guide for your planning. It denotes the lesson's purpose and the executive function area of focus. It will also guide you to consider when you might best use the lesson reactively and proactively. The "When to use this lesson" prompt explores the if/then options when you've observed a need and are ready to teach related skills. This includes recognizing upcoming school or life demands for which these skills could be useful. Other helpful guidelines included are the potential lesson audience, a lesson length estimate, and any notes or potential adaptations.

Some of these lessons need a bit of information specific to your class. For example, when you teach students backward planning (page 199), you will use real examples of tasks and assignments from your class. Or, when you teach students how to digitally organize, you need to know what digital files and spaces are common for them. In this way, these lessons won't feel disconnected or like extra work for you and will better your students' executive function in application to your classwork.

As you teach these lessons, you'll learn the right pace, adaptations, or additional elements needed for your class. Feel free to experiment with the lessons at the end of this book. You can't do this wrong.

Key Points

The key points from the chapter include the following.

- Executive function lessons provide a structure to inspire, teach, and support students in growing executive function skills.
- Executive function lessons include mindful connections to student lives as well as visuals to capture skills for reference and future use.
- The executive function lesson format is available for you to create lessons that best serve your students' needs.

Potential Actions

After reading the chapter, consider taking these potential actions.

- Choose an executive function lesson from appendix A (page 167) that introduces metacognition or general executive function awareness and test it.
- Highlight the teaching points in the lesson list that speak the most to you.
- Complete the following sentences. These reflections will help you identify potential executive function needs, which can inspire lessons to teach the missing skills.
    - I wish my students knew how to . . .
    - I'm tired of reminding my students to . . .
    - I think school would be easier for my students if they could . . .

Journal or Discussion Questions

After reading the chapter, answer these questions in your journal or within a book discussion group.

- What are some easy opportunities for teaching executive function lessons?
- What do you imagine might be challenging in teaching these lessons? What strategies might help address these challenges?
- To whom can you turn for feedback on your lesson writing and implementation?

CHAPTER 4 UNDERSTANDING EXECUTIVE FUNCTION COACHING

Melanie has all her materials spread out in front of her. The freshman English class is quiet except for the sound of typing and a handful of students quietly dictating their thoughts. The whole room is abuzz with focused productivity. Melanie is following the vibe, looking very busy, but when I walk behind her and glance at her screen, the blinking cursor is lonely on the empty page. I bend down to talk to her quietly.

"Hey, you. It looks like you might be stuck. What are you noticing?"

Melanie scrunches her face and sighs. "Yeah, I'm just having a hard time getting started."

"That happens sometimes, but we can always test out some ways to help our brains get started. What have you tried so far?"

"I don't know," Melanie says. "I mean, I've read the prompt like thirty times. I kind of know how I want to answer, but I just can't get moving."

"Reading the prompt is an awesome idea," I reply. "Sometimes, people like to rewrite part of the question to help them form the beginning of the answer."

CHAPTER SNEAK PEEK

By the end of this chapter, you will understand the following.

- What executive function coaching is and why it's transformational
- How and when to hold a coaching conversation that's planned or on the fly
- Common pitfalls and ways to handle "I don't know"
- Examples of coaching questions and sentence stems

"Oh yeah, I could try that," Melanie says with a little more enthusiasm. "But I feel like I spent all my energy already."

"Sounds like you're tired." I ask her, "Where do you think you spent your energy?"

"On that other assignment, the outline. Now, I have all this writing to start. I just don't get why my brain is so lame."

I can tell Melanie is comparing herself to her peers, most of whom seem to be busy typing their essays.

"I'm hearing you say that you spent your brain battery on the outline. You said that it was the other assignment, as if they were separate. Can I challenge your thinking a bit?"

Melanie looks confused, but she agrees.

"Tell me about the outline. What did you have to do for it?"

"You assigned it, Miss Kesty. You know what I had to do."

"Good point," I laugh. "But I mean what was the purpose or the job of the outline? Why do you think I 'tortured' you all with it?"

"I don't know," Melanie says, but her eyes dart upward, indicating that she's thinking. A few moments later she ventures a guess. "The outline is like a different way to write the essay. Like a short version."

"It's possible your brain is seeing the outline and the writing as totally separate," I say, then begin coaching Melanie through the thinking process. "It makes sense that when you feel like you have two hard jobs to do, your brain might feel overwhelmed or tired. I think we've discovered something. It sounds like you may not yet be able to use the outline as a tool for writing. I assigned the outline to help your brain get ready for the writing as if it is the skeleton and you add muscles and skin as you write. What do you think about partnering up, so I can show you how to hack the outline to make writing way easier?"

Melanie and I copy and paste her outline into the essay document. I show her how to add transitions to smooth out the outline choppiness, and after half an hour, one-third of her essay is done, and the rest is on its way. But her changed outlook is our biggest celebration.

I ask her, "How are you feeling now? What do you think went right?"

"I didn't realize I was making the work so much harder for myself" Melanie responded. "I feel way better about writing now."

"Can I add to that?" I ask. Melanie nods. I say, "You stuck with yourself and took some time to think about your own thinking. Because of that, you know your brain a little better, and you have a strategy that will work for you in this class, the rest of high school, and in college."

"Yeah, I don't feel so stuck now." Melanie smiles.

Coaching conversations like this feel like transformational magic. They can be nuanced and subtle or spontaneous and unpredictable. In this chapter, I want to empower you with the coach's lens and toolbox. In addition to creating an executive function–friendly classroom and directly teaching executive function skills, coaching can be an incredibly impactful vehicle for facilitating student growth.

Many definitions of coaching, like definitions of executive function, describe what coaching does: It creates transformation, supports the growth of individuals, and drives institutional change. I agree with and celebrate these assertions, but they leave a vague sense of, "Yeah, but how?"

I define *coaching* in the classroom as the perspective and practice of engaging in a curious conversation that aims to develop a student's self-awareness, content competence, and executive functions. Perfectly clear, right? OK, maybe not yet. But stick with me. By the end of this chapter, you will be excited to test out some of the curious conversations and utilize the coaching questions with your students! The magic, the transformation, the growth? They will be inevitable outcomes of your coaching.

This chapter will help you with several aspects of student coaching, including learning why coaching for executive function skills is essential; figuring out what makes coaching, coaching; understanding the three phases of coaching; developing effective coaching questions; recognizing question and coaching opportunities; making coaching executive function friendly for yourself; handling students saying "I don't know"; and using questions and coaching statement stems.

Recognizing the Vital Impact of Executive Function Coaching

When I was learning to play pickleball, I thought I was probably the worst player in the world, and the shame flushing red in my cheeks reflected my self-doubt. Seriously? Every other hit was wild, straight into the net or way, way off the court. I tried to play it off, cover it with humor, but inside, my guts were replaced with the hot lava of embarrassment, and I wished this was the kind of game where you could just get "out." It was good coaching that changed everything.

"Balls don't lie!" I heard from behind me. The coach, Jill, stood with a smile that said she'd spotted a newbie. "When they go wild, it means you've used the wrong angle. Try this." She modeled how to angle my paddle, allowing me to feel and reflect on what the more effective way to hold the paddle really felt and looked like in my hand. "Let's try a few. I'll hit you some, and you return them, holding the paddle just like that."

I'm not a professional pickleball player, as you may have guessed. But I'm better now. I have better strategies and get better results. I stuck with the game because I had the right support. I know how to experiment and reflect on what works for my game. More importantly, I have a coach's voice in my head, prompting me to use the strategies she taught. I needed Jill's expert feedback in real time to adjust my approach and grow. She met me in my pickleball *zone of proximal development*, to use psychologist Lev Vygotsky's (1978) concept, pushing me just above where I was independently competent and providing tools to keep leveling up with practice.

Executive function coaching works like other types of coaching for our students. Coaching students builds individual competence by providing a customizable experience in which we can tailor tools and questions for students as they explore their needs in real time. Instead of delivering a lesson and hoping students figure out how to apply their learning, the coach saddles up next to the student during their application, illuminating and supporting the learning process. You can think of executive function coaching as a vehicle for teaching students the hows that support their success. Examples include how to learn, how to manage the steps of the activity, how to effectively manage their time and attention, and how to know when they need help, all within the context of real-world application to your classroom curriculum. Coaching helps students do double duty, completing their work and learning about their brains and the tools that best match their needs. Coaching can feel greatly rewarding and effective for teachers and students, helping solve real-world problems while building student capacity.

You may have heard that Malcom Gladwell (2008) recommends ten thousand hours of practice before one becomes great at something. That figure, it turns out, was largely simplified when it was widely shared, but within the idea lies a significant lesson: We need deliberate practice to improve our skills. *Deliberate practice*, a term coined by psychology professor John Hayes, describes the act of focusing on specific skill development, using practice and feedback to improve (Clear, n.d.b). Hayes's research illuminates that the greats, known to be the top performers in their fields, build small skills, purposefully and over time. Coaching offers a vehicle for deliberate practice. When we coach, we can help students identify their missing executive function skills, co-creating strategies and opportunities to practice until they are independently able to perform that skill. Just like a sports coach can pinpoint where an athlete is missing a skill, we, as teachers, can explore students' executive function skill sets with an eye for missing or underdeveloped areas. Then, just as a coach may assign drills or sheltered practice, we can offer students tools and the opportunity to apply them to assignments, reading, studying, or other required school tasks. And, in case you were worried, the ten thousand hours Gladwell (2008) cites reflect data on the people who achieved remarkable "phenom" levels of skills. To become competent, we need fewer hours but are still best served by deliberate practice.

Another key benefit of coaching, rather than just directly teaching executive function skills, is that it invites students to seek, adapt, and adopt their own strategies. After being exposed to strategies in lessons, coaching provides the sheltered practice and instant feedback that students need to make their skills their own. In fact, according to John Hattie's (2023) meta-analysis of the efficacy of instructional practices, feedback for students is more effective for student performance than direct instruction. While students are engaged in coaching conversations, they are also becoming aware of both their executive function needs and the types of strategies that work well with their neurology. Coaching creates a space where students can explore their thinking and experiment with approaches, with the safety and support of a coach to guide them.

As a natural extension of improved self-awareness, students' self-regulation often improves through coaching. Where they once may have become dysregulated and waited for a teacher to intervene, with coaching students can begin to recognize and meet their own needs. Coaching allows students to observe the signs they are becoming dysregulated and learn the patterns leading to these moments. Coaching can also invite students to identify and test strategies to reduce the frequency and duration of their dysregulated moments as well as find tools to reregulate when they need to. Telling students to "calm down" or "just focus" leaves them with unmet needs and positions them to attempt to ignore their dysregulation. Coaching, on the other hand, can help students learn about and work with these moments so they are better equipped to navigate life's emotional ups and downs.

A final win for executive function coaching is its lasting impact. Coaching conversations expose students to a new way of thinking and problem solving that is adaptable to all areas of their lives. As students explore tools and strategies, they add to a growing personal toolbox they can pull from in other classes and future experiences. Willingham (2009) asserts that we remember what we think about, or, as he more eloquently states, "Memory is the residue of thought" (p. 54). Coaching extends students' thought time on critical metacognitive and executive function tasks, increasing the likelihood that they will internalize and remember what they've created in a coaching conversation.

Figuring Out What Makes Coaching, Coaching

For teachers, coaching students differs from our usual teaching in several ways, and shifting into coach mode can take some practice. We're accustomed to telling students what to do, sometimes on repeat, and getting into the curious questioner mindset of a coach can be a clunky transition. You may find yourself biting your tongue when students are so close to a great idea but not yet seeing it or pausing to regain composure when a response surprises you. It's all part of the coaching adventure, and the results will inspire you to push through the potential discomfort as you watch your students thrive. Being aware of how coaching differs from your usual teaching will help your brain mindfully transition into coach mode, making your coaching moments more effective.

The first way coaching differs from our usual teaching is that it positions us as guides rather than instructors, asking far more questions and giving few directives. When coaching a student or group of students, we still have knowledge to impart, but we enter the conversation without a lesson plan or predetermined end goal. We treat students as self-experts, asking questions that require their inner explorations and creating solutions. While we may step in to share ideas, our coaching is not based on imperatives; that is, we will not demand the "right" answer or the "right" action. Instead, we help students explore their own thinking, values, and experience to determine their next steps and tools. Students who have typically relied on heavy instructions and repetitions will especially benefit from the coaching opportunity to own their success.

To think of it in different terms, ADHD coaches Casey Moore and Cameron Gott (2018) describe taking a stance of "curious accountability." They note that a coach may approach a conversation seeking to help a student explore actions or inactions in a way that raises self-awareness, which drives the continued ability to develop new skills and tools. Students who learn about their brains, their learning processes, and types of tools that work for their unique neurology are primed for lasting behavior change. In other words, through coaching, they will have built a personalized internal navigation system.

A second way coaching differs from teaching is that it is reciprocal and evolutionary in nature. It is the opportunity to walk alongside your student as a thinker, helping them begin to observe, celebrate, and extend their cognitive processes. Your questions and statements will naturally evolve with the student's responses. This is hard work. Coaching can feel like intense listening and can take some heavy cognitive lifting on your part. Forming questions in response to the student's replies will take practice, including practicing with peers. Coaching question stems and statements can support this (page 103).

Coaching also differs from teaching as its emphasis is on perspective. A coach focuses on the student instead of results, holding a student's success as a goal but without an attachment to student actions. A coaching perspective stretches us to be neutral, curious observers, momentarily (and as much as possible) stepping outside of the reality that our students' performance reflects on us as professionals. Table 4.1 (page 92) offers a side-by-side comparison of the differences between a coaching perspective and a teaching perspective.

Over time, you may learn to weave in and out of coach and instructor modes, especially as you begin to spot the coaching opportunities that unfold with your students. It may help to support your own executive function growth process by acknowledging some of the potential challenges of taking a new approach in your pedagogy. You may find that you're employing strategies to support future you, just like your students do, as you experience some bumps in the road of learning.

Students who feel safe and open may respond in surprising ways. As you'll learn in this chapter, it's important to try to remain warm and neutral in your word choice, tone, and facial expression. This is easier said than done! I was once coaching an eighth grader who had more than ten vocabulary worksheets overdue. He was facing summer school and had a newfound determination to dig into strategies and make a good plan with me. We narrowed our plan's focus to his completing at least five of the vocabulary sheets in the next two days because their point value would safely move his grade into passing. He chunked and scheduled his steps, and we ensured he had the resources he needed by planning for any obstacles we could predict. Filled with pride for his growth, I asked what I thought was my wrap-up question: "What's your plan for getting started on this first one?" Deadpan, he said, "Oh, I think for all of them I'm going to cheat." I think my face maintained my commitment to neutrality, but I smiled knowing he was feeling safe enough to be honest. We continued our conversation, explored the potential ramifications of using his friends' answers (his version of "cheating"), and dug into why he thought he needed to take a shortcut or cheat. The opportunity allowed me to help him find even better resources so that he could easily complete the vocabulary worksheets independently. Fumbles like these can be huge moments in coaching conversations. They allow us, as coaches, to grow our skill set and respond consistently. In addition, they give us a deeper peek into a student's thinking, opening doors for resources and strategies that would have remained closed if the student had simply responded as expected or out of blind compliance.

Table 4.1: Coaching Versus Teaching Perspectives

Coaching Perspective	Teaching Perspective
• Student focused • Neutral, open questions • Tools but no specific plan or objective • The guide • Curious	• Student and results focused • Questions seeking specific responses • Specific lesson plans • The expert • Definite

Your coaching conversations will *feel* different. Your usual instructor hat may be, at least metaphorically, replaced with an adventurer's sun hat, and the usual certainty of the right answer will be replaced with curiosity. Coaching conversations are often a spontaneous exploration of student need and creation of strategies, giving real-time support to a student's needs. There will also be moments you plan for coaching conversations, noting a pattern of student need or anticipating an upcoming new demand.

Coaching can entail a quick exchange, a few metacognitive questions, and possibly a strategy suggestion over three to five minutes as you walk the classroom during independent work time. These conversations may also be a bit longer, possibly in a private moment with a student at your desk or outside of class hours, offering an opportunity to strategize about something more complex or emotionally charged. Being able to switch into coach mode will be a game changer. When students seek your help, you will be able to ask transformative questions that put them in charge of their strategies, internally developing an understanding of their brains and growing their executive function.

Coaching conversations create a transformative space that has the following required elements.

- **Time:** Coaching conversations can range from a few minutes to over an hour. They will often be part of a series of explorations, and your students may need several opportunities to explore and strategize with you before they see lasting results. Coaching can be slower than direct instruction, as we cannot predict how long a student will need to find their strategies.
- **No judgment:** Coaching is predicated on relationship and safety. Just like in your usual classroom setting, coaching conversations require students to feel connected and safe. They must understand that you will meet their replies with curiosity and openness, withholding judgment so they are free to be honest and open.

- **Self-regulation:** Coaches hear all kinds of replies. Sometimes they are silly, surprising, upsetting, or evoke emotional reactions from us. Coaching requires that we can get into and stay in a coaching mindset, aware of our own needs and our nonverbal communication. If we are distracted, upset, or rushing, students may interpret our dysregulation as signs that our conversation is not important or won't go well. Monitoring ourselves in coaching is a requisite component, and you will get better at it over time.
- **Flexibility:** Coaches often have questions prepared but not assigned. They may have an area they'd like to explore and support with a student, but they will be prepared to follow the students' lead in that exploration.
- **Coaching not instructing:** In coaching, we're seeking to understand, giving feedback, and helping with reflection. Much of this is without giving direct instruction for the "right" answer or the "correct" way to do things. When offering ideas or suggestions, we stay in coach mode (versus instructor mode) by asking if the student is open to ideas or offering a few solutions and allowing them to choose which one to try.

Over time, you may find that you switch seamlessly between instructor, giving direct lessons and information, to coach, encouraging exploration with gentle guidance. Both roles are important to your students, and both represent the blending of the art and science of pedagogy.

Understanding the Three Phases of Coaching

Coaching generally goes through three main phases in a flexible and dependable cycle. Those phases are (1) rapport, awareness, and a goal; (2) strategies; and (3) accountability and action. While the transition between phases won't likely be obvious to your students, it's important you're aware of the goal of getting students to plan for a solution or strategy of their choice at the end of your conversation.

Phase 1: Developing Rapport, Awareness, and a Goal

The beginning of any coaching conversation is going to include building or affirming rapport, gathering information (awareness of context and student needs), and exploring a goal for the conversation. In this phase, coach and student may catch up or connect through updates or short anecdotes. I have some students who love to swap nature observations and others who like to tell me about their executive function wins for the week. Rapport and connection with students usually lasts just a few minutes.

Once you're feeling connected, it's time to establish awareness of the student's current need. This could apply to an assignment, such as writing a research paper or checking in on a process, like writing in general. Often, you may use declarative statements such as "I notice . . ." or "Your calendar shows this assignment is due on . . ." to confirm the facts and help students begin to also notice potential areas of need. Clarifying questions may help both you and your student notice a pattern or priority worth exploring. Once you've uncovered a potential goal for your coaching conversation, ask the student if they agree that coaching may be helpful in that area. The following is an example of a phase 1 conversation.

Teacher: "Your body language is expressing some stress. Are you able to explore that with me?"

Student: "I just have so much to do."

T: "Makes sense you'd feel stress with a lot of things to do. Would it help to team up and make a plan?"

S: "I guess so. But I don't have a lot of time."

T: "OK, I understand. And luckily, most strategies won't take a lot of time. You're saying you have a lot to do. Where are you keeping your to-do list? In your brain, written down, or online? Or maybe they're coming from lots of places."

S: "Mostly, they're in my brain or on Canvas. I don't know where my planner is."

T: "No biggie. Lots of people use tools other than planners. This time of year, most students are pretty overwhelmed with work. Can I tell you about a couple of strategies to help you feel better and make a plan?"

S: "OK."

This initial phase of coaching can be quick and is often a space where you reinforce trust and safety. Hearing from students what they need both informs the next phase on strategies and may provide ideas for future whole-class executive function lessons.

Phase 2: Choosing Strategies

After identifying a coaching goal, phase 2 sees you both exploring needs and potential approaches. In this phase, we ask coaching questions designed to help students become aware of their current strategies and elevate their self-awareness. Students begin to explore what's going well and what is challenging about the situation, and we extend their thinking and challenge their perspective by offering new ways to consider the circumstances and themselves as learners. We may ask students to tell us what their thoughts are on the challenge, what they've tried, and what they think their brains might need. The question stems for self-awareness that follow later in this chapter are great resources for beginning phase 2.

Midway through phase 2, it's helpful to summarize what you're hearing. By now, students will have recognized their needs and challenges, possibly narrowing to a need for a specific strategy. Summarizing here helps students crystallize their thinking and feel validated before generating a solution. The midway summary may sound like, "I'm hearing you share that [skill] is tricky, and it might be because you're not sure how to . . ." or, "You've identified that your goal is to get [task] done today, and you've found that one of the hardest parts about it is . . ." Following up with "Do I have that right?" gives students a chance to hear their own thinking and to clarify anything you summarized incorrectly.

My personal favorite part of coaching is the tail end of phase 2. We're in brainstorm mode, ideating solutions and generating ideas. This is often where our students surprise us by announcing they've remembered a perfect strategy that they had forgotten or can see how a current tool, used in a new way, will help. If students are stuck here, we can ask if they are open to suggestions and share potential solutions from our classrooms, personal toolboxes, or ideas from their peers. The end of phase 2 can feel exciting, and it will be tempting to leave the coaching conversation on this high. However, phase 3 is an essential component that ensures your student acts and provides a vehicle for loving accountability. The following is an example phase 2 conversation with a student who is feeling overwhelmed. It also shows an example of a brain dump and sort.

Teacher: "I imagine you've been overwhelmed before. What have you done that's helped?"

Student: "I just kind of push through it. I guess working with my friends helps a little bit. Sometimes, I also don't do some of the work that's not worth a lot of points."

T: "Sounds like you have some awesome strategies. Partnering up can help us feel focused, and sometimes our friends can help when we get stuck. In a little bit, maybe you and Tessa can partner up? But, before you go, I'm wondering if I can help a bit more. It seemed like when you were overwhelmed and stressed, you were almost frozen. What did you notice about that feeling?"

S: "It's like my brain shuts off. I can't think, but I know I need to work. I hate it."

T: "Our brains do that sometimes, and it sure is unhelpful, huh? I've stolen some good ideas from other students, to help them get unfrozen when they're stressed. One of them is a brain dump and sort. Want to try that?"

S: "Sure."

T: "All right, it doesn't have to be fancy. Do you want to write, or would you like me to capture your ideas? I'll use some scratch paper."

S: "Will you write it?"

T: "Sure, but I want to make the invisible visible. When you're stuck on your own, you can write your brain dump, you can speak-to-text, or you can ask someone else to capture your ideas. OK, the first part of the brain dump is what it sounds like. You dump out everything that's on your mind that's stressing you out. It doesn't have to be only school stuff."

S: "OK, actually one of the things that isn't school stuff is I need to return my homecoming shoes and get new ones. But I don't know when I'll have time."

T: "Got it. OK, what else?"

S: "Ugh. School is a lot. I have the lab for this class, two assignments in English that are almost done, I have work for my ACT tutor, the volunteer dinner this weekend, a math study guide for a test, and two late homework assignments in history. Oh yeah, and I see the extra credit in this class and the test corrections in Spanish."

T: "Nice. We've captured the tasks you need to do. How do you feel?"

S: "It's weird, but seeing the list makes me feel like it's not all that much."

T: "Isn't it funny how our brains might say it's so much, but when we see it, it seems manageable? That's part of why brain dumps can help. Next, let's swipe through the list and look for the things that we can put on pause. Are there any that stick out as maybe not so important that you can let go for a while (or forever)?"

S: "My homecoming shoes. I just remembered my mom and I are shopping later. That's not a big deal. And the ACT tutor work isn't due until next week."

T: "Cool. Some people like to park the tasks they'll do later somewhere else, so they're not causing stress, but they also don't forget them. Where do you think you could write them for future you?"

S: "In my notes app."

T: "OK, do that real quick. Now, let's go through and ask ourselves about priorities. You can look for the things that are worth the most points or are the most stressful or urgent. Those become the first things in your plan."

S: "Definitely English. Those assignments are fast, and my grade could use some help. The math study guide matters because the test is in a few days."

T: "Brilliant, got it. The plan I'm hearing you develop is that you'll start with English, then move to your math study guide. Run through the rest of your list like that. I'll swing back by to see what you came up with."

As you can see, the strategy conversation relies on our interactions to keep the forward momentum; our questions or observations give students the opportunity to reflect and problem solve, with our guidance. It may be tempting to end the conversation here, after identifying a potential strategy. However, phase 3, accountability and action, is vital to ensuring students follow through with their intended strategies.

Phase 3: Taking Accountability and Action

On the heels of finding a great potential strategy (or two), phase 3 guides students into implementation. The dopamine rush of ideating and feeling hopeful about better results is amazing, but it can distract us from the reality that, when applying our newfound strategies, we may feel a bit less enthused. It's only wishful thinking if we stop at strategy identification. We must use phase 3 to pull students through the wishing and into the doing.

In this phase, we're getting down to logistics by creating a concrete, often visual, plan for the steps to actualize the strategy. You may ask students leading questions like, "How will you remind future you to do [task]?" or "How many reminders do you want to set so future you is ready to rock?" (Both of these assume the student will remind themselves in the future.) Additionally, questions that help students make a plan, such as, "What time will you do [task]?" or "Where do you plan to do [task]?" help students visualize and create a plan that is concrete and doable, based on actual plans rather than blind faith.

Phase 3 also provides a chance to anticipate and plan for potential obstacles standing in the way of students and their goals. Students may want to plan for an effective space and time of day to work, as well as tools to raise or lower their energy, depending on what the task demands of their energy. A common obstacle is students realizing they don't quite understand part of their assignment or strategy but doing so at a specific time when help is not readily available. We can guide students to identify the right now and later resources they have available to them, as well as challenge them to consider, "What will you do if you get stuck or need help?" or even, "How will you know you've hit the point that you're stuck or need help?"

Common student actions in phase 3, often prompted by coaching questions, include setting alarms, identifying steps, calendaring steps, and identifying ways to hold themselves accountable to using their plans. The following is an example of a phase 3 conversation.

> **Teacher:** "How'd the list go?"
>
> **Student:** "I figured out that the big things need to happen tonight, but that will work. After that, it's smaller things. I feel like I can think again. I'll see if Tessa wants to finish the lab reflections with me."
>
> **T:** "Before you ask Tessa, let's see if we can do future you one more favor. Your list is now organized, and I'm hearing you say that you feel like it's not so overwhelming. Let's take it one step further. When and where will you finish the big things tonight?"
>
> **S:** "Oh, good question. I have practice after school, then my brother has piano practice, which is so loud. I have about two hours before practice, and I focus really well at the library. Can I text my mom and ask if I can stay there to work?"
>
> **T:** "Sure. That sounds like a great plan. You can use the same strategy of asking yourself when and where you'll finish the other tasks. It helps make sure you really do the things you want to get done."
>
> **S:** "Thanks."

This final phase of a coaching conversation asks students to envision and plan for their next steps. Instead of hoping they will "just remember," students are asked to clarify what they will do after your conversation and when they will do it. This trains them to think in terms of their future selves, planning for their success and even creating options for support in the future.

Developing Effective Coaching Questions

Does it feel like we ask questions all day? (See what I did there?) Probably! So, what makes a coaching question different? To start a coaching conversation and establish a goal, you're likely going to ask questions that seek specific circumstances and facts. These types of questions may feel more familiar and are not necessarily "coaching" questions. For example, you may establish a goal with a student based on factual due dates or missing work. Once you've identified an area of need with your student, you'll move into the second and third stages, where you ask questions more specifically designed for coaching.

A few key elements are present in most executive function coaching questions. First, executive function coaching questions are generally open ended. They invite many ways of answering and do not seek to be quickly resolved with only a few words. Open-ended questions may focus on the content, the process, or the perspective on an assignment, challenge, or other identified need. For example, a coach may pose questions such as the following to ask students about these different concerns.

- "How can you tell the author intended to . . . ?" asks about content.
- "How might you keep track of the ideas you want to capture in this paragraph?" asks about process.
- "What are your thoughts about your writing here?" asks about perspective.

When students say that overwhelm or stress are what they need help with, challenge them to go a little further. Is it the vast amount of work? Is it that they don't know where to start? Maybe they lose track of time or have busy schedules with competing priorities? Overwhelm is often demonstrative of a stress response, where students may not be able to think as critically while in limbic activation (Pedersen, 2021). This means that examining what is causing the overwhelm can be much more difficult while they are feeling overwhelmed and stressed. Allow the student to reregulate if needed before your coaching conversation. During coaching, your questions will help illuminate both the potential cause of and solutions for the overwhelmed feeling.

Quick, open-ended questions may start with or include the following.

- "Why . . . ?"
- "What do you think about . . . ?"
- "How can you tell . . . ?"
- "What makes you think that . . . ?"
- "What do you notice?"

A second key element of an executive function coaching question is that it assumes ability and competence. While many coaching questions are formed to be free of bias or elements that may lead to a "correct" answer, some questions may have a built-in positive regard for the student. The questions may assume students will find an answer, asking, "What solutions can you think of?" rather than, "Can you think of a solution?" Similarly, coaching questions with a positive bias can express an unwavering belief in the student by already envisioning the student as triumphant over the current challenge, such as asking students, "How will you remember to . . . ?" or "What's your plan for . . . ?" Carefully crafting questions that enlist students on their own teams can have a deep impact, helping students bypass potential impediments by leading them through.

A third element of a coaching question is its authenticity. It's not a command in disguise or a rhetorical or sarcastic response. Coaching questions are genuinely seeking honest replies, unattached to the student's response while still highly committed to the student's overall success. Examples of the types of questions to avoid include commands like, "Why don't you just . . . ?" or "Don't you think you should . . . ?" Rhetorical or sarcastic responses are also not usually helpful, although you'll be able to recognize when humor is accepted and helpful. Rhetorical and sarcastic questions to avoid can sound like, "What did you think would happen?" (after a negative result), "Aren't you just . . . ?" and "Did that seem like it would work?"

Open-ended, authentic, and assuming ability and competence, coaching questions are often answered in wonderfully genuine and even surprising ways. Because we do not expect specific or "right" answers, these questions often open doors of insight into students' inner lives.

Recognizing Question and Coaching Opportunities

Beginning to coach students' executive function skills offers you a parallel experience to that of your students, and a key first step is recognizing *when* to practice your new skills. There are some moments when coaching will be too cumbersome, as when a group of students shares a need that may be better served with a lesson, or simply moments when you don't have the time to explore a student's thinking process. Other moments, however, will be prime opportunities to dig in, recognize a challenge, and co-create a strategy for lasting impact.

Coaching conversations can be impromptu or planned in advance. You may recognize moments that are open for coaching but not have the time to coach. Therefore, in these cases, make a note to coach the student when it works for both of you in a more planned experience. Sometimes, you may end up with notes to yourself to coach several students on similar topics. When that's the case, you are recognizing a pattern of student need, which may be served well in a small coaching group or executive function lesson. Consider the following actions as you begin to find coaching opportunities.

Notice Patterns

When a student or small group of students is struggling with a pattern of behavior, there's a good chance the challenge is rooted in a missing executive function skill. Noticing student patterns, especially the patterns that are bothering you, is a great way to also illuminate a potential coaching moment. Giving directions on what to do (or not do) has probably reached the end of its efficacy, and coaching offers the chance to address challenging patterns in a new way. In my experience, students who rebel against being "told what to do" often respond better to problem solving with a coach. Examples of patterns that are great open doors for coaching include difficulties with initiating and sustaining work, missing work, losing focus in most lessons, above-average disorganization, or avoiding certain types of class activities (for example, written work, projects, or group work).

Reduce Prompt Dependence

Prompt dependence describes when students are unable to begin, adjust, sustain, or even return work on their own without significant prompts from adults. Students who are prompt dependent may need several reminders when working independently, although they seem genuinely interested in completing the work. These students often lack navigation tools to get through the process of studenting. Coaching can help students reduce prompt dependence by growing their self-awareness, helping them see the moments they can look to themselves for strategies rather than waiting for external signals. Coaching also helps students make tools for self-management obvious and easy, empowering them to independently practice until they are competent.

Know the Skills Required for Each Classroom Phase

Students who are struggling with executive function skills may need coaching during the three main phases of independent work: (1) getting started, (2) sustaining effort, and (3) completing an assignment or assessment. Each of these phases demands different executive function skills and presents a chance for us to explore and develop these skills in application to real work in our classrooms.

- **Getting started:** When we ask students to initiate work, we are also asking that they can do the following steps.
    - Deconstruct the task into understood, actionable steps
    - Identify and gather necessary resources
    - Position themselves for focus
    - Advocate for misunderstanding or needed resources
    - Self-regulate to match the mental energy needed to transition from learning and listening into working independently
- **Sustaining effort:** Students need to be able to do the following to sustain effort and attention.
    - Self-regulate for energy and focus

    - Adjust their approach or find additional resources as they notice their progress
    - Evaluate periodically whether their responses and actions satisfy the prompt or requirements
    - Manage distractions
- **Completing an assignment or assessment:** The final phase requires that students can do the following.
    - Self-assess for completeness
    - Recognize "good enough" and move past perfectionism
    - Identify the steps for returning work
    - Communicate about returned work
    - Track their completed work as part of their grade management

Knowing the skills required for each main phase of independent work illuminates many areas where we can boost the identified skills with environmental supports, lessons, and targeted coaching questions. This awareness also shows us just how many underdeveloped skills may be getting in the way of student performance, offering new hope for supporting targeted student skill growth.

Provide Opportunities to Regulate

Students who already are or become dysregulated will not be ready for traditional learning. Their brains will be activated in areas outside of the prefrontal cortex, where executive function is most prevalent, and they may need time and tools to enter a state of regulation (Pedersen, 2021). This can open an opportunity for coaching, as they may want to regain composure but not yet know how. In these moments, consider offering students a moment to reflect on their body and brain signals of dysregulation, personal tools to calm themselves, and perspectives and self-talk phrases that will serve them in future moments of emotional dysregulation.

Reflect at Key Checkpoints

Natural checkpoints, such as grading periods and the end of a term, provide a great chance for students to reflect on their experiences, tools, and potential changes moving forward. A coaching conversation leads this reflection from awareness to application. We can guide students through the coaching phases, even as a group, so that they are not only aware of their reflections but also have actionable steps to apply what they learned.

Making Coaching Executive Function Friendly for Yourself

Knowing the profound impact of executive function coaching is exciting, and you may be eager to start! As with all pedagogical changes, coaching for executive function skills will stretch and challenge you. Let's use our own executive function skills of awareness, planning, and organizing to make coaching brain friendly and help you avoid some of the common pitfalls when coaching. The following actions will help you do just that.

Make Space Your Ally

Just as we considered in chapter 2 (page 35), your classroom space can be an executive function–building ally, and it's no different when you're coaching. Consider that you may end up coaching during different moments of the day, next to students as they work, back at your desk, or even outside the door for privacy. This requires being aware of your options for coaching spaces as well as having a plan for the rest of the class while you are coaching for a few minutes. Some teachers find that using a signal for when they're available or not available can help reduce interruptions during a coaching conversation. Others like to keep an extra chair near their desks so students can easily join them for a coaching conversation. Make a mental movie of what you, the student you're coaching, and the rest of the class will be doing and what furniture or materials you will be using during coaching moments. You can have the required setup and resources ready to go, reducing the barriers for future you.

Have Question Stems Handy

Many of my coach colleagues like to say, "Your brain is a factory, not a warehouse," as a reminder that it's unreasonable to try to memorize important things. You can honor this truth by using the questions and coaching statement stems that appear later in this chapter and keeping them handy in several locations in your classroom. The list can help you plan, adjust your approach during coaching, or get you started when you feel stuck in a coaching conversation. It may also serve as a physical prompt; just its presence may remind you to do some coaching while students work independently!

Leave Space for Directives

One of the most common concerns teachers share with me about coaching often sounds like, "Wait, if I no longer tell students what to do, then how will they ever learn?" This makes sense. Our traditional education model is largely instructive, and opening to the vast world of student ideas is a big shift. There is room for directives in coaching. You can state facts, "Your essay is due Monday," as well as state questions for forced choice, "Of the three strategies we explored, which one are you committed to trying?" We're not abandoning our instruction with coaching but expanding it. We're engaging students to explore and innovate but with our ready guidance every step of the way. Just like a sports coach will instruct when they notice a player making a mistake, a teacher coach may offer solutions for specific needs. The difference is in the consultation; coaching will enlist a student's deep participation, allowing for quick feedback and practice.

Know Coaching Is Slower Than Giving Commands

Coaching requires a bit of a tradeoff because it's often slower than simply telling a student what to do. Students may need time to become aware of their challenges, explore solutions, test them, and reflect on them. That's a lot more steps than hearing and enacting a teacher's direction. Keeping this difference in mind can help you feel less frustrated with the coaching process. Your students will grow in lasting ways through coaching, but it takes a bit longer. It's normal to feel like you didn't co-create the just-right strategy or that your student just isn't getting it (yet). Rest assured that every coaching session is meaningful in that it sends two powerful messages to your student: (1) they are worth a deep investment of time and energy, and (2) the coaching process of becoming aware and solving problems is available to them. With that perspective, it can be easier to ride the wave of coaching wins and stagnations. When you coach, you and your students can't lose.

Start With Areas That Feel Exciting or Neutral

Since coaching may feel brand new and clunky, consider starting with the students or executive function areas that light you up. Are there tools you know will help and you want to coach on them to start? Are there students who are "this close" to having a good system or approach and may need that extra feedback and practice? Remember that we often teach classroom routines or new skills in the context of fun for students, and this approach is available to you too. Any practice in coaching will hone your skills and boost your confidence, so why not choose some areas that inspire you to start?

Partner Up With Another Teacher

Teaming up with others to observe and be observed coaching takes guts, but its potential for growth and connection may be worth the leap! Consider finding ways to give and get feedback as you learn to have executive function coaching conversations. Just as the quick feedback of coaching ensures students' growth, your getting and giving feedback about coaching makes you a more aware, more skilled coach. If you're not available to physically observe one another, consider making an audio recording (with parent and student permission) to listen to together. It can help you to hear yourself, celebrate your wins, notice your wobbles, and come up with potential new ways to improve your coaching practice.

Know What to Avoid

As much as a great question can unlock a student's brain, a question perceived as hurtful can shut a student down. It's helpful to honor that you may *think* some sarcastic comments (because you're human) and to challenge yourself to keep them only as thoughts. Responses to avoid are those that may be emotionally charged, are overtly confrontational, assume negative intent or low capacity, or position a student to become defensive. Examples of questions and responses to avoid include the following.

- "Why can't you just . . . ?"
- "Don't you think you should . . . ?"
- "How come this student can, but you can't?"
- "What did you think would happen?" (sarcastically)
- "That was a dumb choice (or action)."
- "Did you really think [choice] would work?"
- "Why don't you care?"
- "Why don't you pay attention?"
- "Why can't you listen?"
- "Why don't you try harder?"

Adjust Coaching for Individual Personalities

Coaching is cognitive heavy lifting for you and your students. As such, you may need to provide yourself and your student with a slower pace, more wait time between responses, or follow-up questions. Another piece to consider is who is doing the talking. A sign of a good coaching conversation is when you find yourself doing about one-third of the talking, with your student doing the rest. This may take time to develop and can vary from day to day. You may have students who hardly talk and some who hardly pause; there's room for both experiences, and you'll certainly find ways to approach each, honing your questions for your shyer students and finding gentle ways to interrupt or pause students who may talk without stopping.

Plan to Observe Body Language

Students' words and nonverbal communication both send messages during coaching, and it can help to watch students as they reply. As you'll learn next, students will give us signs of what they are experiencing, possibly exposing why they may say they "don't know" and showing us a potential path forward.

Handling Students Saying "I Don't Know"

You might wonder how to handle a coaching situation when students say the three dreaded words "I don't know." "I don't know" can feel like a roadblock when coaching a student. As you try to reroute a question, it might be tempting to assume the student isn't interested, isn't trying, or possibly genuinely has no clue how to respond. Too many "I don't knows" from a student may leave you feeling like coaching isn't working or the student won't ever engage with you. As with any new skill set, coaching will feel clunky and awkward at times, and the "I don't know" moments will be some of the toughest. However, there is hope because we can explore the possible origins of "I don't know" and match them up with response types. We can play with factors and strategies to give our students what they need to engage with coaching. In my experience, I have yet to meet a student who will commit to "I don't know" for the entirety of the school year. With our unwavering belief and persistence in finding the coaching environment and questions that work for each student, we will help unlock new self-awareness and reflection tools for our students.

Knowing the origins of a student's "I don't know" can determine the best way to reply. For example, a student who simply missed the question needs a repeat, but the student who is embarrassed in front of peers needs a private place to talk. It can be incredibly tricky to know a student's metamessage, which is their underlying meaning. However, I've discovered the following patterns and indications of these patterns that help illuminate what students may be experiencing.

- **I missed the question:** Sometimes, students reply with "I don't know" because they didn't attend to the question or forgot it quickly. Rather than admit they missed the question, they may respond automatically, saying they don't have a response. Many students have a history of being shamed for not paying attention, so it may feel safer to pretend to be ignorant rather than honest about a lapse in attention or memory. If you suspect a student missed the question, it's OK to ask them if they'd like you to repeat it, or allow some time and then ask again. Signs I've observed that indicate my students missed the question include a sudden "wake up" look on their face, where they seem to jolt into the present moment, or noticing their attention or alertness fade for a moment.
- **I don't understand the question:** Sometimes, "I don't know" reflects that students haven't or can't process the question as originally asked. They could be unaware that they don't understand the question and, instead, offer a

quick reply to stop the interaction. In these instances, it can help to ask them if the question made sense or if they'd like it phrased in a different way. Signs a student didn't understand the question might include a marked change in the pace and content of their replies. For example, they go from solid answers to "I don't know" or short answers. They may also have a confused look, however brief, as they reply to you.

- **I feel ashamed of my answer or scared to tell the truth:** We know executive function is closely tied to morality in many cultures and classrooms. A student who replies with "I don't know" may be covering some shame or fear they feel about revealing an executive function deficit. They may have a history of being told to focus or try harder, and they may expect—and want to avoid—a similar response from you. In this case, you have the following options: (1) allow more time and space to develop trust in your relationship, (2) adjust your approach to share possible answers from other real or fictitious students, or (3) probe a bit to see if answering feels strange or scary to them. Signs that a student is emotionally reluctant to respond could include changes in their body language, facial expression, or vocal tone or volume. You can also gauge emotional reluctance if you know a student's educational history, which may include previous conflicts or blame for their needs.
- **I'm processing something else, possibly something emotional, and need a second before I respond:** Sometimes, students reply with "I don't know" to buy themselves a bit of time. Too many coaching questions in a row can feel overwhelming, and a student saying they don't know can pause the rapid-fire questions, letting teachers recalibrate their reply. Students also may be distracted by an intruding thought or emotion and need a moment to process it, so it's out of their working memories. In these cases, it's OK to ask if they need a moment. This can help them build self-awareness around their own signals of overwhelm or distraction. You can plan to resume coaching after a few seconds or take a break and come back later or another day. Possible signs a student needs processing time include looking or turning away from you, changes in voice tone to indicate possible irritation or overwhelm, and physically making space between you.
- **I don't want to answer in front of people; it's embarrassing:** Teen brains are particularly tuned to their peers, which is an appropriate developmental evolution (Siegel, 2014). However, this may drive a student to avoid answering something potentially embarrassing in front of their peers. Students may cover with "I don't know" to avoid having to continue a conversation or share something private or shameful. Signs a student is

feeling embarrassed could include looking around them, flushing in the face, responding quietly, or showing nervous gestures. In this case, it's important to have options for private coaching spaces. You can also offer students a chance to come back later or respond through writing or other means, allowing them the out for the moment. Forcing a student to reply when they do not feel socially safe will backfire because they may give a false or pat reply or disengage in the present moment and possibly in the future.

- **I'm actually out of ideas or can't find the idea in my brain:** Sometimes, "I don't know" is literal. Students may be stuck, out of ideas, or hit a roadblock that needs your help to overcome. Signs they are out of ideas can include showing high interest in the conversation, confused facial gestures, or looking up or to the side in thought. In these cases, it's appropriate to ask if the student is open to new ideas. You can direct them to resources in the classroom or from your lessons, share novel ideas, or suggest ideas from peers.

The more you get to know your students and the more comfortable you become with coaching, the better you will be able to discern what a student's "I don't know" may mean. While the specific response will be determined by the potential need driving the "I don't know" statement, there are several options for your reply, as exemplified in table 4.2.

Table 4.2: Ways to Respond to "I Don't Know"

Reframe It	• If you did know, what might you say? • If you had to help a friend with a similar challenge, what would you suggest? • What do you know for sure won't work? (Ask the opposite.)
Try a Different Route	• OK, let's see if we can figure it out with a different question. • I can try to ask that a different way. • Where do you think you could look for help figuring this out?
Clarify	• Something got wonky here. Can you tell me more about feeling like you don't know? • It seems like something might have stolen your brain. Want me to ask again?
Offer Solutions	• Seems like this is tricky. Can I offer a few ideas? • I've worked with lots of students who get stuck here too. Can I tell you a few of their ideas?

Visit ***go.SolutionTree.com/lifeskills*** *for a free reproducible version of this table.*

Responding to "I don't know" will feel clunky at first. You will also likely feel like *you* don't know sometimes; I know I do, even after years of executive function coaching! The one constant to keep in mind is *we stick with the clunky moments.* We "roll with the resistance," as my therapist friend says, allowing the awkward moments to be part of the experience. Our bumpy coaching moments can become models of persisting when things are new, cognitively demanding, or not yet mastered. Even when students say they don't know or become emotionally dysregulated during our interactions, we can pause with phrases that acknowledge the challenge and demonstrate our commitment to finding solutions.

Using Questions and Coaching Statement Stems

Shifting from giving directions to encouraging exploration can be tricky. Like practicing any new skill, it can help to have a reference. The coaching questions and statements in the following sections are available for you to try out in your coaching conversations with students. They are organized by phase of the coaching cycle, so you can move students through gaining self-awareness and setting a goal (phase 1), choosing a strategy (phase 2), and creating self-accountability and taking action (phase 3). You may notice that some of the phrases and questions apply to more than one phase of the coaching cycle. You may also notice that you'll have some favorites. Consider keeping the list of questions and declarative statements handy in a few places around the room so they're available when you need them in planned or impromptu conversations.

Questions and Coaching Statement Stems for Phase 1

A key component of executive function coaching is developing students' self-awareness, including their understanding of their own brains, how they think (metacognition), and what types of environments and strategies work best for them. Open-ended questions, like those in table 4.3 (page 110), can afford students the opportunity to stop and reflect, often for the first time, on their experiences as learners. Not only do they become aware of the answer to the question, but also, asking the question makes students more aware of the process of inquiry about self. Keep these questions with you as a guide when coaching students.

Questions, Coaching Statement Stems, and Declarative Statements for Phase 2

After you've explored students' needs, it may be time to shift into a more solutions-focused mindset with coaching. This is often where you mix declarative

Table 4.3: Question Stems and Statements for Phase 1—Developing Rapport, Self-Awareness, and a Goal

Observations or Circumstances	Questions and Coaching Statements
Student is stuck or seems uncomfortable	• What's going right? • What are you noticing right now in your body or brain? • It seems like you've had a shift in how you're feeling. What signs is your body showing you? • It seems like you've had a shift in how you're thinking. What signs are your body or brain showing you?
Student is making progress or starting to plan next steps	• What's going right? • That seemed to go well. What do you think went right? • Where do you picture having a tricky moment? • What might support or limit future you? • What does this make you think about yourself as a learner? • Sounds like you've figured something out. Let's state it in a way that tells about your brain: "I have a brain that . . ." • Which parts are still kind of fuzzy or unclear? • Which part are you dreading or feels overwhelming? • Which part seems easy to you? What about it makes it feel easy?
Student is emotionally dysregulated	• I notice you're having some feelings about that. Tell me more. • It seems like your body or brain might need . . . What are your thoughts?
Open-ended questions	• What are your thoughts about [assignment, test, peer conflict]? • How can you tell? • What are your thoughts? • Tell me more about what you understand about . . .

Visit ***go.SolutionTree.com/lifeskills*** *for a free reproducible version of this table.*

statements (facts or observations stated neutrally) with questions aimed to help students develop strategies. You may provide students with potential strategies and models, but offer these as invitations, not directives. In this line of coach questioning, you will usually follow up with questions to confirm commitment to a strategy and, as listed in table 4.4, explore the student's plan for enacting their plans or strategies.

Table 4.4: Question Stems and Statements for Phase 2—Choosing Strategies

Observations or Circumstances	Questions and Coaching Statements
Defining the problem	• It seems like you've identified that . . . is challenging right now. • OK, I hear you saying you might want some strategies to work on . . . • Would you like to team up and see if we can plan for . . . • I'm hearing you say . . . Do I have that right? • Let me see if I heard you right. • It sounds like you've identified [feeling]. Tell me more.
Creating solutions	• You've had tricky moments like these in the past. What worked back then that you might want to try now? • I had another student struggling with the same kind of thing. They tried [strategy]. Is that something that sounds like it would work for you? • I've stolen a few good ideas from students over the years. What do you think about . . . ? • Can I offer some potential ideas and you can tell me what sounds good to try? • I have some ideas from other students. Can I share a few and you can pick what might work for you?
Planning for potential hurdles or reflecting on challenges	• Let's practice what . . . will look like. • Sounds like that didn't go as well as you thought. What do you think was wonky? What would you like to try differently?
Open-ended statements	• Tell me more about . . . • Some people like to . . .

Visit ***go.SolutionTree.com/lifeskills*** *for a free reproducible version of this table.*

Questions and Coaching Statement Stems for Phase 3

The questions and coaching statements in table 4.5 will help you create accountability without imperatives because you're helping students plan to use the tools they've identified would help them best. You may want to pause to let the students take their first action or set their reminder before ending the coaching conversation.

Coaching can feel like magic. As a reward for slowing down and exploring with a student, you both get to learn about that student's thinking and also often develop strategies that feel organic and easy for the student to internalize. Even when the strategies created are not wholly effective, which is a normal result when we experiment with strategies, the student still learns about their brain, available strategies, and the process of problem solving. In essence, when you and your students engage in curious coaching conversations, you can't lose.

Key Points

The key points from the chapter include the following.

- Coaching to develop students' executive function involves using a coach's mindset and tools. It is a curious conversation that grows students' competence by increasing self-awareness and strategies.
- You can use coaching on the fly or in planned moments.
- There are many ways to respond to (and understand) when students say "I don't know."
- Coaching questions and statement stems are useful tools to help you engage in coaching conversations.

Potential Actions

After reading the chapter, consider taking these potential actions.

- Print or digitally save the coaching questions and stems for your easy use.
- Plan to coach one student as an introduction to coaching. On the same day, plan to take five to ten minutes to reflect on the experience.
- Team up with your grade-level or subject team to plan coaching together. You may consider each testing a coaching conversation and planning to reflect on it together. Or you may want to schedule observing one another.

Table 4.5: Question Stems and Statements for Phase 3—Taking Accountability and Action

Observations or Circumstances	Questions and Coaching Statements
Helping a student plan to see their strategies through or get started	• How do you plan to get started on . . . ? • What are three ways you could . . . ? • What would help you get started? • What's your plan for . . . ? • How will you remember to . . . ? • How can you make that (new strategy) easy for future you? • You've identified a great strategy. How will you be sure to . . . ? • What would feel good to have done? • When will you start . . . ? • Where do you want to work on. . . ? • What might help future you when you work on . . . ? • What do you want . . . to look like?
Helping a student anticipate potential hurdles	• What do you think might be tricky when you use that plan or strategy? • How can we plan to support future you? • How can you use examples of your past strategies and success to help yourself moving forward? • What kind of environment does your brain need to be able to work on . . . ?
Helping a student move through resistance	• Is there something easy you can start with to get your momentum going? • Would you like to start with the hardest task, since you have me here to help right now? • In the past, you've noticed that . . . is pretty challenging for you. What strategy do you want to use when . . . gets tricky again?
Open-ended statements	• I noticed that when you . . . it seemed to . . . • Let's practice what . . . will look like. • Have you considered . . . ? • Some people like to . . .

Visit ***go.SolutionTree.com/lifeskills*** *for a free reproducible version of this table.*

Journal or Discussion Questions

After reading the chapter, answer these questions in your journal or within a book discussion group.

- Reflect on a moment when you had excellent, impactful coaching. What went right? What were the components you can identify that really made that interaction successful?
- How do you feel about students saying "I don't know"? Do you tend to give them an answer right away, assume they aren't trying, or have varied responses? How do you plan to respond when students reply that they don't know?

CHAPTER 5
EXPLORING EXECUTIVE FUNCTION DEFICITS

A dear friend, who is not a teacher, grimaces as she asks if she can ask me something privately. She's embarrassed to admit it, but since her son's ADHD diagnosis, she's wondered if the doctors got it wrong, or worse, if her nine-year-old is faking his symptoms. She explains that he doesn't seem to actually have problems paying attention when he wants to. "The kid can watch videos about plastic building bricks or build with them for hours," she laments. "But it's like his butt is on fire when it's time to sit and do homework." These observations are real and raw for my friend, but she is not alone. Most of us have observed, in ourselves or in our students, the inconsistencies of executive function challenges. We may have wondered why sometimes, in some contexts, things seem to go just fine, but in others, we or our students just fall apart. We observe the contrasts between different days, times of days, classes, situations, and settings and think, "Well, if it was truly a problem, we'd see it everywhere!"

My friend's assumptions are common; when we observe differing executive function abilities across contexts and times, it's not a far leap to assume the difference is related to

CHAPTER SNEAK PEEK

By the end of this chapter, you will understand the following.

- Why executive function skills are inconsistent and sometimes confusing to observers
- The conditions and circumstances that impair executive function
- How to assess executive function skills
- The stealth manifestations of executive function deficits

effort, however incorrect that is. I believe that because executive function is impacted by a myriad of factors and the skills are interconnected, the likelihood that executive function will be constant throughout our lives is incredibly low. For example, sleep and hydration both impact mental performance, including the use of executive function skills (Aubrey, 2018; Randolph, 2020). Our logical brains assume that if a student can do something once, it shows mastery that becomes a new baseline, and we expect the student to perform at that level moving forward. Yet, with a quick reflection, we can see the flaws in that assumption.

Let's pretend you're a busy teacher, getting through another busy Monday. Over the weekend, you were able to get into the zone and jam through updating grades and answering emails, condensing three hours of work into one. Your brain was on fire. You got to work early Monday morning and have about an hour to jam again before students arrive. You sit down to work, and, what's this? Where is your brain spark now? You open an email, but its title reminds you that you forgot to reply to your sister's text, so you grab your phone to text her back. While your phone is open, a shopping app alerts you that you didn't check out your cart. OK, you start doing that quickly. A few minutes later, you're standing at the whiteboard, ready to write the day's agenda, and the bell rings for class. Your autopilot, distracted brain is genuinely shocked that the hour has passed, and you wonder again, what happened to fire brain?

Having a big executive function win feels amazing, but it is not the same thing as mastering an executive function skill. These spikes in capacity are positive signs of improvement and are part of the very nonlinear experience of change (Slade, 2024). It's to be expected that our capacities ebb and flow throughout and between days, since ever-changing factors such as hydration, stress, and fatigue impact executive function (Aubrey, 2018). Because *executive function* describes the mostly invisible mental work we all do, our option for observing it is to monitor behaviors. But we know that behaviors are the tip of an internal iceberg, possibly not revealing the trials and errors, the strategies, and the tenacity that lead to the observable action.

In this chapter, we will explore the nuances of executive function, including what conditions impair executive function, assessing executive dysfunction, understanding stealth manifestations of executive function deficits, and making a plan and a promise. By the end of the chapter, you will have a greater understanding of the broad impact of executive function and a set of diagnostic tools to identify executive function needs in your students.

Noticing Executive Function Impairments

Neurology researchers joke that the human brain is the eighth wonder of the world, and I tend to agree. As much as we use brains, we still know relatively little about them. A hallmark of the human brain is its inconsistency. So many factors impact our brain's performance, it can be hard to predict or depend on our brain's capacities. Often, the environment and the student's interactions with it can make executive function deficits easier or more difficult to observe. As my friend described earlier, her son can "pay attention" to plastic bricks but struggles with homework, reflecting inconsistent attention abilities depending on the task. Consider the following scenario.

> Forget game face: The confusion is radiating from me. Angel sits at his desk, kicking the band on the legs of his chair, a mint crunching between his teeth, his favorite gel pen nearly rolling off his desk. We've employed all the engagement and activation strategies that usually work, yet he hasn't added a single letter to his essay and it's due in about an hour. This is the same eighth grader who wrote nearly two pages in an hour yesterday, mentioning on the way out that he "really got in the zone." Today, it's like his brain has been replaced, and I'm perplexed. How can the same student perform so very differently one day to the next?

For students like Angel, the day-to-day variability of performance can be frustrating. From the outside, it could look like a lack of effort, making it easy to assume that his not writing that day was due to lack of desire to do so. However, the lens of executive function clarifies what many in education, like Greene (2010) and Emily Kircher-Morris (2021), repeat: Students do well when they can. Our safest assumption is that students struggle or fail to perform when they don't have the skills or variables that they need.

Angel has ADHD. His brain struggles to manage his attention, his focus scattering in response to external and internal stimuli. His body needs a high amount of movement to feel regulated. And he's a teenage boy with a human brain. The "zone" he slipped into the day before could have been a result of a successful recipe of factors—maybe he slept well the night before. Maybe he hydrated, exercised, was less distracted by the outside world, felt interested in and capable of the work, ate well that day, and employed the right strategies. The following day, when it was harder for him to write, any one (or likely several) of the ingredients in his previous recipe for success could have been off.

"I feel like my brain broke today," Angel tells me, and my heart hurts with him. I see the difference in him, and I can imagine the battle he's engaged with inside of his head, with an invisible "enemy." Although he can play with factors and tease out what really seems to impact him, that takes time and concerted effort, luxuries he lacks under this essay deadline.

With the detective perspective, we are called to see through a new lens, changing our role as educators to helping students write the tech manuals for owning their unique brains. We help them become aware of, experiment with, adapt, and then adopt strategies and variables that generate their personal success. Our students, and the world we live in, are changing constantly, so it is not our job to lock in their success formula forever; no one would be served well by a permanent solution to evolving challenges. Instead, we help them explore and understand the factors and strategies that best serve their brains and bodies, empowering them with a toolbox for life.

Understanding Conditions That Impair Executive Function

In the introduction (page 1), we explored how our brains develop back to front, making our executive function skills, mostly taking place in our prefrontal cortexes, the last to fully integrate between ages twenty-five and thirty (Randolph, 2020). By their ages alone, our students have underdeveloped executive function skills. But age is not the only factor to impact students' executive function because both permanent and temporary conditions impair executive function (Cleveland Clinic, 2024). While we cannot control most of the variables that impair executive function, it's important to recognize where we can show students both understanding and support.

Many neurological conditions that impact the brain are associated with executive dysfunction. They may affect the prefrontal cortex or delay communication between parts of the brain. Neurological conditions known to impact executive function include cerebral palsy, ADHD, autism spectrum disorder, learning disabilities, traumatic brain injuries, Creutzfeldt-Jakob disease, dementia, and multiple sclerosis (El Wafa, El Latif Ghobashy, & Hamza, 2020). Mood or mental health disorders such as post-traumatic stress disorder, anxiety, and depression can also impair executive function; although, the mechanism for these is likely an activation of the limbic system, which serves to make communicating with the prefrontal cortex (our executive function hub) less effective (Feller et al., 2020).

Students with significantly impaired executive function present a mind-bending challenge for teachers because we see students who look and mostly act similarly to their same-aged peers. However, their brains' capacities for some executive function skills, like impulse and emotional control, working memory, and time management, could be more aligned with those of students up to three grades below, or 30 percent to 40 percent below their same-age peers (ADDitude, n.d.). A fifteen-year-old sophomore, who can engage with grade-level work, may also have some executive function skills at the level of a seventh grader, along with some at the eighth, ninth, or tenth grade levels, too. That gap and variance between executive function skills and a student's age can be profoundly frustrating for all involved. The student will feel like they've maxed out effort but still miss the mark, and teachers will feel duped that the student who understands grade-level content also can't manage independent work time or use a calendar system. Additionally, as we learned in chapter 1 (page 13), executive function and IQ are independent of one another. Students can be gifted learners with high IQs and also have executive function skill sets at similar levels to students three grades below. As one parent told me, "It's like he has a Ferrari engine with a Honda Civic car body; the mismatch is mind boggling!"

Each brain is different from the next. The neurodiversity movement asserts that brains come in a wide variety of styles and that neurodivergent brains—those that differ from the accepted "norm" —are not incorrect because of their differences. Some brains may have multiple neurodivergent conditions; it's not uncommon to have both autism and ADHD, for example. As you read about the brain differences in the following sections, consider what a student with one or more of these conditions experiences in the classroom, based on their neurology. This empathy walk can deepen your understanding and even spark ideas to reach and support your neurodivergent students.

Students With ADHD

Students with ADHD do not have a deficit of attention. Instead, their attention is inconsistent and sometimes difficult to manage (Dodson, 2024). Psychiatrist William Dodson (2024) describes ADHD as an "interest-based nervous system," meaning brains with ADHD respond with increased and more sustained attention when something is interesting, new, or exciting. This is not the same thing as actively choosing to pay attention to something. Brains with ADHD actually send neurotransmitters (chemical messengers) in response to outside stimuli. The reverse is also true. Brains with ADHD will not consistently send out neurotransmitters if a stimulus doesn't activate their nervous system, making focusing and sustaining effort incredibly hard. As many students and loved ones with ADHD have shared, it's like they are at war with themselves internally, their brains wanting to do a task but unable to generate the required "focus juice" to do so. Students with ADHD have differences in the activities of their neurotransmitters, particularly dopamine, and some of the regions of the brain, like the thalamus, which manages impulses

(WebMD, n.d.). It is genetic and does not reflect poor parenting, impaired morality, or students "not trying hard enough."

While we use the term *ADHD* broadly, the condition is categorized into three types: (1) ADHD-hyperactive, (2) ADHD-inattentive, and (3) ADHD-combined presentations (American Psychiatric Association, 2013). Students with ADHD-hyperactive experience high levels of physical and mental activity and impulsivity, while students with ADHD-inattentive struggle with managing their attention (American Psychiatric Association, 2013). As you may assume, the combined presentation describes when students experience both hyperactivity and difficulties with attention.

ADHD can also impact other areas of a student's life. Impulsivity, emotional dysregulation, and rejection sensitivity are also reported by people with ADHD (Dodson, 2025). Executive dysfunction is a hallmark of ADHD, compounded by the need for sustained attention to use many executive functions. In the classroom, students may become overstimulated by sensory input. They also may go inside their own minds for stimulation when the environment is not providing stimulation.

You will likely have students with ADHD in your classroom each year. Connect with them to understand their experiences, needs, and unique perspectives. These often nonlinear thinkers may reveal themselves as great problem solvers and contributors to class discussions, as their unique brains can often appreciate many potential paths of thought.

Students With Autism Spectrum Disorder

Autism spectrum disorder describes a neurological and developmental disorder that manifests as difficulties with communication and social interactions, as well as rigid or repetitive patterns of behavior (Mayo Clinic, 2018). It is described as a spectrum because of the range in intensity and symptom manifestation (American Psychiatric Association, 2013). Asperger's syndrome was folded into autism spectrum disorder in the fifth edition of the *Diagnostic and Statistical Manual of Mental Disorders* (American Psychiatric Association, 2013). Many adults are using the terminology of being "autistic" instead of saying "a person with autism." Your student may have a preference, and it's important to honor that.

Students with autism may not correctly interpret or respond to social or environmental cues for them to adjust their behavior or respond to stimuli (WebMD, 2018). They may interpret speech literally, struggling with sarcasm or idioms (WebMD, 2018). Often, students with autism have high sensory needs and low sensory tolerances (American Psychiatric Association, 2013). In addition, they may need to self-soothe with sensory input or avoid sensory overload (Boroson, 2022).

Students with autism spectrum disorder may need support learning to speak or to communicate their thoughts effectively and with awareness of social norms (Boroson, 2022). In the classroom, they may struggle with group work or interacting with peers and teachers (Boroson, 2022). Autism spectrum disorder is closely associated with executive function deficits; in fact, much of the research on executive function comes from autism studies (American Psychiatric Association, 2013). People with autism can vary in intelligence, as it is not an intellectual disorder but can occur along with intellectual disorders. It's important not to assume low capacity when a student struggles with self-expression.

Your students on the autism spectrum may share some traits with one another, but expect that they will vary, as all students do. These students often benefit from similar executive function supports to your students with ADHD. Students with autism may also need guidance navigating social communication, such as cueing them in group discussions or helping them draft emails that hit the desired social tone and message. You may find that your students with autism provide unique and thought-provoking questions and perspectives, including their personal learning and executive function strategies.

Students With Specific Learning Disabilities

A specific learning disability (SLD) describes a neurodevelopmental disorder that impairs one or more of the three major academic realms: reading, mathematics, and writing (American Psychiatric Association, 2013). According to the U.S. Department of Education (2004), diagnosis of an SLD requires meeting the following criteria.

- A student has academic difficulties persisting for six months or more, despite interventions.
- A student has skills lower than expected when looking at their capacity.
- The student's struggles are not exclusively related to identified disadvantages, such as poverty, insufficient instruction, lack of English proficiency, or hearing or vision problems.

Some SLDs impact executive function directly and some impair executive function because they draw resources away by attempting to overcome the processing disorders (Zeigler Dendy & Hughes, n.d.).

Specific learning disabilities include, but are not limited to, dyslexia (reading difficulties), dyscalculia (mathematics difficulties), and dysgraphia (writing difficulties; U.S. Department of Education, 2004). Students with SLDs are not less intelligent; their brains have processing challenges that make learning or expressing their learning difficult, unrelated to their IQ (American Psychiatric Association, 2013). Students with SLDs may benefit from instructional interventions to provide different ways and more time to learn (CAST, 2024a).

Chances are high you also have students with SLDs in your classroom. These students' executive function needs will vary, but many SLDs impair executive function. Similar to students with ADHD and autism, students with SLDs benefit from accommodations and instructional approaches that minimize the impact of their learning differences while supporting the skill development. An additional consideration for students with SLDs is to carefully consider the academic areas impacted by the SLD, adjusting both how students receive and demonstrate their learning. For example, a student with dysgraphia may need to take notes differently, like audio recording a lecture. The same student may also benefit from the option to verbalize their answers instead of writing them or to use speech-to-text software for assessments. Students with SLDs may already know about and share learning strategies, adding a richness and experience to your executive function discussions and your classroom in general.

Other Factors Impacting Executive Function

Temporary or lifestyle conditions can also impact executive function. Many of these factors are outside of our direct control, yet being aware of them can help in many ways. First, we can connect lagging executive function with life conditions rather than assuming a student is lacking effort or values. A natural extension of this awareness is to move into our detective perspective where we're looking for variables to adapt. Next, we can help students become aware of what can help or hurt their brains and executive function. We can also empower families to know about and change some factors that improve executive function, and we can speak up for the systemic changes often necessary for families to access resources to sustain positive changes. Lifestyle and temporary conditions that impact executive function include the following.

- **Hydration:** Researcher Mindy Millard-Stafford analyzed over thirty studies and found that "when people are mildly dehydrated they really don't do as well on tasks that require complex processing or on tasks that require a lot of their attention" (Aubrey, 2018). In fact, one study showed a 12 percent increase in errors, which could mean a big difference in engagement and successful completion of work for our students.
- **Long COVID and other illnesses:** A systematic review explains that the mechanism for changes in executive function after a COVID-19 infection is unclear, but numerous studies indicate negative changes to executive function after healing from the acute phases of COVID-19 (Panagea et al., 2024). Several other conditions, including neurodevelopmental disorders

like cerebral palsy, traumatic brain injuries, and tumors also can impair executive function (Cleveland Clinic, n.d.).

- **Nutrition:** Children's and teens' brains are undergoing myelination (forming the myelin sheath around their neuronal axons) and synaptogenesis (the creation of new synapses). Several nutrients, such as iron, Omega-3 polyunsaturated fatty acids, zinc, iodine, and B12 and folate, are critical in phases of significant, rapid growth, and a lack of these nutrients can be detrimental to students' development (Costello, Geiser, & Schneider, 2021).
- **Lack of sleep:** Disturbed or inadequate sleep is connected with poorer inhibitory control and working memory, with possible indirect impairments of cognitive flexibility (Chen, Wang, Wang, Zhang, & Wu, 2021). In short, brains that lack quality sleep may struggle with impulsivity, working memory, and flexibility in navigating the day's cognitive demands.
- **Limbic activation:** Stressed or emotionally dysregulated students' brains are experiencing a stress response from their limbic system, the well-known fight, flight, freeze, or fawn reactions. In this state, students' brains prioritize survival and prepare the body for action, deprioritizing the prefrontal cortex in favor of quick reaction functions, like running (more blood flow to the legs) and noticing danger (eyes get bigger to let in more light; Archambault Besson, 2017).

It can feel defeating to see the list of factors that impair our students' executive function, knowing that we can have little impact on many of them. However, students' sensitivity to these factors also indicates that their brains are malleable; if such factors can have negative impacts, so too can others have positive. As brain health expert and author John Randolph (2020) explains, "We have the ability to proactively rewire our brains if we adopt positive habits, live in certain ways, and engage in novel and stimulating activities" (p. 27). You've got the novelty and mental stimulation covered in your lessons, and the small adjustments and big awareness you're gaining in this book will help your students (and you) adopt the positive lifestyle habits.

Assessing Executive Dysfunction

Assessing or identifying executive dysfunction can involve formal and informal means, both of which have limitations. Formal assessments are sometimes criticized for a lack of applicability to a real-world scenario. For example, a test for sustained attention may be novel enough to capture a student's attention for the moment, possibly inflating the results to make it appear as if the student has more control over their sustained attention than is functionally true. Formal assessments are also harder to access equitably. Private assessments are expensive for families, and assessments done at school may be available only to a limited number of students, likely those on or being considered for an IEP. Please see appendix B, "Formal Executive Function Diagnostic Tools" (page 229), for more information about formal assessments of executive function.

Informal assessments, on the other hand, are accessible to any teacher or parent wanting to observe or interview a student. However, a lack of standardization can mean informal assessments are less reliable and may miss important information. These criticisms are not to scare you away from assessing students' executive dysfunction but to make you aware of what lies ahead—it can be challenging to get a full and accurate picture of a student's executive function skills. I'd argue that this is completely OK because these skills evolve and grow over time and are inconsistent within each of us. A gestalt view may be enough for us to innovate support and move our students forward.

As we explore informal assessments of executive function, remember that these tools are not meant to diagnose students with specific disorders, but rather to understand the areas of student need. Formal assessments that go beyond the typical tools used in the classroom often require parent permission for use. Your school psychologist will be a great resource should you have questions about formal assessments. The following section provides more information on informal assessments.

Informal Assessments of Executive Function

Informal assessments describe those that are classroom or school based and not normed (that is, they are not taken by a large sample of students to check for biases and validity). Informal assessments are already happening in your classroom. For example, every time you observe a student or reflect on the class's understanding, you are gathering quick, informal data that drives your decisions and actions.

When informally assessing executive function, we seek to understand the student's challenges and possibly tease out the executive function deficit behind them. Figure 5.1 helps you connect the student struggles you observe with possible skills deficits. Students may not be aware of why certain competencies currently elude them, and unfortunately, the journey of uncovering executive function deficits requires a fair amount of executive function. Helping students discover their executive function strengths and struggles models the process for students and develops their executive function, but it can take time and a fair amount of hypothesizing.

Informal assessment can take the form of interviewing a student, reflecting on a coaching conversation, looking at student work or performance in class, observing a student, or using informal rating scales to collect feedback from students, families, and other teachers. As is the case with formal assessments, our informal data becomes the basis for planning our classroom adjustments and interventions. Although gathering this data can take a bit of time, using that data to identify and prioritize our actions saves time and guesswork; we're better able to meet a student's need when we understand the need first.

Observed Student Challenge	Possible Executive Function Needs
Off task in class most of the time	• Ability to manage attention • Planning work or time • Task initiation • Sustained effort on task
Missing or late work	• Planning work or time, inside and outside of school • Calendar and work management systems • Reminder systems to return work • Prioritizing and handling overwhelm
Disorganization	• Time management (including time to organize) • Task initiation • Systems to become organized • Systems to stay organized
Poor test scores	• Attention and note-taking in class • Memory strategies • Study strategies • Time management during assessments
Poor writing (sometimes in contrast to effective speaking about a topic)	• Managing overwhelm • Chunking work and sustaining work over time • Avoiding procrastination and rushed work • Idea organization strategies
Emotional dysregulation	• Awareness of body signals • Tools for meeting sensory needs • Communication strategies • Self-calming methods

Figure 5.1: Observed student struggles and potential needed skills.

The reproducibles "Student Executive Function Skills Reflection" (page 135) and "Teacher Executive Function Skills Reflection" (page 137) at the end of this chapter have rating scales for teachers and students to reflect on executive function strengths and struggles. The reflections can provide great data for making personal or class goals, or discovering areas of need that you can support with your pedagogy. For the student reflection, allow students to reflect on their present skills in each reflection category. Consider adding your own skills to the chart or allowing students to add skill areas they'd like to reflect on and possibly grow. Date the reflection so students can compare it with future reflections. It may help to remind students that this reflection is not graded and that low scores indicate areas of potential growth, not failings.

Understanding Stealth Manifestations of Executive Function Deficits

Most of our examples so far have been in the context of student academics, but as you know, executive function extends to all aspects of life. The skills that make a strong student often transfer to making someone successful at work or at home. Here, we explore the stealth manifestations of executive function deficits, where the connection to executive function may not be direct or obvious.

Social Impacts

Many students with executive function deficits struggle with the invisible demands of creating and maintaining friendships. Consider the experience of Sophia, whose experience of isolation is not hers alone.

> **"I'm so lonely," Sofia, a sophomore, confides in me through tears. "I thought high school was supposed to be all friends, all the time. It's not like that for me."**
>
> **"What is it like?" I explore.**
>
> **"Well, I talk with everybody at school. I get along with everybody. But on the weekends I'm alone. It's like I forget to text friends back, and I'm awful at making plans. I feel like I know everybody but kind of can't make actual friends. So I hang out at home."**

Social connections require executive function. Students must manage priorities well enough to have open time to socialize. They must remember details and dates related to their friendships, initiate and plan activities, and respond to communication. In conversations, students must track the topic, not interrupt, and add related comments or questions.

A student's executive function struggles can cause their peers to assume lack of effort or desire to connect. Friends may feel hurt or let down by lack of follow-through, and students with executive function deficits may not understand the cause of peer conflict or drifting apart. For example, a student who never returns texts will likely stop receiving texts from others, leaving him feeling isolated and his peers feeling neglected. Because the cause of the unreturned texts isn't apparent, peers will assume it's a lack of desire or effort, and to protect themselves will often distance themselves from the nonreciprocating friend.

Unfortunately, executive function deficits that cause social challenges add to the problem with executive function. As Randolph (2020) explains in *The Brain Health Book*, "Increased social activity is associated with better executive functioning, quicker thinking speed, and improvements in some types of memory" (p. 114). Although it can be frustrating and may need some strategies to improve, socializing is important for our students' executive function.

Social isolation is processed in the same area of the brain that processes physical pain. You read that correctly. As researchers Naomi I. Eisenberger and Matthew D. Lieberman (2004) state, "Physical pain—the pain experienced upon bodily injury—and social pain—the pain experienced upon social injury when social relationships are threatened, damaged or lost—share neural and computational mechanisms." When students with impaired executive function suffer a negative consequence in a relationship, their brains experience a cascade of chemical reactions that alert them to danger, similar to what may happen if they injure their bodies. Understanding the brain's experience can give a new perspective on the importance of social interactions and connections for our students. Figure 5.2 demonstrates some of the skill manifestations in social settings.

Executive Function Skill	Social Manifestation
Time management	• Being on time for social events • Honoring the social expectations for the duration of social events, like staying at a party or in a conversation
Working memory	• Tracking a topic of conversation • Maintaining memory of a social request (helping a friend, bringing an item) • Remembering names of new people
Initiation	• Starting a conversation • Making plans • Reaching out to show support

Inhibitory control	• Refraining from interrupting in conversation • Avoiding blurting rude comments • Staying in the expected space during social interactions

Figure 5.2: Social manifestation of executive function skills.

The great news is that building executive function skills like planning, organizing, and time management will benefit students' relationships and social skills. However, they may need support applying what they see as academic strategies to other realms of their lives. This can be accomplished by varying the examples you provide when teaching executive function skills. Teens welcome home and social examples, which are both relevant and a great way to capture their attention.

As teens mature, they form their identities, in part by using feedback and comments from peers, teachers, parents, and society (Siegel, 2017). Knowing this, it's important we continue to look through a lens of developing executive function, assuming an observed skill deficit rather than commenting on a student's character. Many adults with ADHD, autism, and other learning difficulties have shared with me that they worked hard to realize they weren't lazy, disorganized, or numerous other negative labels, as many had told them in the past. They had taken to heart what adults and society told them as children and only in adulthood, on learning about their challenges and finding effective strategies, did they realize that they could let go of the labels and see themselves through a more positive lens.

How We Can Help With Social Challenges

Other quick adjustments and strategies to support students' executive function for social success include the following.

- Mindfully seating and grouping students for successful interactions
- Scaffolding group work and expectations to be clear and individualized; checking in and intervening when necessary so that students with executive function needs are meeting mini-deadlines and completing their portions of group work
- Monitoring student communication and potential isolation in your classroom
- Providing reflection opportunities after group or partner work to help students become aware of their social strengths and struggles
- Adding school social events to your classroom calendar for student reference

Avoidance and Apathy

In the world outside of school, students receive messages about their value based on their skills. For example, a student who is on time consistently will be praised for being punctual, while a student who struggles with time management may hear that they are lazy or disrespectful. Students who are highly organized may be told they are responsible, while our disorganized students may be criticized as messy or immature.

In school, students may experience a similar assumption that executive function deficits stem from a weak character. In *Overcoming the Achievement Gap Trap*, Anthony Muhammad (2015) describes how school systems can unknowingly harm students through the concept of meritocracy, rewarding achievement and talent while believing that "the disinterested and less talented fail" (p. 39). This is likely not the intention of individual teachers, nor is it part of any district mission statement. Yet, functionally, by grades and awards alone, schools are set up to reward the best. The less visible flipside is experienced by all of those who are not the "best." They often feel unseen, incapable, and demotivated. Why try when it's clear you won't make it to the top?

Mason comes to mind when I think of a student who deeply cared about his success but projected the opposite. At school, Mason missed deadlines and struggled to get started in class. He took poor notes and very rarely asked for help from anyone. His report cards reflected comments like, "If he cared more . . ." and "Mason is capable but doesn't try . . ." These statements deflated him. At one point, he remarked to me, "I'm done trying in history. The teacher thinks I don't care, so I guess I just won't care." Mason's home experience, in contrast, was a full-throttle effort. He'd work into the early morning hours on homework and unfinished classwork, often stuck but unsure how to get help. He wasn't comfortable asking teachers who assumed he didn't care and was especially cautious about asking for help too close to the deadline. He dreaded a teacher's reply that "he should have started sooner" or that "he should have paid attention in class." Mason was all too aware of these struggles but saw no solutions on offer at the time.

Faced with the possibility of being left out due to their challenges, students may employ the protective mechanisms of avoidance or apathy. Unaware that a strategy may change their school experience, a student may attempt to lower the risk of failure by avoiding academic endeavors that are not sure to bring success. This lower engagement may look like disinterest, which is reinforced by teachers and parents who may remark that they don't seem to try hard. Although internally these students know they try hard, they may move into an apathetic facade, appearing not to care how well they do. Our brains seek safety, sometimes taking the easier paths to it, like apathy and avoidance, even though these coping strategies hurt us in the end.

How We Can Help With Apathy and Avoidance

Our first step to help students who appear apathetic or seem to avoid academic tasks is to monitor our own assumptions. What story have we crafted about the student, based on what we've observed? What could an alternative story include? Where are we assuming intent or effort?

Once we've identified the potential areas where we've possibly shortchanged an aloof student, it's time to engage with them. A great place to start is a coaching conversation that explores their self-concept and beliefs about themself as a student and about school. What does the student find particularly challenging? What do they think may be impeding their progress? Are there things teachers have said over the years that ring true as areas of need, but they're not sure how to address them?

> "My teachers say I don't listen," Emy shares through tears. "I do listen, but my brain doesn't listen to me." Emy shares with me a common student experience: She hears her teacher's directions, then "One thousand other ideas come in too. Sometimes, I forget what she said, or sometimes I get started but then get distracted" (Personal communication, January 5, 2024). Like many students, Emy is motivated to listen to and follow directions. From the outside, however, it may look like she's not attending, since she often needs reminders after agreeing to complete a task. When you see what you might initially consider noncompliance in your classroom (when students fail to follow through with directives), consider that there are many reasons a student may not "comply." Students may be distracted, have trouble with working memory, be emotionally dysregulated, unsure how to complete the request, overwhelmed by the number of steps, or various other reasons. Instead of noncompliance, it's more likely that students who are not following directions completely, immediately, or well are demonstrating executive function needs.

As we start to shift our assumptions of effort, we embody the belief that students do well when they can. The way we interact with them changes, and we may ask questions or offer suggestions that are strategy-centric rather than effort-centric. We may replace "you should" with student-led explorations of potential strategies. We may start to recognize and reward small steps and growth, offering feedback throughout the journey instead of saving it for completed work.

Self-Care

Self-care describes the requisite actions and skills for showing up healthy and ready for school, like sleeping enough (and waking up on time), eating well, maintaining hygiene, managing personal belongings, and exercising. These are sometimes referred to as *vocational skills* during IEP discussions. Self-care requires a whole lot of executive function. To meet our bodies' daily needs, we must also be able to plan, prioritize, initiate, manage distractions, complete many steps, and manage time, just to name a few skills. Think about your morning routine before driving to school; although it's likely (mostly) internalized now, you once had to learn it and may have relied on repetition, strategies, and reminders.

Many families hesitantly share with me that self-care is particularly tricky for their child with executive dysfunction. They notice that while their child seems to be able to do anything—often very challenging things like rebuild an engine or deliver an incredible speech—they struggle intensely with their daily hygiene actions. As one parent shared, "This kid could invent a new cure for cancer, but he never brushes his teeth." Others have described how their children's time management and working memory make the mornings before school a mad dash: "She goes up and down the stairs so many times, then she gets in the car only to have to run back in the house."

For some students, executive dysfunction may slow or even prevent their internalization of their self-care routines, making "automatic" steps like getting dressed or putting on deodorant effortful. Although we can't see if from the outside, showing up to school may be the result of significant effort and time, draining students' energy before the first bell rings. Additionally, these students may have arguments and struggles at home before they even start their school days and possibly show up at school less prepared and distracted by unmet physical needs. Their lack of preparedness may be noticed by peers or even penalized by teachers, who intend to help students remember to be prepared by giving detentions or other negative consequences. Figure 5.3 illustrates how executive function skills manifest in the self-care realm.

Executive Function Skill	Self-Care Manifestations
Time management	• Being on time for school and appointments • Accurately estimating the time for self-care tasks • Managing time efficiently for self-care tasks • Transitioning easily between fun and self-care
Working memory	• Staying on task and being efficient in each space • Following through on multistep directions • Packing school bag or lunch without forgetting things
Initiation	• Transitioning from relaxing or fun activity to self-care activity • Starting self-care with time to complete it • Cooking meals or preparing food when hungry
Inhibitory control	• Resisting junk food • Honoring bedtime • Avoiding impulsively using drugs or alcohol

Figure 5.3: Self-care manifestation of executive function skills.

How We Can Help With Self-Care

What students with executive function deficits need isn't more negative consequences; the stress of rushing, struggling, and still being a little (or a lot) unprepared is already negative enough. Instead, students need *different.* They need us to have a variety of tools to help them learn the executive function skills needed for at-home steps, and they need us to show them how their skills apply in different environments. Students need us to hear their struggles and validate them, allowing them space to explore solutions instead of positioning them to respond to our criticism or punishments. Students whose executive function skill deficits impair them at home need us to have options available at school so they can borrow what they need and move on with learning, avoiding falling behind due to a difference in their brains and skill set. And, they need us to help them and their parents adopt detective perspectives so they can understand, strategize, and augment their struggles at home.

Making a Plan and a Promise

I often end my professional development presentations with a plan and a promise where learners commit to an action step and devise ways to promise its success to their future selves. In this way, trainings, much like your learning in this book, lead to new actions rather than being nice but fuzzy information that floats in your brain without actualizing.

As you've explored executive function deficits more deeply, plan to take an action inspired by this chapter. Do you want to further explore some of the factors that cause executive function deficits? Tell your students about the adjustments they can make for better executive function? Or, are you motivated to take action to support some of the stealth manifestations of executive dysfunction, like social communication or self-care? See if you can choose one or maybe two actions to take.

Next, employ some of your own executive function by making a promise to your future self, envisioning the successful implementation of the plan. Figure 5.4 will help you do so. How do you remember to take the action? How do you address any potential hurdles? How do you keep the plan and positive changes motivational and front of mind so they last? This promise process helps distill your intentions into more likely actions, requiring your brain to take just a few steps beyond writing something on a to-do list. It actualizes your promise to future you and guides you to plan how you will see that promise through.

I plan to:

I will make this happen by using the following strategies:

I will take these actions on (date) __________ at (time) __________.

I will remind myself by:

Figure 5.4: A plan and a promise.

Visit ***go.SolutionTree.com/lifeskills*** *for a free reproducible version of this figure.*

Key Points

The key points from the chapter include the following.

- Executive function deficits are inconsistent and will show up differently across times, settings, and contexts. They can be confusing to observers and even within our own brains.
- There are many permanent and temporary conditions associated with impaired executive function, many of which our students experience.
- There are several assessments to gauge how well executive functions work. In addition, observation and student interviews are also powerful assessment tools.
- Executive function deficits manifest in nonacademic ways, many of which we can support through understanding and addressing students' needs.

Potential Actions

After reading the chapter, consider taking these potential actions.

- Explore the executive function assessments available. Choose one you would like to use to collect data about your class or a student.
- Practice observing a student's executive function skills in action. Keep notes of what you notice or realize during this process.

- To maintain your problem-solving perspective, make a reminder note for yourself to consider the many ways that a student's executive function may be impaired.
- Complete your plan and promise. Leave it somewhere prominent so it reminds you of your commitment to action.

Journal or Discussion Questions

After reading the chapter, answer these questions in your journal or within a book discussion group.

- As you read about the potential confusions or frustrations surrounding executive function challenges, what came to mind? What are some of the private wonderings you've explored? How have they changed in light of your new understandings?
- When have you observed inconsistent executive function skills across times, settings, or contexts? What are the differences that could explain the incongruence of skills?
- Which of the stealth manifestations of executive function deficits resonated with you? What will you do with your new understanding?

Student Executive Function Skills Reflection

Reflect on your present skills in each reflection category.

Name:

Date:

Skills at School	Not Yet (1)	Just Starting (2)	Mostly on My Own (3)	Totally on My Own (4)
Email teachers on my own				
Know *when* to ask for help				
Know *how* to ask for help				
Pack my backpack				
Manage homework time				
Use a calendar (digital or physical)				
Create a to-do list				
Solve friend conflicts				
Work in a group				
Take notes				
Pay attention in class 80 percent or more of the time				
Study effectively				
Write an essay				
Read 60 to 100 pages a week				
Get to school and classes on time				

Page 1 of 2

Skills at School	Not Yet (1)	Just Starting (2)	Mostly on My Own (3)	Totally on My Own (4)
Add Your Own				
Add Your Own				
Add Your Own				

Teacher Executive Function Skills Reflection

Use the following reflection to measure a student's current levels of performance in each skill area. Date your reflections so you can compare them with future skill development. Any occurrences of 1s or 2s that emerge as patterns can become areas of coaching or direct executive function instruction.

Name:

Date:

Skills at School	Not Yet (1)	Just Starting (2)	Mostly on My Own (3)	Totally on My Own (4)
Email teachers on their own				
Know *when* to ask for help				
Know *how* to ask for help				
Manage their belongings				
Manage homework time				
Use a calendar (digital or physical)				
Create a to-do list				
Solve friend conflicts				
Work in a group				
Take notes				
Pay attention in class 80 percent or more of the time				
Study effectively				
Write an essay				

Page 1 of 2

Skills at School	Not Yet (1)	Just Starting (2)	Mostly on My Own (3)	Totally on My Own (4)
Read 60 to 100 pages a week				
Get to school and classes on time				
Add Your Own				
Add Your Own				
Add Your Own				

Page 2 of 2

CHAPTER 6
PLANNING EXECUTIVE FUNCTION SUPPORTS

A colleague of mine is excellent at organizing; her spaces are beautiful, logically arranged, and consistently in order—a contrast to the papers, books, and sticky notes that decorate my workspaces. She is also excellent at teaching the organization process, which I observed her walk through with a freshman midyear. The student's spaces were chaotic: a backpack full of papers, old food, random school supplies, and a sock; her laptop desktop and Google Drive were sprinkled with files, some named and some untitled. I witnessed the rush of overwhelm as the student unveiled her messy spaces and braced for my colleague's judgment. (I imagine she's heard how messy she is numerous times over the years.) However, my colleague surprised us both by taking a few deep breaths with the student, likely to regulate her emotions. Then, she handed the student a visual for the process of organizing. Her steps were clear, had a few sketches to make them approachable, and seemed to make sense to the student. What started as a potentially long, overwhelming process quickly became a clear, traversable path when structure was offered.

Chances are, now that you know a bit about executive function and have some

CHAPTER SNEAK PEEK

By the end of this chapter, you will understand the following.

- The three heavy-hitter areas for executive function support and intervention
- Planning executive function supports
- How (and why) to involve students
- Accommodations for executive dysfunction

growing belief in its profound impact, you're feeling ready to use your knowledge. However, the process of choosing your strategies may feel a lot like cleaning a messy space—overwhelming! Remember that chapter 2 (page 35) is a great place to start, giving ideas for classroom environment, presentation, and assessment changes that support executive function needs for students. Both chapter 3 (page 73) and appendix A (page 167) present lessons to teach executive function skills to your students directly. But what if you want to be more deliberate with your approach or have a group of students who needs more targeted interventions? This chapter is for you.

Many schools work with a response to intervention (RTI) or multi-tiered system of supports (MTTS), which involve both general and special educators in providing academic and behavioral interventions to students. This multistep process involves layers of our own executive function and would feel nebulous (and therefore difficult to start) without structure. In this chapter, we add structure and clarity to your plans for building students' executive function! Learn how to use your data, prioritize with different lenses, and create plans and possible accommodations that serve your students' executive function needs.

Before we move on, there's a mighty elephant in the room that we need to address. You're a general educator and the "intervention" piece may seem more like it would be in the wheelhouse of your special educator colleagues. I get it. There are two perspectives I'd like to share. First, most of your students with 504 plans and IEPs probably spend most of their academic time in your classroom, and so it behooves you to have a full toolbox of strategies to support them effectively. Educators Kristen M. Bordonaro and Megan Clarke (2024) share the following in their book *The Collaborative IEP*:

> As teachers, we want to support students, and our first inclination is often to pull the student to a smaller setting where we can give more individualized instruction or a different skill for them to be successful. However, that is comparable to learning to drive a car by riding a bike in your driveway without any obstacles. The experience is entirely different." (p. 18)

Supporting struggling learners in your classroom provides them the opportunity to practice their new skills in the most relevant context.

Second, you can consider this chapter your playbook for growing students' executive function. It shares many strategies for intervening with more intensive student needs, but it also seeks to simply provide a structure for using your learning from the book. In this chapter, you will learn how to create a plan for executive function interventions and better understand accommodations in your classroom, 504 plans, IEPs, and gifted programs. This chapter also gives you assessment tools, reflections, and ideas for interventions that reach students with and without recognized disabilities.

Creating a Plan for Executive Function Interventions

At the risk of getting a bit meta, planning for executive function interventions takes executive function. We must schedule (and keep) the time to go through the process, evaluate students' needs, prioritize our steps based on our data and the feasibility of time and resources, and enact our plans. Let's consider a shift in perspective: When you use the classroom adjustments from chapter 2 (page 35), when you teach executive function lessons like those in appendix A (page 167), or when you engage in a coaching conversation with a student, you are indeed providing executive function support, and potentially also an intervention, as described in many RTI and MTSS models. Instead of adding to your plate, let's systematize your executive function support so that you may be more deliberate in your approach and possibly monitor your impact.

While skill sets associated with mathematics and reading are easier to ordinate (for example, we must learn that every letter makes a sound before we can learn prefixes), most executive function skills will not organically fall into a set order. Teachers often find that students need several skills that relate to one another or have so many deficits that it's hard to choose where to start. To add to this challenge, prioritizing and organizing the intervention plan for executive function skills requires a teacher's executive function and can feel overwhelming.

There is no perfect order to teach, accommodate, or coach executive function skills in any classroom. However, there are ways to organize the changes you plan to make to support your students' executive function growth. Start by considering the three heavy hitters that impact executive function and student experience: (1) working memory, (2) classroom environment, and (3) emotional regulation. These are foundational for students to be able to access and improve their executive function.

Addressing these heavy hitters can create a foundation for future growth as well as alleviate unnecessary barriers. Recall exploring all three—working memory, classroom environment, and emotional regulation—in chapter 2 (page 35). In this chapter, we extend our awareness of them and organize methods of self-assessing our approaches in these areas. Let's review what these areas include and why they are so essential for students' executive function.

- **Working memory**: It's like the whiteboard in our brains, where we hold and manipulate information. Freeing up working memory allows students to retain content and solve problems more efficiently. Working memory drives students' capacity to follow directions and process multistep tasks. It supports their note-taking, conversations, and writing by maintaining ideas for the time needed to produce a sentence, question, or other interaction of learning.

- **Classroom environment:** It's equally important, as it can support executive function when the space is predictable, easy to navigate, and rich with visuals to support student engagement, such as calendars and lists of steps for common processes. The environment can also proactively prevent student executive function struggles, like distractions, sensory overload, and student confusion.
- **Emotional regulation:** It makes communication with our "thinking brain" (the prefrontal cortex) more effective. Stressed or emotionally dysregulated brains often focus on surviving what they interpret as a threat, leaving very little mental energy available for rational thinking or learning (Pedersen, 2021). Providing tools for students to self-regulate can empower them to more readily meet their own needs and re-engage with learning.

Figure 6.1 shows the heavy-hitter areas and intervention ideas for each one.

As you read in chapter 2 (page 35), there are several ways to choose and prioritize which executive function skills you support. You may consider the urgency of a needed skill set, attune to what you are reflecting on ("I wish they could just . . ."), or use the natural demands of the calendar to determine what's most timely. Individual student intervention plans will likely be based on the student's data and needs, while whole-class interventions may be created to meet the demands of the content or time of year.

The process of planning executive function interventions includes three basic components or phases: (1) awareness, (2) skill building, and (3) reflection. Grade-level, subject, or coteaching teams and individual teachers seek to understand the executive function needs of the student group, create plans to teach and support these skills, and systematically reflect on the plans, adjusting as necessary. If this cycle seems familiar, it is! While students use a cycle of awareness, strategies, and reflection to build their executive function, we teachers can use a similar cycle to *plan* building executive function in our classrooms, as figure 6.2 (page 144) demonstrates.

In the awareness phase, teachers examine the adjustments needed to address some of the biggest factors impacting executive function, including classroom setup, students' ability to emotionally regulate, and the protection of students' working memory. Teachers also use multiple ways to assess executive function, as covered in

Heavy-Hitter Area	Intervention Ideas
Working memory, classroom environment, and emotional regulation	• Directly teach the skills. • Involve students in making classroom adjustments. • Provide a variety of tools for students to independently meet their own needs.
Working memory	• Make visuals of the steps of common processes. • Label parking spaces where classroom items are stored and where work must be returned. • Offer sticky notes and various ways for students to quickly capture their ideas. • Consider chunking instruction or pausing to allow time for students to process information.
Classroom environment	• Make access and navigation easy and clear. • Create spaces for self-regulation and focus. • Make time visual and concrete with clocks, calendars, timers, and so on. • Make distractions harder to access. • Develop systems to keep the classroom organized. • Decrease sensory distractions, when you can.
Emotional regulation	• Teach and allow tools for self-regulation. • Support students' monitoring their energy and emotional levels. • Engage with school staff to create spaces and people who can support students in moments of emotional dysregulation.

Figure 6.1: Intervention ideas for working memory, classroom environment, and emotional regulation.

chapter 5 (page 115), and use the data to prioritize three areas of executive function to focus on. Extending from the awareness phase to the skill-building phase, teachers create a plan to build skills, including teaching students to become self-aware and learn and use strategies (see the reproducible "A Plan to Build Executive Function: Interventions for Your Class or Individual Students," page 160). In the final phase, reflection, teachers regularly communicate to monitor and reflect on the efficacy of the plan. Of course, adjustments will need to be made as part of the learning and intervention process. The following sections describe the awareness, skill-building, and reflection phases in more detail.

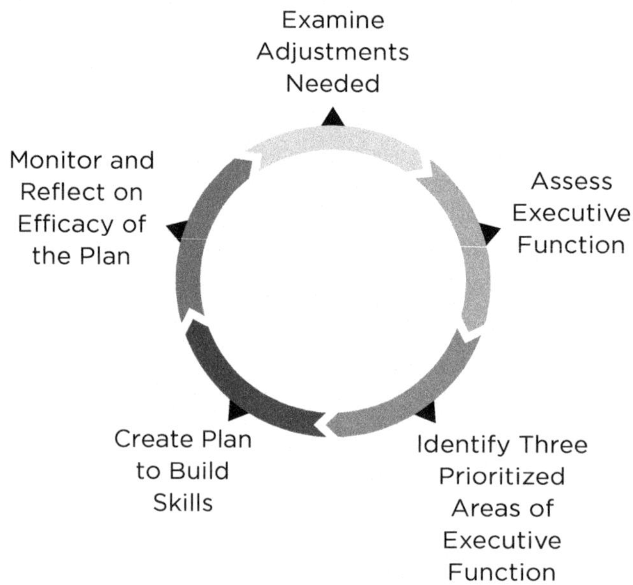

Figure 6.2: Cycle for planning executive function building in the classroom.

Awareness Phase

There are many ways you can collect data about students' executive function challenges. Sometimes, a coaching conversation with a student can spark strategy ideas and experimentation. Other times, you will want to plan to systematically develop your students' executive function skills. During this awareness phase, remind yourself to stay curious and nonjudgmental of your pedagogy. You are taking a snapshot of where you and your students are and looking at it through the lens of executive function (Weathers, 2024). This is a moment to take stock of where you are, knowing in the next phase you'll get the chance to move toward where you want to be.

Figures 6.3 and 6.4 (page 146) provide checklists to reflect on some of the elements that impact executive function in your classroom. You may notice that working memory, one of the heavy hitters, is not distinctly called out in a reflection list; rather, it is embedded in both classroom environment and emotional-regulation lists.

Use the list in figure 6.3 to collect observational data about your classroom environment and reflect on what you notice. This is an opportunity to recognize both the strengths of the executive function–supporting elements in the classroom as well as some that are weaker or absent. The notes sections provide space to reflect on your observations and record any changes you'd like to explore moving forward.

Time is concrete and visual

- Schedule for the period or day
- Digital and analog clocks
- Timers
- Calendars
- Bell schedule
- Class and school events
- Due dates

Notes:

Distractions are minimized

- Students' phones are away
- Systems are in place to manage devices
- Areas are mostly clear of visual clutter
- Areas are mostly clear of auditory clutter

Notes:

Classroom walls are useful to students

- Anchor charts highlight key content and skills
- Steps for common routines are concrete and visually represented
- Verbal instructions are also made visual for common tasks or long-term projects
- Opening and closing routines are predictable and visually represented

Notes:

Classroom setup is helpful to students

- Classroom items are labeled for easy navigation
- There are parking spaces (labeled areas where things are to be returned) for shared resources
- A resource area provides common references, school resources, a school calendar, and other student tools for all to access
- Steps and resources for logging in to online or digital spaces are clear and accessible

Notes:

Figure 6.3: Classroom environment list for executive function.

Visit ***go.SolutionTree.com/lifeskills*** *for a free reproducible version of this figure.*

Spaces

- Students have an area to go to reregulate (or a process for taking a moment outside of the classroom)
- Students have a variety of spaces to work and focus
- Emotional awareness is represented in the classroom space (on the walls, with student voice on bulletin boards, and so on)
- Students can advocate to change seats to support focus or regulation
- Students have access to a trusted support person when in crisis

Notes:

Tools

- The classroom has a process for expressing emotional or regulation needs that allows students to get what they need in the least disruptive way to instruction, such as the following:
    - Hand signals
    - Use of a pass
    - Hand raising
    - Accessing peer help
- Fidget toys or other sensory tools are available for students to use (examples include quiet objects of varying sensory feedback, Velcro strips on desks, glitter jars, and more)
- There are multiple ways to engage, including the following:
    - Verbal statements
    - Writing
    - Submitting digitally

Notes:

Student Awareness

Students know how to do the following:

- Begin and end class
- Capture their to-do list items

- Process common activities
- Get help when needed
- Communicate with teachers
- Check their grades
- Work with their peers

Notes:

Figure 6.4: Classroom setup for emotional regulation and engagement observation list.

Visit ***go.SolutionTree.com/lifeskills*** *for a free reproducible version of this figure.*

Use the list in figure 6.4 to observe the emotional regulation supports and opportunities available to your students. The notes sections provide space to reflect on your observations and record any changes you'd like to explore moving forward.

Strategies Phase

After reflecting on the data you collected, the strategies phase lives up to its name: You plan and test out targeted strategies to support students' executive function. The data may lead you to adjust an approach to strengthen a heavy-hitter area (working memory, classroom environment, or emotional regulation). Or, the data may inspire you to directly teach executive function skills that revealed themselves as student deficits.

As mentioned in chapter 2 (page 35), prioritizing what to address and when depends on several factors, including urgency, prevalence,

As you learned in chapter 2 (page 35), one easy but impactful shift to support students' executive function is to offload their working memory by making the classroom routines clear and predictable. Standardizing how class periods begin and end can be a powerful support for students' executive function on the school and classroom levels. Leaving room for teacher individuality and creativity, create a predictable routine for students to prepare for and begin learning, as well as a routine to end the period by reviewing, cleaning up, and capturing their to-do tasks. Weathers's (2024) book *Executive Functions for Every Classroom* provides models of predictable routines that consist of shared elements like a warm-up question and a learning reflection and describes their impact. He writes that a predictable routine "that is implemented consistently every day and ideally shared between colleagues, can reduce the cognitive load for students, freeing up working memory to help students focus and learn, ultimately setting them up for success" (Weathers, 2024, p. 55).

or intensity of the challenge you seek to solve. When you plan and test out your strategies for supporting students, consider limiting your changes to one to three at a time. That way, you avoid overwhelm and can more accurately reflect on which change made the most impact.

If part of your strategies phase is to offer accommodations to identified or even all students, remember you can do so without an official plan. Universal Design for Learning (CAST, 2024d) describes the model for offering students variety in processing, receiving, and expressing their learning, celebrating the availability of accommodations that are naturally available in the classroom.

Reflection Phase

Reflecting on the impact of and experience with your strategies is the final step in the intervention cycle. Make time to consider both how students responded to the changes and how the changes felt for you to implement. Intervention strategies that are taxing or time consuming may be unsustainable over time. Collecting feedback from students, your colleagues, and sometimes parents can help you paint a full picture of the impact, as well as provide new insights into the potential next cycle of strategies and interventions.

The reflection phase most often leads to revisiting a previous phase. That is, when data shows your intervention was impactful and successful, you may be thrilled to return to the data collection phase to choose new focus areas for strategies moving forward. If the data indicates a need for adjustment to your intervention, you will likely return to the strategies phase, making small changes to your plan and implementation. Each time you reflect, you grow in both your awareness of your impact and your ability to adjust your approach to effectively meet students' needs.

Understanding Classroom Accommodations, 504 Plans, IEPs, and Gifted Programs

The spirit of accommodations is to offer a change that empowers an individual to engage, learn, and express their learning by decreasing or avoiding the negative impact of their limitations. Accommodations are often important parts of 504 plans, IEPs, gifted programs, and interventions, but they can also be a response to other recognized needs, including situational needs and for students without official diagnoses. For example, a student with a broken dominant arm may need accommodations for writing until their cast comes off. Or, you may notice that a student without an IEP or 504 plan benefits from moving while they work, so you offer them an exercise ball as a seat. Many times, teachers accommodate gifted students by offering extensions or differentiated work. These same students may be twice exceptional, meaning they have both high IQs and some learning or behavioral needs, a situation we will explore later in the chapter. For students with disabilities that impair major life activities, accommodations will often be part of their college experience as well.

The prevalence of accommodations does not mean they are clear cut, understood, or easy to develop. Misunderstandings abound about what an accommodation is versus a modification, and some teachers (and even students themselves) share with me that they worry accommodations will give some students an unfair advantage. Given the challenges around developing accommodations, it can help to have a formula for creating your own accommodations and a list of potential accommodations. Therefore, we will explore some of the most common misunderstandings about accommodations, as well as ways to develop accommodations and involve students in the process.

Many students may have executive dysfunction related to their disability. ADHD, autism, and many processing impairments associated with specific learning disabilities can impair executive function skills. As we've explored, these impairments can result in up to a three-year gap in skills from students' peers, meaning students can understand grade-level content but may have the executive function skills of someone three grades below (ADDitude, n.d.). This gap can be incredibly frustrating for students and confounding for adults. For example, the teenage student who can talk your ear off about a physics concept is the same one who isn't yet able to remember to complete and finish their work. Interventions and accommodations help students fill these gaps so their executive function deficits are not hindering their academic success.

Dealing With Accommodation Objections

The most common objection to accommodations I've heard is, "Why give the student accommodations when they won't have that in the real world?" The spirit of this objection is valid in that we don't want students to become reliant on circumstances and tools that may not be available to them after they graduate. However, many accommodations are available in the real world in college, trade or tech school, and the workplace. Some accommodations are easy enough for students to incorporate into their daily lives, benefiting from the exposure and practice during their time with us. For example, think of the subtle use of fidget toys or allowing themselves to use timers or chunk their work. When you or your teammates find yourselves considering the real-world objection, think about the following.

- Is there a possibility that this accommodation or a version of it will be available in college or the workplace?

- Is the student aware of their needs and accommodations? Engaging students in choosing and using accommodations empowers their self-awareness and enables them to own the need moving forward (Hamblet, 2023). They will be more likely to seek similar accommodations independently if they understand which and why they receive accommodations.
- Are we exploring a modification (a significant change to the curriculum or performance) that may be masking a student's actual performance?

A second, maybe more subtle objection to accommodations reflects the misunderstanding of the separation between intelligence and executive function. I've heard teams hesitate to offer accommodations to gifted students, relaying that a student who is that smart "shouldn't need accommodations." The data on and testimonials from twice-exceptional students debunks this myth (Kircher-Morris, 2021) because IQ and executive function are not connected. Twice-exceptional students display asynchronous development; their high IQs do not seem to align with their lagging executive functions or other learning needs. It's important to be mindful not to fall into the trap of tangling intelligence with executive functions. In fact, as you may remember from the introduction (page 1), brains that are slower to thicken the cerebral cortex tend to have more time to develop a high IQ, but that delay results in delayed executive function as well (Kircher-Morris, 2021). In short, no IQ score or participation in an advanced curriculum can eliminate the need for accommodations and support of executive function.

> Caryn is a mom of a twice-exceptional student who has a high IQ and ADHD. She reflects that the several-year process of creating and honing accommodations for her son was "exhausting, frustrating, and lonely." She often heard that her son was too smart to need accommodations, or worse, that he was not a good fit for advanced classes because of his ADHD. Over the years, she encountered a few teachers who really understood and naturally supported her son, using accommodations to get around his executive dysfunction and clear the hurdles created by having a brain with ADHD. In those classes, her son excelled, validating the power of the right accommodations. (Personal communication, November 20, 2024)

In addition, think about the process of learning any new, challenging skill. When we do, we often use cues, tools, and tricks as we learn, which may decrease in frequency as we become more adept at the skills. Allowing students accommodations as they grow their executive function is no different because they are empowered to learn and develop their skill set when we use accommodations to meet their needs and remove the barriers related to their lagging executive functions.

Thoughtful construction of an accommodations list is worth the effort. The small changes accommodations provide can alleviate the needs that come with learning challenges and disabilities, allowing students the opportunity to engage with grade-level curriculum and grow their executive function skills on their timeline. In my experience, students share that accommodations simply remove some of the extra mental work necessitated by their disabilities or learning needs.

Developing Accommodations

You can think of accommodations as solutions to the challenges that present themselves due to a student's needs. Sometimes, these challenges are inherent to the disability, and sometimes they are a result of the friction between how the student operates and what the environment demands. For example, a student with ADHD whose body needs to move for their mind to stay engaged may need accommodations to allow movement inside a seated classroom, which is a need conflicting with the environment. The same student may not need movement accommodations on the soccer field because the environment is set up for them to meet their own needs within the context of available options. When developing accommodations, answer the following questions.

- How does the disability or challenge impair the student's experience?
    - Interview the student and parents. Ask, what patterns of challenges seem to impede you? What do you wish was easier or available?
    - Observe the student in the classroom: How do they move, interact, and engage in the environment?
    - Read the psychological report, doctor or specialist recommendations, or vetted information about the disability. What accommodations make sense given your understanding of the student's needs?
- What does the environment demand or limit?
    - Consider physical access impediments and the kinds of movement required or allowed.
    - Consider addressing distractions or spaces to use for better focus.
    - Walk through a typical period as if you are a student with that learning need or disability. Consider the potential environment-based challenges and the accommodations that could help ease those challenges.
- How can the student meet their needs, or how can you adjust the environment, learning input, or student output so the student is no longer impaired?

- Consider physical and digital tools that may be useful.
- List people you can consult about the student's disability.

Keep in mind that you do not need to develop a formal, individual plan to offer accommodations to your students. In fact, you are likely doing so without conscious awareness. As you become experienced with matching accommodations to student needs, it may become second nature to adapt and accommodate with the flow of your students.

Involving Students in the Process

Let's say you've identified a student who needs deeper support. While you prepare to create a classroom intervention plan, be sure to consider involving the top expert: the student themself. Involving students in learning about their brains, choosing accommodations, and developing goals increases student buy-in and helps students "develop the executive function skills of self-monitoring, self-regulation, and self-evaluation" (Kircher-Morris, 2021, p. 102). The disability rights refrain, "nothing about me without me," reminds us that students must be included in discussions and plans about their learning experiences (Chasteen, n.d.).

While some portions of meetings may not be appropriate for younger students to attend (for example, going over a detailed psycho-educational evaluation), teams must make time to ask the student questions and update students on potential plans. Interviewing students before a meeting can often shed light on their perspectives, experiences, and needs, often saving the team time and guesswork in finding what will best serve the student. Inviting students to attend or even lead their meetings increases students' self-efficacy and is often considered best practice in preparing students to transition to postsecondary life (Hamblet, 2023).

After developing the intervention plan, it's essential to involve students in tracking and celebrating their progress. Because initiating and scheduling meetings may require executive function skills that students are still constructing, it is helpful to routinize and schedule regular check-ins with them, as figure 6.5 shows. Brief weekly meetings can ensure students are using their tools, strategies, and accommodations and meeting their academic demands and goals. A word of caution: It is easy for these check-ins to become grade focused, resulting in a to-do list and stress for a struggling student. Although our intentions are positive—to help our students do well in their classes—the focus on achievement can derail the intended purpose of supporting the whole student in developing executive function skills. One way around this pitfall is to use an agenda or other dependable structure, like the one in figure 6.5, to guide your time together.

Name: ____________________

Date: ____________________ Time: __________

Reflect

- What's going right?
- What strategies are working?
- What patterns or needs are you noticing?
- Is there a particular assignment or assessment you could use some help with?

Plan

- What's your plan for addressing identified challenges or completing identified assignments?
- What do you need to communicate with teachers this week?
- How will you remember to take these actions?

Figure 6.5: Student check-in agenda example.

Another opportunity for student involvement is to have them create what Kircher-Morris (2021) calls *microgoals*, which are student-led and student-assessed goals that support progress toward a larger goal. For example, if the student's larger goal is to return more work on time, a microgoal may be to first document the work on a list or calendar. For example, a microgoal in support of improving work return would be to increase the number of minutes they are on task during independent work time. According to Kircher-Morris (2021), microgoals are "process-oriented, fluid, student-tracked, and intrinsically driven" (p. 102). They are created collaboratively with students who reflect on, monitor, and adjust them mostly on their own. Microgoals help students internalize the coaching process of awareness, strategy utilization, and reflection. They also offer the chance to celebrate the smaller positive developments that may otherwise be overlooked. Microgoals are not written into any official student plan; instead, they are shared areas of focus between you and a student, an illuminated step on the way to their larger goals.

The accommodations in figure 6.6 (page 154) represent several options available to support students' executive function needs and growth. This is not an exhaustive list, but it can serve as a model or a starting point for conversations with students about how to best meet their needs.

<table>
<tr><th colspan="2">Accommodation List</th></tr>
<tr><th>Accommodation</th><th>Rationale</th></tr>
<tr><th colspan="2">Environment</th></tr>
<tr><td>Sensory accommodations and self-regulation:
• Provide students with the opportunity to take sensory breaks using identified sensory tools in a designated area or method at their desk, and using a timer to manage the break.
• Allow students to use a fidget toy to help regulate attention and energy.
• Allow students to move to a space in the classroom (or designate a space on campus) where they can take a break to calm or refocus. Use a timer and pass to manage the process.</td><td>Self-regulation can be aided by sensory input adjustments, such as decreasing stressful sensory input or increasing calming input. For example, a student may need to take a break to reregulate after a particularly noisy experience. Another student may need to use a calming sensory tool, like a fidget toy or visual stimulus, to create a sense of calm to focus on work.</td></tr>
<tr><td>Provide students with breaks to run errands or otherwise walk on campus when feeling restless.</td><td>Students may need to move their bodies to regulate and be able to focus. Planning for this can keep students engaged and positively connected. Without the opportunity, students may become restless or disruptive, or may make excuses to leave the room.</td></tr>
<tr><td>Provide students task cards for repeating demands.</td><td>Task cards (lists of steps of common student actions or problem-solving processes) offload a student's working memory. Students can access the visual of the steps rather than hold it all in their working memory.</td></tr>
<tr><td>Allow student-led seating to reduce distractions and sensory inputs.</td><td>Consulting students on where they sit affords them the chance to choose the best location for focus and sensory experiences.</td></tr>
<tr><td>Time accommodations:
• Use clocks, timers, and calendars to make time visual and concrete.
• Use timers to support transitions and independent work time.</td><td>Making time concrete and visual helps students manage their time and sequence their actions.</td></tr>
</table>

Accommodation List	
Accommodation	**Rationale**
Learning Input (Assignments and Engagement)	
Break assignments into chunks, ideally with students leading the chunking, assigning each chunk a due date.	Large assignments can overwhelm a student's brain, leading to avoidance or procrastination. Small, doable steps, however, empower them to take action and complete components of each larger task. Working with students to chunk assignments will teach them the mental process to do so.
Allow students to use headphones to control the sound during independent work time.	Brains that struggle with attention will often scan the environment for novel sounds. Allowing headphones helps students maintain predictable sound when working, reducing distractions. Headphones can be noise-canceling only or have approved music.
Provide books as PDF files or audio.	PDF and audio versions can enable students to have texts read aloud to them. Students may adjust the speed to help them with pace or retention of learning. Pairing audio with reading visually can help maintain focus and increase comprehension.
Check for understanding by having students demonstrate the task or restate the directions in their own words.	Students may not be aware that they're misunderstanding directions (often over-complicating a task) until they attempt the work at home, independently. Allowing them to interact with the work in a sheltered practice situation (at school) ensures they'll be able to do the work on their own, at school and at home.
Develop and use a private cue to remind students to attend or redirect attention to lecture or task.	Students who struggle with maintaining attention in class may need a private reminder to come back to focusing on a lecture or activity. Keeping it private reduces embarrassment and maintains a positive student-teacher relationship.

Figure 6.6: Executive function accommodation ideas. Continued ▶

Accommodation List	
Accommodation	**Rationale**
Provide students a check-in at the end of the period, to check they have written or typed the day's homework and important upcoming dates.	Writing down dates and assignments is necessary for student success and is often difficult for students with executive function needs. Providing a check-in can be a safety net for their success and get them in the habit of checking that they've captured their lists and dates.
Learning Input (Group Work)	
• Mindfully partner students for group work. • Support student groups by assigning roles and clarifying each group member's responsibilities and due dates. • Allow students the option of working alone instead of in a group or partnership, at teacher discretion.	Executive function deficits can mean students are late or miss work, struggle to engage in group work, or have difficulties communicating (interrupting or not following through), often creating a negative dynamic in a group. Partnering a student with a peer who is a strong communicator or who the student trusts can help avoid negative social consequences related to impaired executive function.
Learning Output (Assessments)	
Test timing accommodations • Give extra time for assessments. • Test over multiple days (same test in parts and only one test per day).	Students' brains do double duty when they process directions and content. Extra time allows them to give their best effort and do so at their pace.
Provide the option to take tests in quiet space.	Reducing environmental distractions can improve focus and test performance.
Provide the option to verbalize answers rather than write them. Provide the option to scribe a test.	Different ways to express their understanding on an assessment can help students assess content rather than reflect a mix of their content knowledge and academic struggles.
Provide the option to have the test read aloud.	If not an assessment of reading, having a test read aloud for a student (often a digital option) can help bypass visual processing challenges and support attention to the test.

Accommodation List	
Accommodation	**Rationale**
Learning Output (Homework and Classwork)	
Reduce or remove penalties for late work.	Provide this option with awareness, as some students need the clarity and urgency of a deadline to activate. Removing academic penalties for late work can help students avoid grade penalties resulting from executive function needs.
Learning Output (Notes and Writing)	
In-class accommodations: • Allow students to take a photo of notes, assignments, or exemplars. • Provide students with a copy of a peer's or teacher's notes. • Provide students with skeleton or cloze notes. • Do not grade notes. • Post teacher materials online for reference, as available. Or, share slides ahead of class for students to print at home.	Students may not be able to take notes completely yet, so photos can act as backup while they master these skills. Visuals are very helpful and can allow students a reference for later work. During lectures, it can help students to have preprepared notes they can annotate while listening rather than try to write everything during a lecture.
Provide speech-to-text options, including designated spaces for using speech-to-text software at school.	Students may speak faster or more clearly than they write. Allowing a speech-to-text tool (and providing the opportunity to use it) helps students with lagging written expression skills maintain pace with their peers.
Allow student to submit photos of work digitally to reduce work management needs.	Allowing the student a digital means of returning work on paper expands their options and avoids struggles with organizing their physical belongings.
Provide the option to type instead of hand write notes, work, essays, and tests.	Many students are faster at typing than writing; typing may enable students to take notes or express their learning more efficiently.

Continued ▶

Accommodation List	
Accommodation	**Rationale**
Instructions accommodations: • Have students highlight signs and symbols in mathematics. • Encourage students to number the steps of prompts and problems.	These approaches help students to differentiate and clarify instructions. This can lead to more complete and accurate work.
Miscellaneous	
Remove language of "on student request" for accommodations (for example, students will receive extra time for a mathematics test *on student request*).	Students may not be able to accurately predict when they will need extra time or other accommodations, due to some executive dysfunction. Requiring permission ahead of time limits access to accommodations.
Communicate regularly with students and families about missing work and upcoming larger assignments and tests.	Often, students with lagging executive function find out about missing work once it's very late and has been graded as a zero. Giving families a heads-up while there is still time to act allows the student a chance to adjust their approach and seek family help as needed.
Provide access to assistive technology, such as the Glean app (https://glean.co), recording pens, note-taking apps, and lecture recording devices.	Assistive technology abounds to support students' executive function. Consult your district's expert on assistive technology. Many of the tools they have are available districtwide or are inexpensive, effective ways to empower students.

Visit ***go.SolutionTree.com/lifeskills*** *for a free reproducible version of this figure.*

Creating plans to develop students' executive function will take some of your executive function too. You can plan for individual students or your own class following a process of first becoming aware of the needs and potential adjustments, then teaching executive function, and finally reflecting on students' growth. Just like your students' executive function skills, your skills in supporting and purposefully addressing executive function will grow with time and experience.

Key Points

The key points from the chapter include the following.

- Three starter heavy-hitter areas for executive function interventions include working memory, classroom environment, and emotional regulation.
- Creating an intervention plan involves observing and collecting data, using strategies, and reflecting on the plan's impact.
- There are many accommodation options for executive dysfunction.

Potential Actions

After reading the chapter, consider taking these potential actions.

- Plan one or two adjustments to your classroom environment that may support executive function.
- Consider the routines or processes that repeat in your classroom and create a visual reference of the steps.
- Collaborate with your colleagues to explore support ideas at the school or classroom level.
- Identify a student for whom you want to increase supports. Involve the student in creating ideas for support and microgoals.
- Use the accommodation ideas in figure 6.6 (page 154) when planning or classroom adjustments.

Journal or Discussion Questions

After reading the chapter, answer these questions in your journal or within a book discussion group.

- Explore the heavy hitters of working memory, classroom environment, and emotional regulation. What small changes can you see making in one or two of these areas?
- What were your thoughts as you read the common objections to accommodations?
- Are there accommodations in figure 6.6 (page 154) that you'd like to employ for your whole class? How will you begin?
- What did you realize or wonder as you read the chapter?

A Plan to Build Executive Function: Interventions for Your Class or Individual Students

The following questions and reflections guide you through the three steps of using interventions to develop students' executive function. Consider this tool an anchor for your journey, a space you can come to when you feel like you need more structure for the process, or even when you feel overwhelmed. This tool can also guide you through implementing strategies you've learned in our journey together, allowing you a format for organizing your thoughts and plans.

Phase 1: Awareness

Let's look at how to address each of the heavy hitters in the classroom.

Working memory: How are the routines of the day offloading student working memory? Is there consistency across your periods and days in how students begin and end the day? Is the way they return work and receive feedback consistent? Is the way they communicate with teachers or check grades also consistent? The more routine, practiced, and known these aspects of the school day are, the more we free up working memory for students to use learning content.

Describe some classroom routines and how to make them visual and concrete.

Classroom setup: The classroom checklist in figure 6.4 (page 146) is a great place to start becoming aware of the classroom environment and its support of executive function. Now, consider walking into the classroom as a student.

How are you able to navigate?

What do you reference?

Is it clear how to help yourself if you were lost in a process during the day?

When thinking about navigating the classroom as a student, describe some common observations and classroom needs.

Emotional regulation: Figure 6.4 (page 146) provides a starting point for considering the available classroom emotional-regulation accommodation.

Are there spaces to go or methods students can use to calm down when they need to?

Does the class have sensory or self-soothing items available?

How are students made aware of the systems for emotional and sensory regulation in class?

Describe classroom tools and methods for students' emotional regulation.

Look at Your Data

- Classroom observations
- Feedback from students and parents
- Executive function student and teacher checklists

Needs emerging from an analysis of classroom data include:

Phase 2: Skill Building

After examining your class data, determine the executive function skills you will build in all students or an individually identified student.

Prioritized executive function skills include:

Classroom Instruction and Practice of Skills

When? (Which dates?)

How will you teach the skills? (With which materials? Using which approaches?)

How will the students practice the skills? (What will the skills look like in each class? How will you monitor students' progress? How will you celebrate students' growth?)

What accommodations can support identified skills? (What might students with significant executive function needs require to learn and use the skills?)

Phase 3: Reflect and Support as a Team or Individually

Describe the feedback you hear from the following.

Your peers:

Students:

Parents:

What do you observe in your classroom regarding student engagement? Student behavioral concerns?

What does initial data look like for monitoring skills growth?

What adjustments or new teaching are you planning to propel the growth further?

Epilogue

I once saw a man on the television program *American Outdoors* who could identify birds by their calls, and I knew I needed that superpower. I became a volunteer guide at Mission Trails Regional Park and can now identify a few dozen birds by their sounds. I can also identify many native plants, animal tracks, and even scat, which is not as gross as it sounds. Moving through the world is different now because the aspects of nature that are illuminated to me will never be invisible again.

Today, you may feel the same way about executive function. You can't *not* see it now; its presence is illuminated and acknowledged in many aspects of your life. What was once easy to miss or felt elusive is there for your exploration and experimentation. This executive function awakening can be the start of a shift to sustainable, long-term upgrades to how you interact with your craft and especially with your students.

I will likely never recognize all birds by their sound alone. So, too, we will never have the executive function development formula dialed in perfectly for our students or ourselves. But now that we are aware and have a full toolbox of strategies and lessons, we can proceed down the path with trust.

We trust ourselves. We trust that what we notice, assess, and even intuit that students need is good enough to get started. We trust that our own executive function shortcomings are gifts in disguise, providing empathy and a real-life model of growth for our students. We trust that our best efforts and even our experimentation with strategies are exactly what our students need.

We trust our students. We trust that our students are their own best self-scientists. We trust that their shortcomings are reflections of need, not effort, and that they are only a strategy away from a new unfolding. We trust that our students have capacities and grit within them that will continue to reveal themselves long after they've left our classrooms. We trust that our students will grow the seeds we've planted with them during our short times together.

We trust the process. We trust that the process is designed to be exactly as messy and nonlinear as we find it. We trust that we improve our teaching in the same ways students improve their academic skills: by testing out, adjusting, and reflecting on experimental approaches. We trust that although we often won't see immediate changes in executive function skills, they are happening reliably and beautifully below the surface. And we trust that our new awareness and small changes are really all it takes to transform our students' lives.

Your new executive function–empowered world awaits. You've got this.

APPENDIX A
EXECUTIVE FUNCTION SKILLS LESSONS

These executive function skills lessons are intended to be used in any order, based on identified student needs, as part of a study skills class or resource specialist program, or in anticipation of executive function demands, such as final exams. The following list shows the eighteen lessons in this appendix.

- **Metacognition:** These lessons support students in developing awareness of their learning, executive function, and unique needs.
  - Practice on purpose will help you grow any skill (page 169)
  - Collect and use brain tools to make learning easier (page 172)
  - Think of your working memory like a whiteboard (page 175)
- **Self-regulation:** These lessons help students recognize and manage their energy, focus, and emotions.
  - Remember that stressed brains struggle with thinking (page 179)
  - Make space your ally to get things done and feel better (page 182)
- **Organization:** These lessons help students develop systems to manage their physical, digital, and temporal spaces.
  - Use differentiation to visually organize physical and digital spaces (page 186)
  - Use the pile, sort, purge, put back, photo, plan (PSP4) organizing strategy (page 189)
- **Time (Attention) Management:** These lessons develop students' awareness and effective use of time.
  - Plan work time with warm-ups and cooldowns (page 193)
  - Recognize your brain stealers to earn back your time and focus (page 196)

  - Use backward planning to meet deadlines (page 199)
- **Studying and Grades:** These lessons teach students to study, improve grades, and initiate work.
  - Perform a test replay to earn a better grade next time (page 202)
  - Find points vampires to give your grades a quick boost (page 207)
  - Use active studying to score better on assessments (page 210)
- **Planning and Prioritizing:** These lessons teach students to manage workload by prioritizing and planning their actions.
  - Motivate by making the task clear, social or fun, or urgent (page 213)
  - Use capture, schedule, and remind (CSR) systems to manage your work (page 216)
  - Use brain dumps to decrease overwhelm and help create a plan (page 219)
- **Social and Collaboration:** These lessons teach students to communicate and collaborate effectively.
  - Use the nice-ask-nice formula for easy emails (page 223)
  - Hack group projects (page 226)

Practice on Purpose Will Help You Grow Any Skill

Objective: Students will be able to state how intentional practice builds skills and identify areas they plan to practice and grow their skills.

Executive function areas: Self-awareness and metacognition

When to use this lesson:

- You notice students seem to be giving up or scoring poorly on assessments
- In advance of assessments where skills and memorized information will be necessary

Lesson audience: Whole class, small group, and individuals

Estimated time: Twenty minutes

Notes and adaptations: This is an introductory lesson that establishes the basis for enacting growth mindset: We get better with deliberate practice. Consider borrowing examples of students growing from practice in many areas of their lives—academic, athletic, social, or extracurricular. Be sure to validate all examples students share; it is likely they will have video game examples and honoring what matters to students can maintain your connection.

Connect and Open the Lesson

This morning, I arrived at school and was turning off my car when I realized something a little scary: I had no memory of driving here. I assume I was a safe driver, and when I think about it, I do remember stopping at the last few lights and watching a cute dog on his morning walk. But it's like the path to school and even driving itself are so automatic in my brain that I didn't notice driving here. My brain and body took over because I've practiced coming here so many times.

In contrast, when I was first learning to drive, nothing was automatic. Practicing driving took all my focus, and I needed lots of reminders and help. I had to slowly get more skilled in parking lots and on quiet streets before I drove in the city or the freeway. And it took a few years before driving really felt automatic for me.

You're learning how to learn and the content in your classes. Most of it is new to you, so it won't feel automatic.

Teaching Point

Today, I want to teach you that you can practice on purpose until something you're learning feels automatic.

Practice Together

Practice on purpose means you plan for things to take time and make adjustments as you get better at new skills. Let's think about something you're learning for fun. You might be learning to play an instrument or trying to beat a level in a game. You practice on purpose whenever you play, and you might even spend extra time looking up videos or tips to help you improve faster.

What we often forget, though, is that we can practice any skill on purpose, including student skills. Think about writing. You had to practice your handwriting when you first learned, then you had to practice your spelling words. As you've grown, it's become less obvious that you're still practicing skills because they're interconnected and there are a lot of them. But when we think about practicing on purpose, it can help us feel more hopeful and motivated when we're faced with hard tasks.

What are some things that used to be super hard to do but now feel automatic? You can think back to when you were very little, if you'd like.

Today, what are some classes or academic tasks (like studying or writing) that seem really hard?

Take one or two examples from students.

OK, a lot of you agreed that writing is hard right now. How would you practice writing on purpose? Where would you look for tips? How would you make it kind of fun or exciting to get better?

Invitation to Use the Skill

Sometimes, your homework will give you enough practice. You'll know you're getting it if you can do all or almost all of the assignment without help or looking at a resource. You'll also know you need to practice on purpose when the learning feels bumpy and you only remember part of the steps, or you don't yet feel like you can do it on your own.

Ideas for a Visual

- Create an interactive "Practice on Purpose Examples" bulletin board: Students can add their ideas to the board after the lesson and throughout the span of time the board is displayed.
- Display this teaching point: "Brains need practice to feel solid in a new skill. I can practice on purpose."

My Reflections and Improvements for Next Time

Collect and Use Brain Tools to Make Learning Easier

Objective: Students will learn to identify the tools that best help them at school and at home, creating a system for capturing the tools and creating reminders to use them.

Executive function areas: Metacognition, strategy awareness, and self-awareness

When to use this lesson:

- You notice students are new to executive function, lack self-awareness, or struggle to persevere through challenges
- In advance of future executive function lessons, self-reflections, or an increase in academic rigor

Lesson audience: Whole class, small groups, or individuals

Estimated time: Fifteen to twenty minutes

Notes and adaptations: Keep in mind that students will need several reminders to use the tools they identify; it won't usually be enough to state a tool or strategy without intentionally designing reminders of when and how to use it. The conversation in this lesson can be a powerful way to reach students, who may learn from each other's strategies. This is often a foundation lesson, establishing the language of brain tools for future reference in lessons and coaching conversations.

Connect and Open the Lesson

My friend is a mechanic and a lover of bargains. The other day, he found a super deal on a new toolbox, so he bought it. When he realized he didn't need his old toolbox, he gave it to me. I was excited, but when I set it up, I realized that my hammers, screwdrivers, and cutting tools didn't fill it. There are whole drawers in the toolbox that are empty right now.

Just like I'm having to gather tools to fill my toolbox, you're learning brain tools to make studenting easier.

Teaching Point

Today, I want to teach you that you can collect and save brain tools that make school and life easier.

Practice Together

For illustrative purposes, I've used studying as a context for listing brain tools; the emphasis is on the prevalence and awareness of tools, not the tools themselves. Try to capture all ideas, as you're aiming to demonstrate the vastness of brain tools, not evaluate the tools at this time.

> **One thing that's been tricky for a lot of you lately has been studying. You hear from teachers all the time that you need to study a lot, but we teachers sometimes forget to show you how. Let's work together to think of the brain tools you already use to make studying work for your brain. As we list them from everyone, be on the lookout for tools you'd like to collect and put in your own brain toolbox.**

On your interactive bulletin board or whiteboard, create a list of brain tools for studying, with space to add on in the future.

Invitation to Use the Skill

> **Identify your top three studying brain tools. They can be ones you use or ones that inspired you today.**

Ask the students the following questions.

- **Where will you keep your tools so you remember them?**
- **How will you make these tools obvious to future you so you have them when you need them?**
- **How and when can you tell you will need them?**

Ideas for a Visual

The following are some ideas for creating an anchor chart or similar visual.

- Create a chart of brain tools for studying with the class.
- Display this teaching point: "I can collect and save brain tools that make school and life easier."

My Reflections and Improvements for Next Time

Think of Your Working Memory Like a Whiteboard

Objective: Students will learn to consider their working memory, its natural limitations, and strategies to support it, in application to daily academic and life activities.

Executive function areas: Metacognition, strategy awareness, and self-awareness

When to use this lesson:

- You notice that students often seem distracted; students are having a hard time following multistep directions; students are missing parts of prompts
- In advance of increased independence requirements or multistep processes

Lesson audience: Whole class or small groups

Estimated time: Twenty to thirty minutes

Notes and adaptations: If students need more examples to understand the impact of distractions on working memory, consider exploring what it feels like to try to work when hungry or sick (interoceptive information is distracting and using working memory space) or the challenges of switching between their phones and schoolwork. Keep in mind that some brains are prone to distraction, like those with ADHD, and it is not a behavioral or character flaw. Rather, it's neurological and something that these strategies and awareness can help.

Connect and Open the Lesson

Have you ever walked into a room and thought to yourself, "Why am I here?" Or maybe you've seen an adult at home do that. The part of your brain that keeps track of the stuff you're actually paying attention to is called your working memory. Think of your working memory like a little whiteboard with notes on it. That mental whiteboard is what helps you think in class or keep track of plays in a game.

The tricky part is, this working memory whiteboard in your brain is kind of small because it can only hold three to seven memories, and it is erased and rewritten easily and all the time.

Your working memory whiteboard holds everything you're actively thinking about, such as this lesson, how you feel in your shoes or sitting in the chair, your best friend's outfit, the smell in the room—all the things. And, just as I listed those things, you

probably thought about them. They went on your working memory whiteboard. Oh, but there's a tradeoff. For anything to get into your working memory, usually something else must go. Your working memory whiteboard is constantly erased and rewritten, and that process takes a lot of energy.

Think about when you (or your parents) need to find an address while you're driving somewhere. When this happens, many people turn the music down or off because the quiet means sounds won't take up space in your working memory. There are other tricks to help your working memory too.

Teaching Point

Today, I want to teach you that you can protect and support your working memory, which acts like a whiteboard in your brain.

Practice Together

Think about when you want to remember a list or a phone number. What do you do?

Students will likely give variations of the answer "repeat it to yourself."

Repeating something to yourself is an example of helping your working memory. If you repeat something, it's like rewriting it on your mental whiteboard. Let's write that down as a way you support your working memory. What else do you do when you need to remember something?

Potential answers could be the following.

- Quiz myself
- Write it down
- Set a reminder
- Make a mnemonic
- Create a song

Awesome. We've got a good list of ways to make working memory a bit more effective. Now, let's think about how to protect it. We know distractions and incoming information, like sounds, can erase parts of our whiteboard. When might we need to protect our working memory? What might we do to protect it?

Figure A.1 is an example of a chart created with students.

Support Working Memory	Protect Working Memory
• Repeat things to myself • Quiz myself and practice recall • Write things down • Set a reminder for future activities • Use or make a mnemonic • Create a song to condense information	• Limit distractions • Turn down sounds • Get into a space where things aren't moving around me • Use headphones to limit sound • Tell others I need to focus

Figure A.1: Strategies for supporting and protecting working memory.

Invitation to Use the Skill

> ***You'll likely recognize the moments you need to protect or support your working memory because you'll know something is important, or you'll feel the burn of forgetting and trying to find something again in your mind. How will you remind future you to try one of the strategies we thought of today?***

Ideas for a Visual

- Create with students and then post a chart, modeled after the one in figure A.1, demonstrating ways to support and protect working memory.
- Display this teaching point: "You can protect and support your working memory, which acts like a whiteboard in your brain."

My Reflections and Improvements for Next Time

Remember That Stressed Brains Struggle With Thinking

Objective: Students will learn how stress impacts the brain, including how it impedes problem solving.

Executive function area: Self-regulation

When to use this lesson:

- You notice students are dysregulated but not necessarily aware of it; students are resistant to using self-regulation strategies and the stress level is high
- In advance of high-stress times (for example, finals)

Lesson audience: Whole class, small groups, or individuals

Estimated time: Twenty to thirty minutes

Notes and adaptations: Consider showing students a video of Daniel Siegel's hand model of the brain and "flipping your lid" as context for the lesson (Siegel, 2017). In the following Connect and Open the Lesson section, you may need a different lesson opening if your school is in a state that does not change between standard time and daylight-saving time.

Connect and Open the Lesson

The other day, I was running really late for an appointment with the principal before school. My brain was imagining everything that would happen because I was late. Would I get fired? Would the principal be so upset she wouldn't talk to me? Would she make my evaluation look bad after being late? My brain was really stressed.

While I was driving, I kept worrying. I got to school about fifteen minutes later than my appointment. I walked as quickly as I could into the office, but the principal wasn't there. Almost no one was. And then I looked at the clock. I was forty-five minutes early because of the time change. My brain was so stressed that I couldn't think to look at the clock in my car. I missed the chance to use tools to calm down, and because my brain stayed so stressed, I didn't realize that I was totally fine.

Teaching Point

Today, I want to teach you that stressed brains have a hard time thinking. Therefore, calming down your brain can help you think of solutions when you're stressed.

Practice Together

Let's discuss. What are some moments when you really feel stressed? In those moments, what does your brain feel like? What are the thoughts or actions you usually have? Have you missed anything that would have helped you because you were so stressed?

Now that we recognize that stressed brains struggle with thinking, how will you remind future you to calm yourself in moments of stress? It may also help to think of the stressful moments you can predict and plan to avoid asking your brain to do hard thinking at that time.

Invitation to Use the Skill

You'll know when you're stressed, but your brain may not realize that it's not thinking so well. Consider a few ways you may remind yourself in the future that you need to be calm to think well.

Ideas for a Visual

- Create an interactive board where students can add their calming techniques to share with each other.
- Display this teaching point: "Stressed brains have a hard time thinking, and calming down your brain can help you think of solutions when you're stressed."

My Reflections and Improvements for Next Time

Make Space Your Ally to Get Things Done and Feel Better

Objective: Students will learn how their environment impacts their behavior and how they can engineer their spaces to support focus and effective use of time.

Executive function areas: Self-regulation and attention management

When to use this lesson:

- You notice students are distracted, disorganized, or messy
- In advance of increased student demands, multiday essays or projects, and increased work outside of class

Lesson audience: Whole class or small groups

Estimated time: Twenty minutes

Notes and adaptations: Be careful to avoid language that shames students for living circumstances outside of their control. If you choose to discuss off-campus study spaces, be sure to include public spaces like libraries or local colleges to expand students' options. Remember, not every brain responds well to quiet spaces. Some brains scan a quiet environment for new sounds, increasing the frequency of distraction. These students may prefer to work with music or ambient sound.

Connect and Open the Lesson

The other day, I saw a cartoon where a character's papers and wrappers and cups—his mess—could talk. They said things like, "Clean me up," and "I think I smell bad," which was funny, but it also got me thinking. The spaces around us can distract us. We're getting small messages from our spaces, telling our brains how to act or reminding us of things we need to clean up or get done. Our stuff can't talk in real life, but there are lots of sounds in our spaces that may be stealing our attention. Focusing when we're in distracting places makes us play on hard mode by accident. Each of our brains are distracted by different things, but what we share in common is that we need to change our environments to match what our brains need.

Teaching Point

Today, I want to teach you that you can make your spaces your allies and those allies can help you focus and finish work easier and faster.

Practice Together

> **Let's think about visual distractions for a second. I'll be brave and have us look around the classroom first. What distracts you here? Are there things that you see every day that have become less obvious to you now? Are there things that always attract your attention? One way to manage visual distractions is to limit them. We could take everything off the walls (please don't), but it may feel weird without anything there. Instead, what could you do to limit how much you see when you need to focus?**

Answers might include move away, cover the visuals, or move to a dedicated focus space, like a library or study room.

> **Another distraction that comes from the spaces we're in is sound. Sometimes, our brains register a new sound and momentarily attend to the sound to figure out what it is. This process can happen without us knowing and take a few moments from our focus. We obviously can't take away all sounds, and dead silence itself might not be ideal. The idea is to think about the sound levels and types that help you focus. That might be different depending on the situation. Let's see what we can come up with when we explore the types and volume of sounds that help in different situations.**

Figure A.2 (page 184) shows an example chart of different approaches to sound. Italicized words represent potential answers. Alternative answers are common and acceptable, as different brains react differently to sound.

Invitation to Use the Skill

> **There's no right or wrong way to make space your ally. You will likely have to practice and adjust until you find the setups and spaces that help you maintain focus and energy to complete your tasks. Consider starting with the visuals and sounds that are in your environment when you're trying to work.**
>
> **You'll know you need to think about your working environment when you've been attempting a task for more than about fifteen minutes but haven't gotten started. Another sign is when you're noticing the distractions, but you can do something to alleviate their effects.**

Ideas for a Visual

- Create a chart with students on different approaches to sound, modeled on figure A.2 (page 184), and post it in the classroom.

Activity	Type of Sound Volume of sound	Why It Might Help
Listening to a lecture and taking notes	Quiet environment Sound of teacher as focus Outside sounds limited	• Quiet allows focus on teacher's voice. • Reducing sound input can help you process learning and notes.
Working on my school tasks with words (like essays, reading)	Music without lyrics Medium volume Quiet, no outside sounds	• Music can help motivate. • Omitting lyrics can help your brain process language. • Some brains work best in quiet for writing and reading.
Working on my school tasks without many words (like mathematics, art)	Music with lyrics (or without) Medium volume	• Some tasks are OK for lyrics, if you're not having to process a lot of language. • You may find that predictable sounds help your brain focus (since it's not scanning the environment for new sounds).
Working on physical tasks (like cleaning a room, chores, making a meal)	An upbeat movie soundtrack, video game songs, or other energizing music Possibly a conversation with a friend or someone who's working with you A predictable show or podcast Maybe louder volume	• Our brains respond to the energy of music. It can help you activate to get a task done. • Shows and podcasts can be helpful soundtracks for tasks, if you don't have to look at them while they're on.

Figure A.2: Different approaches to sound.

- Create and post a similar chart that lists visual adaptations in the environment that support focus.
- Display this teaching point: "Space can be my ally. I can engineer spaces that match what I need to do."

My Reflections and Improvements for Next Time

Use Differentiation to Visually Organize Physical and Digital Spaces

Objective: Students will learn different methods of visually differentiating online and physical spaces to streamline organization.

Executive function area: Organization

When to use this lesson:

- You notice students are disorganized and struggle to find things; you're prompting them a lot to get ready; they have to go back and forth from their lockers or backpacks
- In advance of increased academic demands

Lesson audience: whole group, small groups, or individuals

Estimated time: Fifteen minutes

Notes and adaptations: If you work with students in challenging socioeconomic situations, avoid recommending they buy new school supplies to color code. Instead, consider providing colored sticky notes, tape, or other shared supplies for their use. Plan to prompt students to use their systems for a few weeks after the lesson; they may need several opportunities to practice the pause to organize before it internalizing it. Sharing this strategy with parents can help students generalize their skills to all settings.

Connect and Open the Lesson

The other day, I was hanging out with another teacher, talking to her while she organized for the day. She was so fast! She zipped along and seemed to not even need to think about where things go. Sometimes organizing (and staying organized) is hard for me, so I asked her how she made it so easy. She said it was also hard for her, but she found a shortcut: She makes things in different categories look different, so it's easy to know where they go!

Teaching Point

Today, I want to teach you an organization hack. You can make items in different categories look different so they're easy to organize. One great way to do this is to use different colors for different things.

Practice Together

> Let's think about your organization demands. You have many subjects, with papers and digital files. You also have school, social, home, and possibly work things in your schedule. Without a system, your physical and digital spaces can become overwhelming. Let's explore a few examples of making your items look different to stay organized.
>
> **Subjects example:** A great place to start is to choose a color for each subject for the divider tabs in your binder or your folder. When you place all your mathematics in your green mathematics folder, for example, that means that you quickly know both where things go and what to grab in your backpack or locker. Let's take a minute and decide which colors you want each subject to be. We don't have to match each other. Once you've decided, you have choices. For example, you can color in the divider tabs, or add a colored sticky note or tape to a divider or folder you already have. You can also make a note to get new folders, if that works for you.
>
> **Digital folders example:** Just like your physical papers for classes, you can add color to separate your class folders online. I'll show you a model of a few of my folders and how to choose their colors.

This may be an opportunity to lead students to create class folders if they haven't done so already. Look for online video tutorials for setting up folders in Google Drive (https://workspace.google.com/products/drive), Microsoft OneNote (https://www.microsoft.com/en-us/microsoft-365/onedrive/online-cloud-storage), or other digital organization tools to guide you.

> **Calendar example:** Another way to organize is by organizing your time. Calendars are one space where you can use colors or symbols to quickly see the different appointments or tasks you have coming up. Some people like to make different colors for each class. Others make school, social, and home tasks their own colors. There's no wrong way to color code your calendar. Remember, it's a way of seeing your organization system easily, helping you make decisions and plan more smoothly.

Choose one or more of the preceding organizational strategies and lead students to create their own color or symbol system to organize.

Invitation to Use the Skill

> Many times, you'll want to set up your folder, binder, online work, or calendar system when you start the school term. You may also want to do so if you're noticing it's taking you a long time to find things or organize at the end of a class.

Ideas for a Visual

- Add photos of example organization systems to your strategies bulletin board. Students may also take and even share their own photos for reference.
- Display this teaching point: "Make items in different categories look different so they're easy to organize."

My Reflections and Improvements for Next Time

Use the Pile, Sort, Purge, Put Back, Photo, Plan (PSP4) Organizing Strategy

Objective: Students will learn the PSP4 organizing strategy to organize their physical belongings.

Executive function area: Organization

When to use this lesson:

- You notice that the classroom, desks, or students' backpacks are disorganized, or students are losing finished work
- In advance of increased academic demands or a school event for parents

Lesson audience: Whole class or small groups

Estimated time: Forty-five minutes, with time for students to complete the PSP4 organizing strategy

Notes and adaptations: The time investment for this lesson will pay off for you and your students. Consider teaching this lesson after a test or other demanding period, where students need engagement but a small break from content. Some students will need help determining what to keep or purge, and many will need to go through the process a few times before it becomes routine practice. Some students may need help physically designating the space to use for piling and sorting. Their own desktop is a great option. Other ideas include making a circle with masking tape or dry erase marker or using a piece of butcher paper to define the workspace.

Connect and Open the Lesson

I've heard from students in almost every period that they're feeling disorganized. In fact, when I went through and marked missing work online recently, at least ten students emailed me to say they either lost the work or forgot to turn it in because it was too messy in their binders or backpacks. I know a lot of your work is digital these days, but you still have papers to organize and probably your rooms at home, yeah?

Getting organized isn't as easy as just putting your papers in your binder or cleaning up the clothes in your room. It feels overwhelming to a lot of students—and even for me. But, organizing is a skill, and just like the other skills, we can learn to do it and make it easier.

Teaching Point

Today, I want to teach you the PSP4 organizing strategy for getting (and staying) organized.

Practice Together

I'm going to quickly go over the steps, but for most of our time together, we're going to use the PSP4 organizing strategy to organize your backpacks, binders, or both.

1. **Pile:** Our first step will be to collect all the things in one pile. This makes sure we have everything and we don't get distracted finding things. At school, this might be a pile of papers; at home, this might be a pile of clothes or dishes and cups in your room.
2. **Sort:** In the next step, we sort our big pile into smaller ones. My favorite way to do this is to make three smaller piles—(1) Yes, keep it; (2) No, this is garbage, and (3) Maybe, I need to think about whether I need it. Try to move at a medium pace here. You want to move fast enough to not get distracted thinking about the object you're sorting, and slow enough to not accidentally throw away something you need.

   Once you have your three piles, go back to the maybe pile. You can ask yourself (or partner with someone to explore), "Will I need this later to study or turn in?" "Do I use this as a reference?" "Would it cost money or time to make or buy this again?" Your maybe pile will be gone after you move the things to the yes or no piles.
3. **Purge:** When we purge, we dump the recyclable materials in the no pile into the recycling bin and the rest into the trash. Celebrate a little!
4. **Put Back:** You now have only your yes pile. Don't rush this step. Put the items you're keeping back in a place that both makes sense to you and will help future you find them quickly. If it's inside your binder, be sure to use a hole punch and add them in the class section, behind the divider.
5. **Photo:** Many times, it can help to take a photo (or notes) for reference. When you can see what organized looks like for you, it's easier to replicate based on your photo. Save your photo in your digital notes app.
6. **Plan:** Organization works when we keep it up! For our last stage, we plan how we will maintain and update our organization systems. When will we do the PSP4 organizing strategy again? How will we make it easier for our future

selves to maintain the system? Note down your plan, add your next organization session to your calendar, and set a reminder.

Invitation to Use the Skill

Go through the PSP4 steps together. Be sure to help students stay on track with the steps, especially when they are determining what to do with their maybe piles.

Ideas for a Visual

Figure A.3 lays out the PSP4 organizing strategy. Post this for students to refer to in the classroom. You may also want to add photos of different organized spaces and systems, for ideas.

Pile: Gather all the things related to the area or topic of your binder or backpack.	**Sort:** Create piles of Yes/Keep, No/Trash, and Maybe (ask a teacher or peer).	**Purge:** The No/Trash pile goes into the garbage *as you sort*.
Put back: Return the Yes/Keep items to their proper spaces, possibly adding or clarifying labels to make using the system easier moving forward.	**Photo:** Take a photo of what "organized" looks like as a reference for yourself.	**Plan:** After organizing, reflect on the process. What went right? What did you learn? How do you plan to use your organization system throughout the week? How will you remember to use it?

Figure A.3: The PSP4 organizing strategy.

Visit ***go.SolutionTree.com/lifeskills*** *to download the free reproducibles in this book*

My Reflections and Improvements for Next Time

Plan Work Time With Warm-Ups and Cooldowns

Objective: Students will learn to organize their scheduled activities using a template that includes warm-up and cooldown time to more accurately account for entire processes.

Executive function areas: Organization and planning

When to use this lesson:

- You notice students are rushing through work and not leaving time to set up or clean up; student work is often late; students are packing up in a rush or leaving class late
- In advance of increased independence demands or a transition to a more challenging unit or grade

Lesson audience: Whole class or small groups

Estimated time: Twenty minutes

Notes and adaptations: After this lesson, you may want to use the warm-up and cool-down language in discussing your plan for each period. You can extend the learning from this lesson by reminding students to add warm-up and cooldown time when they calendar tasks for your class. Students may need further support in estimating the amount of time to save for warm-ups and cooldowns; consider encouraging them to plan in fifteen- or twenty-minute blocks of time.

Connect and Open the Lesson

The other day my [nephew, son, or friend] was making a schedule for his day. He had a lot to do, so he planned his time in thirty-minute increments. It was a great idea, but then I noticed something. He had planned to be at the gym between 9:00 to 10:30 a.m., do his homework from 10:30 a.m. to 1:00 p.m., then be at a restaurant for lunch at 1:00 p.m. His plan looked great, but he forgot an important part of planning. You must plan for travel, get-ready time, and cleanup time. This can be tricky for our brains, but there's an easy way to think about planning.

Teaching Point

Today, I want to teach you how to think about tasks like workouts or sports practices where there is a warm-up, an activity, then a cooldown. These warm-ups and cooldowns help us make a realistic plan and are opportunities to organize.

Practice Together

> *Most of the time, getting tasks done takes some setup because we need to go where we need to be, have the necessary things, and even get into the mindset to do what we need to do. The setup is like our warm-up.*
>
> *After we finish something, we often need to put away our things, save or turn in files, or move to a new location. These activities are our cooldown.*
>
> *When we can think about our warm-ups and cooldowns, we get the chance to help our future selves. We can think ahead about what we need, how much time tasks actually take, and how to clean up so that we stay organized.*
>
> *Let's look at a typical period for our class to see if we can determine the warm-ups and cooldowns.*

Make a brief sketch of a typical class period together. The discussion may include students answering the following questions.

- How do you enter the room and get set up?
- What do you need to have out and what needs to be put away?
- Are there typical warm-up activities or daily business?
- For the cooldown, how do you jot down your homework and dates?
- How do you organize your materials to be ready to leave the room?

Invitation to Use the Skill

> *You can think about your warm-ups and cooldowns for each class, for homework time, and even for things like work and chores. You'll know you need to plan for warm-ups and cooldowns if you're feeling rushed and things take longer than you planned. You also may need to try this strategy when you know you're going to be really busy, like finals week.*

Idea for a Visual

- Create (or have students create) a poster or large sticky note with this teaching point: "Think about tasks like workouts or sports practices where there is a warm-up (getting ready), an activity, then a cooldown (cleaning up)." You or the students may want to add a visual to draw attention.

My Reflections and Improvements for Next Time

Recognize Your Brain Stealers to Earn Back Your Time and Focus

Objective: Students will learn to identify and manage the elements that distract them to help improve their focus.

Executive function area: Time (attention) management

When to use this lesson:

- You notice students are off task often, or distractions are slowing down their work
- In advance of more independent work, study, or project demands

Lesson audience: Whole group, small groups, or individuals

Estimated time: Fifteen to twenty minutes

Notes and adaptations: This lesson can also be fodder for coaching conversations and asking questions to explore where students' attention goes and how to increase their focus by managing distractions. Keep in mind that students with ADHD may have neurochemical reasons for being distracted, so be mindful you are neutrally describing distraction and avoiding shaming remarks.

Connect and Open the Lesson

Have you ever dreaded doing something because you thought it would take forever, but it was actually really fast? Or, maybe the opposite happened, when you thought something would be really quick, but it took a long time. You might hear people tell you to work on your time management, but I'd like to offer a new idea.

Time management is actually attention management. The time we need to finish something often speeds up or slows down due to our attention or distraction levels. When we think about what helps us focus best, we can help our brains work more efficiently, making work feel possibly quicker or easier.

Teaching Point

Time management is attention management. When you recognize what steals your brain's attention, you can plan ways to avoid distractions and get the most out of your time.

Practice Together

> ***Think of a time when you really felt locked in, focused on something, even if it wasn't a school thing. What was happening around you? What were you doing or, better yet, not doing? Chances are, when you visualize yourself being really focused, you're zoned in on the task, not being taken away from it by distractions. That focused space can feel amazing and make better use of your time. And, the great news is we can plan for it!***
>
> ***Let's explore the usual distractions we face and brainstorm some ways to avoid or limit them when we need to work.***

See figure A.4 for a sample chart about avoiding distractions. The text in the "How to Avoid or Limit Distraction" column shows potential student responses. Honor what your students offer, adding in ideas from here as you see fit.

Distraction Example	How to Avoid or Limit Distraction
Socializing when you have independent work to do	Move to a focus space, alone for a while Ask your friends to also focus, so you're nearby but not talking Take a quick break to talk, and then tell your friends you're working now
Notifications, apps, games, or social media on your phone	Silence your phone Put it where you can't see it Airplane mode Set hours (phone settings) that you can and can't access certain apps or games
Tabs on your browser that are just for fun	Use an extension to save your tabs so you can close them Use a dedicated browser window for work Set and use breaks so you have time to explore the fun tabs too
Student ideas	

Figure A.4: Common distractions and strategies to avoid them.

Invitation to Use the Skill

> **We can continue to practice planning for strong focus. These strategies and ideas are applicable to all your classes. As you test them out, you'll start to learn more about your brain and know how to adjust your world so you're better able to manage your attention.**

Ideas for a Visual

- Add the distractions strategy chart in figure A.4 (page 197) to your wall for reference.
- Consider adding one or both of these teaching points to your strategies bulletin board: "Time management is attention management," or, "When you recognize what steals your brain's attention, you can plan ways to avoid distractions and get the most out of your time."

Your Reflections and Improvements for Next Time

Use Backward Planning to Meet Deadlines

Objective: Students will learn how to backward plan so that they can schedule the important steps to complete an assignment by the deadline.

Executive function area: Time (attention) management

When to use this lesson:

- You notice students are procrastinating, or there are large projects, essays, or tests on the calendar
- In advance of multiday projects or essays, or on the day you introduce a project or essay

Lesson audience: Whole class, small groups, or individuals

Estimated time: Twenty to thirty minutes

Notes and adaptations: This lesson lends itself to continuing in coaching conversations. Backward planning will advance to planning a day, which includes estimating the time a task will take. This could be difficult for some students, so be prepared to offer suggestions of how long to roughly plan for each task. Initially, you'll be setting daily steps or goals without deep consideration for the estimated time (more like a to-do list or mini-goals so they meet the larger deadline). This is one lesson you can ask students to share their "starts" —the beginnings of their answers—to help students who may be struggling to initiate.

Connect and Open the Lesson

This is a great lesson to apply to real life. If possible, use a project, essay, or lab from your class as an example so students actively engage in using the backward planning strategy.

> I imagine our [project or paper name] isn't the only thing that's on your calendar right now. It can feel like a lot to balance, having multiple deadlines, tests, and dates! And, it's pretty common to cope with this overwhelm by not dealing with assignments until the night before they're due: the dreaded procrastination. I get it. But there is a way to work with your brain and help yourself meet deadlines, and it's called backward planning.

Teaching Point

> Today, I want to teach you that backward planning is a way to manage projects, papers, and tests and get them done on time!

Practice Together

Display your project prompt in a format you can write on, as well as a calendar that represents today through the due date. (An alternative is to make a table that serves as a calendar, to demonstrate the strategy's flexibility.)

> Let's look at our [project or paper]. By [due date], you will have [project] done. But what happens in between? Do you wait until the day before the project is due to start? Maybe, but it's likely that would be really stressful. Let's backward plan and schedule small chunks so you'll be on time.
>
> First, we look at the project and read the requirements a few times. We may also visualize the final product, maybe even the process of completing it. We're starting to get a feel for the process we will need to go through, so let's get more specific about the steps.
>
> One strategy is to chunk the assignment into smaller steps. We can number parts of the prompt to find some of our steps. Or, we can go back to our visualization and explore what we will be doing to complete the project. Each "scene" we picture is a step.

Model this with your project or essay, annotating the assignment to clarify the components and steps (see pages 49 and 50).

> Once we see the chunks or steps, it's time to put each one on the calendar. We can go backward from the due date. The last step I see is [name the step]. I'm going to write that step two days before the due date, to give myself wiggle room. The second to last step is [name the step]. I imagine that step will take a few days, so I'm going to back up three days and write it there.

Proceed through the steps, writing them on your model calendar. Ask students to do the same in their digital calendars, planners, or even on a makeshift calendar they create on the assignment sheet.

> Look at our plan! Will it go perfectly? Probably not. You might be early or late for your goal dates, and that's OK. What we know about having a plan with smaller chunks and mini-deadlines is that you're less likely to feel overwhelmed and more likely to get your project done on time!

Invitation to Use the Skill

> You can use backward planning for anything that takes a few days to complete. You can plan studying, essays, even packing for a vacation or planning a party. Backward planning helps take a big

assignment and make it manageable, giving you small steps and clear deadlines.

Ideas for a Visual

- Post the backward plan calendar for each long-term assignment.
- Display this teaching point: "Backward planning is a way to manage projects, papers, and tests and get them done on time!" You can also add the example prompt and calendar to your bulletin board.
- Add the backward planning calendar to the assignment files on your digital learning platform.

My Reflections and Improvements for Next Time

Perform a Test Replay to Earn a Better Grade Next Time

Objective: Students will learn how to reflect on their experience with an assessment to become aware of their strengths and weaknesses and use that awareness to adjust their studying and test-taking approaches.

Executive function areas: Studying and grades

When to use this lesson:

- You notice that students didn't do as well as expected on a test or students are expressing disappointment in their grades
- In advance of assessments, progress reports or report cards, or midterms and finals

Lesson audience: Whole class or small groups

Estimated time: Thirty minutes

Notes and adaptations: Some students may have significant feelings about their test grades. Make space to honor the emotions they experience and the real or perceived pressures they are under. It's helpful to do this exercise together after several assessments, as it gets students in the practice of reviewing—and learning from—their performance. If test corrections are part of your practice, consider adding some of the test replay components to your test correction protocols.

Connect and Open the Lesson

We just took [test name], and I'm proud of each of you. I know it's complicated getting your grades back, as there can be pressure to do well and disappointment when you don't do as well as you thought. Every single test—the high and low scores—gives you a chance to learn how to play the game of school a little bit better, showing you how to adjust your studying and test approach so you do better each time.

Teaching Point

Today, I want to teach you how to do a test replay so you can learn from your tests and adjust how you study and take future assessments.

Practice Together

> **Let's look at [test name] with a curious mindset. We're becoming sports analysts or detectives, looking for patterns and clues.**

Lead students through the test replay, allowing them to reflect, share, and jot down their ideas. When you discuss ideas for next time, consider the following suggestions.

- Match your study approach with the test format.
    - Multiple-choice or matching questions (study approach: memorize using flash cards or use questions at end of chapters)
    - Essays or short answer (study approach: memorize some sentence starters, write practice essays, memorize vocabulary and key facts)
- Schedule time to check in with teacher three to five days before the test.
- Schedule study time for smaller chunks across three to five days.
- Focus on the materials where you know the questions are likely to come from.
- Clear your social schedule the day before the test.
- Set a bedtime two or three nights before the test.
- Join or form a study group.

Use figure A.5 (page 204) as reflective tool for students to use shortly after taking a test. Students may complete this regularly as part of their test-taking experience, and you may refer students to their recent reflections as they prepare for their next assessments.

Invitation to Use the Skill

> **We'll do a few of these replays together this year. You can also use this process after any test, including your ACTs or SATs. It helps get your brain in the mindset of reflecting and adjusting your strategies after every test. You'll likely find this strategy really helpful in college too.**

Idea for a Visual

- Display this teaching point: "Test replays help you learn from your tests and adjust how you study and take future assessments." However, do not post students' actual test replays to your strategies bulletin board.

My Test Replay

After I test, I can reflect on the content and how to take a test in this class (the process).

Brain Dump

What's on my mind after the test?

Deep Dive

What do I remember about the content? (What did the test ask about?)

What do I remember about the format? (How did the test look?)

How do I predict I did?

What was I well prepared for?

What parts felt shaky to me?

What did my teacher seem to emphasize or not cover well? (Ideas for tutoring or after school support)

How did the test compare to my expectations?

What surprised me?

How prepared do I feel I was after taking the test? (circle one)

Not at all Kind of Totally

How much did I study versus how much studying may be necessary? (circle one)

Not at all Not enough Enough A little too much Way too much

The test format was (check all that apply)

- ☐ Multiple choice
- ☐ Short answer
- ☐ Essays
- ☐ Matching

The questions seemed to come from (check all that apply)

- ☐ My notes
- ☐ The readings
- ☐ The practice test
- ☐ The lecture slides
- ☐ What my teacher repeated or emphasized
- ☐ Videos we watched in class
- ☐ I'm not sure

My Plan for Next Time

Study:

During the test:

Figure A.5: Test replay reflective tool.

Visit ***go.SolutionTree.com/lifeskills*** *for a free reproducible version of this figure.*

My Reflections and Improvements for Next Time

Find Points Vampires to Give Your Grades a Quick Boost

Objective: Students will learn to audit their grade reports to find patterns of needs, empowering them to adjust their approaches and improve their grades.

Executive function areas: Grades and studying

When to use this lesson:

- You notice that students are missing work, or their grades are suffering due to patterns of struggle
- In advance of progress reports or report cards

Lesson audience: Whole class, small groups, or individuals

Estimated time: Fifteen minutes

Notes and adaptations: It helps to have fictional student grade examples for a shared model. This lesson can be extended into a coaching conversation, allowing students to explore where they are missing out on points and possibly develop strategies to address the recognized pattern. Examining example student grade printouts can lead to discussions about prioritizing high-value assignments. If you'd like to address this strategy, make a note to yourself to ask questions about it.

Connect and Open the Lesson

Teachers love patterns. We like routines and often use the same ideas, lessons, and assignments year after year. You can use this to your advantage because these patterns are often the paths to boosting your grades.

Let's say a teacher assigns ten points a week for your warm-ups. You may think, "It's only ten points, so no big deal." But if it's a weekly pattern, those ten points will be about 150 points by your report card. Then, those points are a big deal.

It can be tricky to see these patterns without some help. But, once you know how to find these "points vampires," these patterns where you're losing points like a vampire might be stealing your blood, you can give your grade a quick boost by changing your pattern.

Teaching Point

Today, I want to teach you that you can find your points vampires and give your grades a quick boost.

Practice Together

Provide a few fictional student assignment printouts. These may come from your learning management system, where student assignments, tests, and other grades are displayed together, forming a picture of the overall grade.

> **Let's check out this example. Take a look at the overall grade, the assignment grades, and anything that jumps out at you. Where is this student doing well? What seems to be a pattern for them? Where is this student losing points? What do you think might help them boost their grade?**

Continue with further examples. Then, ask students to pull up a grade screen from one of their classes. Ask them to look at the patterns they notice. Are there places they are excelling? Patterns where they lose points? Allow time for independent reflection then gather the class to wrap up.

Ask students to share anything they notice. What do they plan to adjust? How might making that adjustment impact their grade? How will they help themselves remember their adjustments?

Invitation to Use the Skill

> **Anytime you're feeling less than satisfied with your grade or you have a grade that you want to boost, you can look for your points vampires and adjust. Sometimes, when you see your own patterns, you have the chance to improve your grade in what feels like an easier way.**

Ideas for a Visual

- Display this teaching point: "You can find your points vampires and give your grades a quick boost."
- If the patterns in your class are readily apparent, consider adding a visual that demonstrates the percentages or importance of each type of assignment or assessment to students' final grades. You can also adjust your online learning platform so that it clearly indicates the percentage value of each assignment or category (assessments, homework, and so on).

My Reflections and Improvements for Next Time

Use Active Studying to Score Better on Assessments

Objective: Students will learn methods of active studying to increase effectiveness of studying and align practice with what each type of assessment demands.

Executive function areas: Studying and grades

When to use this lesson:

- You notice students are not studying effectively or at all; students are reporting not knowing how to study; test scores are lower than expected
- In advance of assessments, progress reports, or report cards

Lesson audience: Whole class, small groups, or individuals

Estimated time: Fifteen to twenty minutes

Notes and adaptations: While your colleagues may recommend rereading as an effective study technique, focus instead on the benefits and examples of active studying. You may refer students back to their previous test replays (see page 202) and ask them to match the test question types with their study approaches.

Connect and Open the Lesson

Have you ever spent hours studying for a test and still did awful? I know I have! That can be such a frustrating, demoralizing experience. I mean, you put in the effort, but it didn't pay off.

Chances are you've been told so many times to study, but it's likely you haven't really learned how. That's usually the reason we spend a lot of time studying but we don't get the results we want.

Teaching Point

Today, I want to teach how to use active studying to do better on tests and feel better about studying.

Practice Together

Most of the time, when we picture studying, we imagine reading the book or our notes, or clicking through a slideshow. For many people, this passive approach isn't enough and can feel kind of boring. There's a lot of research that says we need to be active in our studying. We need to think about and do something with the information we're learning, or we risk forgetting it for the test.

Active studying can be many things. Let's see what we can add to this chart.

Use figure A.6 as a model chart to complete with students. You may want to have the first two columns filled in to get your discussion started. Then have students add their own active studying ideas. Complete the third column as a class, adding the types of questions best supported by each form of active studying; italicized responses in the third column are potential student answers.

Active studying idea	Why it works	Types of test questions the idea helps with best
Flash cards or Quizlets (https://quizlet.com)	Our brains practice learning and recalling information when we need it. It gives us a chance to repeat the answers we don't know as well.	*Multiple choice* *Matching* *Fill in the blank*
Self-quiz or partner quiz	Our brains practice learning and recalling information when we need it.	*Multiple choice* *Matching* *Fill in the blank*
Practice tests	We get a chance to feel what the test might be like. Previews help our brains see new things as more familiar (and possibly make us less nervous).	*Multiple choice* *Matching* *Fill in the blank* *Short answer* *Essay* *Oral exams*
Practice paragraphs, memorizing sentence frames	We are able to organize our ideas in writing. We get a chance to feel what the test might be like.	*Short answers and essays*
Student examples		

Figure A.6: Model chart to complete with students.

Invitation to Use the Skill

Think about the tests you have coming up. What active studying strategies might you try when you get ready for the test? How will

you remind future you to use these strategies? Would partnering with someone in class or at home be helpful?

Ideas for a Visual

- Add the chart you complete together in figure A.6 (page 211) to your strategies bulletin board.
- Send a copy of the chart home for families to reference or post it on your digital learning space.
- Display this teaching point: "Use active studying to do better on tests and feel better about studying."

My Reflections and Improvements for Next Time

Motivate by Making the Task Clear, Social or Fun, or Urgent

Objective: Students will learn how to motivate themselves to initiate work using urgency, interest, clarity, or specialness to plan their work time.

Executive function area: Planning

When to use this lesson:

- You notice that students are struggling to get started on their work or are sharing feelings of demotivation or overwhelm
- In advance of increased academic demands, more independent time, or group projects

Lesson audience: Whole class, small groups, or individuals

Estimated time: Twenty minutes

Notes and adaptations: Often, when students report feeling unmotivated, they are actually struggling to initiate work. Their intention is to accomplish goals, yet they struggle to do so on their own. You can model this strategy with think-alouds or sharing what you do when you feel tired or need to get moving.

Connect and Open the Lesson

I think I've had at least three students in every class today tell me they're feeling unmotivated lately. It makes sense. When we have lots to do or feel wiped out, it can be really hard to get moving.

I want to challenge your thinking a bit, though. When you say, "I want to get this thing done, but I'm not motivated," that isn't true, is it? You're saying you're motivated because you want to get it done. What you're struggling with is activation—it's getting started. And that's great news. Because there are a few ways to hack your activation and get yourself moving!

Teaching Point

Today, I want to teach you how to use urgency, interest, clarity, and specialness to hack your activation and get yourself moving.

Practice Together

Our brains respond to urgency, interest, and specialness with extra attention; they literally create brain chemicals that help us focus and activate! Making things more clear can also help us activate

because we can show our brains that it's really only a series of small steps to complete. Brains that feel energized and not so overwhelmed have an easier time getting to work.

Let's explore what these hacks look like in real life. I'll give you some ideas for each to get started, and you can share the ways you use, or you might start using, these strategies.

Figure A.7 will help you explore and organize examples for each of the categories that support motivation and activation. Italicized words in the right column depict potential student responses but are not an exhaustive list.

Hack Area	Ideas
Urgency	*Set a timer* *Make it a competition* *Give yourself a deadline for one part* *Plan to finish the work before a scheduled event*
Interest	*Use new markers or pens* *Find something you care about in the assignment* *Reflect on the assignment value (to your life, the world, or your grade)*
Clarity	*Break the assignment or task into small steps* *Annotate the prompt* *Explain the task to someone else to be sure you're clear*
Specialness	*Work in a new place* *Give yourself a fun treat, like hot chocolate or popcorn* *Work with a friend* *Have a playlist or soundtrack for the task*

Figure A.7: Hack areas that support motivation and activation

Invitation to Use the Skill

Whenever you're feeling like it's hard to get started, see if you can use one or more of these hacks. Chances are you'll find the right mix of strategies to help yourself get unstuck and get moving!

Ideas for a Visual

- Add the chart you complete together in figure A.7 to your strategies bulletin board.
- Send a copy of the chart home for families to reference or post it on your digital learning space.
- Display this teaching point: "Use urgency, interest, clarity, and specialness to hack your activation and get yourself moving."

My Reflections and Improvements for Next Time

Use Capture, Schedule, and Remind (CSR) Systems to Manage Your Work

Objective: Students will learn a work-management system in which they capture (list) and schedule their work, then remind themselves of their scheduled work times and deadlines.

Executive function area: Planning

When to use this lesson:

- You notice that students are forgetting assignments or due dates; students are asking questions you've already answered in class; work is consistently late
- In advance of opening a school term or increased student workload

Lesson audience: Whole class, small groups, or individuals

Estimated time: Twenty to thirty minutes

Notes and adaptations: Students' CSR systems will vary, and it may take a few iterations before they find a system that works. You can support their use of the CSR system by creating time and a daily prompt to capture their work for your class, schedule when they'll complete it, and set a reminder. The CSR practice may take three to five minutes daily but will result in more on-time work and less stress for all of you.

Connect and Open the Lesson

Most of my students have been told to "just use a planner," and some of you might use one. Others of you may not. We're not here to shame anyone, and I'm not here to force you to use any particular planner. In fact, we're going to explore all the ways you may manage your workload and your time in a process I call CSR.

CSR means capture, schedule, and remind. These are the steps that you take to manage your workload and time.

Teaching Point

Today, I want to teach you that CSR is a process to manage your work and time.

Practice Together

> Let's look at the parts that make up capture, schedule, and remind, which we will call CSR. First is capture. When you have assignments, to-do tasks, deadlines, and so on, the first step is to capture them somewhere outside of your brain. This could be in your planner or in a space that makes sense to you, like a notebook, a written list, or an audio note to yourself. There are lots of options. The one big point is that you have a system that is the same and consistent; is available to you in all spaces, including school, home, work, and social life; and finally, is something easy and memorable enough for you to use it.
>
> The second part is to schedule when you'll do the task you captured. You might schedule each task, such as math homework from 4:00 to 5:00 p.m. and reading from 5:00 to 5:30 p.m., or you might schedule homework time in the evening around 7:00 p.m. If it's a long-term project, you might add it to your calendar on several days or add smaller steps. When you schedule your work, you're more likely to remember it. However, we have the last part to make sure you do.
>
> The final part of our system is to remind future you to do the task. If you schedule your task in a digital calendar or app, you can add an alarm or notification. If you add it to your paper calendar, you'll need to also set an alarm or a notification in an app, your phone, or a system like Alexa to remind yourself to do the task. You might end up experimenting with how you remind yourself. Some people find that writing things down on paper and then setting digital alarms are right for them, while others do everything digitally. If it's right for you, stick with it!

CSR examples include the following.

- **Capture:** Lists, photos, Google Keep (https://keep.google.com) notes, OneNote (https://www.microsoft.com/en-us/microsoft-365/onedrive/online-cloud-storage), calendars, planners, agendas, online lists, and texts and emails to self
- **Schedule:** Digital or paper calendar, planner, agenda, task cards, to-do lists with specific times, and partner dates
- **Remind:** Alarms, alerts, notifications with specific times, accountability partners, scheduled texts or emails, and planned celebrations

Invitation to Use the Skill

Having a solid CSR system can be a game changer. You get to decide what your system will look like, although it might take a few tries to get it dialed in. Allow yourself to keep experimenting until you find what works best for your brain.

Ideas for a Visual

- Add the list of CSR examples (page 217) to your strategies bulletin board.
- Display this teaching point: "Capture, schedule, remind (CSR) is a process to manage your work and time."

My Reflections and Improvements for Next Time

Use Brain Dumps to Decrease Overwhelm and Help Create a Plan

Objective: Students will learn how to use a brain dump to decrease overwhelm and create a prioritized plan to complete necessary tasks.

Executive function area: Planning

When to use this lesson:

- You notice that students are showing high levels of stress because of concurrent tests or projects in other classes; students have demands outside of school, like jobs or applying for colleges
- In advance of busy times of year, usually toward the end of the grading term

Lesson audience: Whole class, small groups, or individuals

Estimated time: Twenty minutes

Notes and adaptations: Students who think faster than they write may benefit from having a scribe or using a speech-to-text tool. If you scribe for a student, capture their words and avoid commenting on what they share.

Connect and Open the Lesson

You all have a lot going on, a lot that you need to remember, do, and manage. When we have a lot to do or a lot on our mind, it can cause us to feel stressed or overwhelmed. Sometimes that means we'll kind of freeze up and not work as much, even though inside we know we really need to.

We all can use a system to manage stress and make plans when we're overwhelmed. One system is a brain dump, and we're going to practice it today.

Teaching Point

Today, I want to teach you that a brain dump is a way to get out your stress and gently plan to address it.

Practice Together

We're going to do a brain dump together! We'll get all the to-do items—and even some other potential stressors—out of your

> brains. Don't worry, you can keep your brain dump private. Then we'll explore some ways to plan how to deal with what's on the list.
>
> Let's start by getting out what's on our minds. It can be tasks you need to do, for school or outside of school, or for activities you're excited for, worried about, or don't want to forget. I'll give us about a minute and a half to list what's on our minds. If you have a brain that thinks faster than you write, you might want to abbreviate or use a speech-to-text tool.

Encourage students to explore different areas of life during their brain dump: school assignments due soon, assignments that are late, tests coming up, sports, activities inside and outside of school, family calendar items, stressors, and random to-do tasks.

> You don't have to share specifics, but what did you write on your list?

Record students' responses and then continue with the following.

> If any of the ideas your classmates shared reminded you of something, take thirty seconds to add to your brain dump.
>
> Just getting thoughts out of our brains can help reduce stress. But we don't want to stop there. Next, we'll review our brain dump and identify what we aren't going to deal with right now. These are low-priority items because they're not worth a lot of points for your grades or aren't due or happening soon. Cross them off the list or write them in another space for consideration later.
>
> Next, let's look for important items that are your top priorities. They might be big parts of your grades, assignments that are due very soon, tasks that are almost done, or tasks that are big stressors. Choose three to five items that seem very important. These items are where you will devote your time and attention the next time you have a chance to work on them. Schedule them in your personal scheduling system. (Allow time for students to choose and schedule their top three to five tasks).
>
> Let's look at the brain dump one more time. What's left might not be too important but can't be crossed off. For these, we can collect similar tasks and plan to get them all done at once. For example, you could list all the vocabulary assignments and plan to do them back to back. Or, you can add these to your schedule later, since they aren't priorities.
>
> Let's take a moment to reflect on how we feel now that our brain dumps and sorting are done. What do you notice? Was the list as big or small as you predicted? How might this process help you in the future?

Invitation to Use the Skill

> **Anytime you have a lot to do or are feeling overwhelmed, a brain dump can be helpful. You can use the model we used today by dumping all the to-do items out then sorting for what you will let go, what you will prioritize, and what you will schedule. Or, you can adapt it to make it work for your brain.**

Ideas for a Visual

- A model for a brain dump might look like making space for the dump of ideas and tasks, followed by a space to organize the tasks. You may consider including a priority matrix, as figure A.8 (page 222) depicts, or guiding students to identify their priorities based on due date, stress level, or importance to their grades.
- Display this teaching point: "A brain dump is a way to get out your stress and gently plan to address it."

My Reflections and Improvements for Next Time

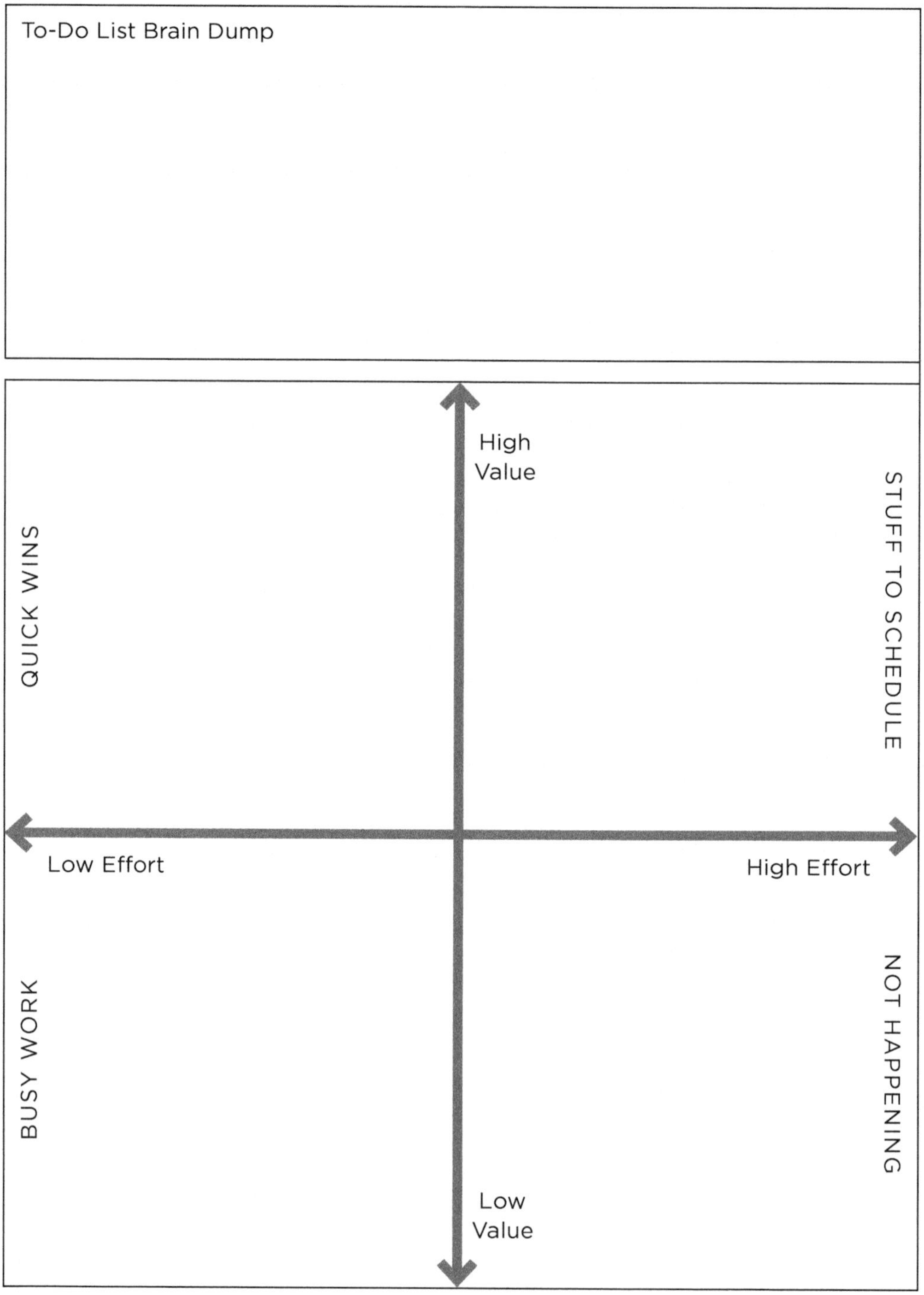

Figure A.8: Priority matrix.

Visit ***go.SolutionTree.com/lifeskills*** *for a free reproducible version of this figure.*

Use the Nice-Ask-Nice Formula for Easy Emails

Objective: Students will learn a formula for creating professional, effective emails in academic and professional settings.

Executive function areas: Social and communication

When to use this lesson:

- You notice students aren't emailing appropriately or when they need to
- At the start of a term or with new students

Lesson audience: Whole class

Estimated time: Ten to fifteen minutes

Notes and adaptations: Consider providing a document with template emails that students can reuse and add to over time. Students who struggle with written work may need more scaffolding, such as sheltered practice of writing emails together or AI tools to help phrase or edit writing. Students with significant executive function deficits may need prompts and visual cues to use their templates. It can help to add "email teacher" to a student's to-do list or schedule for the day to ensure it happens. Additionally, a follow-up task to check email can help ensure students complete the communication process.

Connect and Open the Lesson

Have you ever started to write a new email only to feel stuck on what to say? I just heard from a student who said they'd been trying to email me for two weeks but didn't know the right words to use and felt like it might be easier to just not ask me the question. I get it. Sometimes, teachers need to email parents, you, or each other, and it can feel like an enormous task, so much so that we avoid it. But an easier way to email is to use a formula!

Teaching Point

Today, I want to teach you an easy formula for writing emails, which is the nice-ask-nice formula.

Practice Together

The email formula goes like this: first, say something nice, then ask for something, and finally, say something nice again.

It might look like the following example when writing your teacher.

> Hi, [Insert teacher name],
>
> [Begin by saying something nice.] I hope you're having a great evening. [Then, ask for something.] I'd like to meet with you to ask some questions about the upcoming test. When do you have some time available? [End with saying something nice.] I really appreciate your help.
>
> [Sign your name]

Teachers and your future bosses will appreciate this formula because it's friendly, professional, and clear. Your brain will love the formula because it takes the guessing and worrying out of writing an email. It can almost feel like filling in the blanks, and often it becomes so automatic that you don't think about it anymore.

Invitation to Use the Skill

Let's create a few example emails. We will type them in a shared document so you all will have them for your own use later. How would you use the nice-ask-nice formula to write to a teacher about the following requests?

- To ask a question about an assignment
- To ask about an upcoming date
- To ask for more time or an extension
- To ask about missing work

Ideas for a Visual

- The nice-ask-nice formula can easily become an anchor chart in your classroom. Consider creating (or having students create) a reference that encapsulates the teaching point.
- Share one or two example emails using the nice-ask-nice formula. Consider creating a doc with your example emails and the formula. Later, students can copy the doc and utilize the email templates on their own.

My Reflections and Improvements for Next Time

Hack Group Projects

Objective: Students will learn strategies to successfully work in groups.

Executive function areas: Social, communication, and planning

When to use this lesson:

- You notice that students have conflict or work inefficiently in groups
- In advance of labs, group work, or Socratic seminars

Lesson audience: Whole class or small groups

Estimated time: Fifteen to twenty minutes

Notes and adaptations: Consider embedding support for group work, like mindfully partnering and grouping students, assigning clear roles, and having scheduled check-ins and work-segment deadlines. Students with social needs, such as those on the autism spectrum, may need direct instruction on social communication strategies and support to understand the hidden curriculum of social rules.

Connect and Open the Lesson

Every year, when I ask students to give me feedback on their experience in class, many students tell me how much they hated group work. They said they felt confused about what to do, didn't have the time to get the work done, didn't get along with their group, or ended up doing all the work themselves.

Working in a group can feel hard because it requires some social communication and places you in a situation where your grade depends on others. Hearing from my students made me realize that I was missing part of the puzzle. Group work is just a bunch of skills, and skills can be learned and hacked. Therefore, I needed to figure out how to teach students to actually enjoy and find success with group work.

Teaching Point

Today, I want to teach you some group-work hacks to make your group time feel successful and harmonious.

Practice Together

For practicing together, we will look at these three hacks: make the group work clear, manage the project together, and schedule work *time to activate and get things done. First, we need to create clarity by asking the following questions.*

1. Show students the questions, whether on a chalkboard, whiteboard, or slide.

- *What are we being asked to do?*
- *What are each of our roles?*
- *Who will do which parts?*
- *When will we have our parts done?*
- *How will we communicate?*

The next hack is to manage the group work like any other project by doing the following.

2. Direct students' attention to these steps.

- *Break the work into small steps, assigned to certain people with deadlines.*
- *Schedule the steps for each person.*
- *Set reminders as individuals.*
- *Schedule check-ins halfway through and two days before the group project is due.*

Finally, the third hack is to use the activation magic of body doubling by doing the following.

3. Show students the following steps.

- *Work together in class, when you can, to help yourself feel motivated and focused.*
- *Schedule time to work together outside of class, in real life or online.*

Invitation to Use the Skill

The obvious time to use these hacks is when you have a group project, but there are also other, less obvious times. Think about working on a team in gym class, during a class review game, or when forming or working in a study group. There are many chances to practice your group-work hacks. Keep reflecting and perfecting as you go!

Idea for a Visual

- Make (or have students make) a poster (or on a whiteboard) listing the group work hacks, with additional space for students to add hacks of their own.

My Reflections and Improvements for Next Time

APPENDIX B
FORMAL EXECUTIVE FUNCTION DIAGNOSTIC TOOLS

As Brenda Goodman and Shelly Shepard (n.d.) note, no single test can specifically diagnose executive dysfunction. The formal assessment tools your school psychologist or a student's medical professional may use will gauge how well executive function works for a student. Formal assessments are usually standardized rating scales, collecting feedback from older students, parents, and teachers. Some of the diagnostic assessments your school psychologist may give a student, as for an initial, annual, or triennial IEP, may also include tasks that measure a specific executive function skill, such as inhibitory control. For example, the Stroop Color and Word Test is a formal assessment that explores a student's ability to inhibit an automatic response. Students begin by reading a list of color words, in black print, and then naming color patches; these responses feel automatic and congruent. However, in the third round, students are asked to respond to a color word that is printed in a different color ink (for example, *pink* may be printed with orange letters). Students must inhibit their automatic response to read the word and instead name the color of the printed letters.

Formal assessments provide an insight into some executive functions, most commonly working memory, inhibitory control, planning, attention, cognitive shifting, and processing speed (Kelly, n.d.). Rating scales may collect information about the observed results of executive function, such as how often the student uses a planner, but they are limited in their ability to expose the root cause of observed behaviors. A student who is not using a planner, for example, may struggle with attention and distractibility, forgetting to engage with the planner. Another student who looks similar from the outside may not be using a planner due to deficits in planning and time management skills. Results are best used within a context of understanding the student and can provide insight into possible struggles, relying on the team to connect these insights to the student's current experience and potential strategies to address their struggles.

If your team is looking to collect formal assessment data on a student's executive function, consider the following executive function inventories available to teachers and psychologists.

- **Barkley Deficits in Executive Functioning Scale:** Created by ADHD expert and author Rusell Barkley, the test uses an eighty-nine-item questionnaire and rating scale for individuals and someone close to them. The scales offer insight into students' "time management, organization and problem solving, self-restraint, self-motivation, and self-regulation of emotions" (Stoelting, 2025).
- **Behavior Rating Inventory of Executive Function (BRIEF):** This is a screening questionnaire for parents, teachers, and older students (students age ten and younger are observed by adults but do not complete rating scales). Executive function areas included in the probe are inhibition, self-monitoring, shifting, emotional control, initiation, working memory, planning and organizing, task monitoring, and organization of materials (Gioia, Isquith, Guy, & Kenworthy, 2015).
- **Comprehensive Executive Function Inventory:** Similar to the Barkley scale, the Comprehensive Executive Function Inventory is one-hundred questions that students, parents, and teachers complete, giving a view of nine areas of students' executive function, including "attention, emotion regulation, flexibility, inhibitory control, initiation, organization, planning, self-monitoring, and working memory" (Goldstein, Naglieri, Princiotta, & Otero, n.d.).
- **Minnesota Executive Function Scale:** An app with options for educators and psychologists, the Minnesota Executive Function Scale is a game-like assessment for students. It provides a composite score that reflects students' inhibitory control, cognitive flexibility, and working memory.
- **Delis Rating of Executive Functions:** Available for use by school psychologists and teachers with master's degrees, the Delis Rating of Executive Functions (D-REF) provides rating scales for students, parents, and teachers to provide feedback about a student's current executive function abilities.

Figure B.1 lists the assessments available by skill area. Keep in mind that you will often need signed parent permission to conduct a formal assessment. These resources are intended to support your journey and may become springboards into other resources, voices, and perspectives. You may want to annotate or add to the resources in your book, creating a living list of books, articles, assessments, and lessons that support your students' executive function.

Skill Area	Assessment Names	Notes
Attention	Test of Variables of Attention (TOVA) Integrated Visual and Auditory Continuous Performance Test (IVA-2) Conners Continuous Performance Test II (CPT II) Conners Parent Rating Scales (3rd edition)	These assessments explore a student's ability to pay attention. Other factors, such as slow processing speed or inhibitory control, may impact scores.
Working Memory	Digit Span and Spatial Span subtests of the Wechsler Intelligence Scale for Children (WISC) Working memory tasks in the Woodcock-Johnson Cognitive Battery (WJ-III)	Assessors may ask students to repeat a series of letters, numbers, or movements, in order or backward.
Organization and Planning	The Tower Test of the Delis-Kaplan Executive Functions System (D-KEFS) Rey-Osterrieth Complex Figure Test Tower of Hanoi game	These assessments require students to complete tasks in efficient ways by following rules. Students use planning, sequencing, and organizing information to complete the tasks, which are often timed.
Shifting Attention	Wisconsin Card Sorting Test The D-KEFS Sorting Test Minnesota Executive Function Scale (MEFS) Trail-making tests	Task shifting demonstrates cognitive control and is assessed by asking students to shift between tasks or develop an understanding of a task's rules through trial and error.
Inhibitory Control	Stroop Color and Word Test The D-KEFS Color-Word Interference Test	These assessments ask students to refrain from giving an automatic response.

Figure B.1: Assessments available by skill area.

References and Resources

Adams, M. P. (2013). Explaining the theory of mind deficit in autism spectrum disorder. *Philosophical Studies, 163*(1), 233–249.

ADDitude. (n.d.). *Seven core executive functions in children & teens*. Author.

Aguilar, E. (2013). *The art of coaching: Effective strategies for school transformation*. Jossey-Bass.

American Psychiatric Association. (2013). *Diagnostic and statistical manual of mental disorders* (5th ed.). American Psychiatric Publishing.

Anderson, L. W., & Krathwohl, D. (Eds.). (2001). *A taxonomy for learning, teaching, and assessing: A revision of Bloom's taxonomy of educational objectives*. Allyn & Bacon.

Anthes, E. (2009, April). How room designs affect your work and mood: Brain research can help us craft spaces that relax, inspire, awaken, comfort and heal. *Scientific American Mind, 20*(2). Accessed at www.scientificamerican.com /article/building-around-the-mind on December 16, 2024.

Archambault Besson, N. (2017, September). Climbing out of limbic: When anxiety takes hold, children default to their brain's fear-focused limbic system. And learning stops short. *The ASHA Leader, 22*(9), 54–59. Accessed at https://leader.pubs.asha.org/doi/10.1044/leader.FTR2.22092017.54 on December 17, 2024.

Asbill Law Group. (2020, December 23). *The top 10 reasons people get fired*. Accessed at www.asbilllaw.com/blog/the-top-10-reasons-people-get-fired on December 16, 2024.

Aubrey, A. (2018, July 30). *Off your mental game? You could be mildly dehydrated*. NPR. Accessed at www.npr.org/sections/health-shots/2018/07/30/632480321 /off-your-mental-game-you-could-be-mildly-dehydrated on December 16, 2024.

Baggetta, P., & Alexander, P. A. (2016). Conceptualization and operationalization of executive function. *Mind, Brain, and Education, 10*(1), 10–33.

Barkley, R. A. (2011). *Barkley Deficits in Executive Functioning Scale (BDEFS).* Guilford.

Barkley, R. A. (2012). *Executive functions: What they are, how they work, and why they evolved.* Guilford.

Barrasso-Catanzaro, C., & Eslinger, P. J. (2016). Neurobiological bases of executive function and social-emotional development: Typical and atypical brain changes. *Family Relations, 65*(1), 108–119.

Blanchfield, T. (2024, August 21). *Music for ADHD: Benefits & types to improve focus.* Accessed at www.verywellmind.com/music-to-improve-focus-adhd-6361057 on December 16, 2024.

Bloom, B. S. (Ed.). (1956). *Taxonomy of educational objectives: The classification of educational goals; Handbook I: Cognitive domain.* McKay.

Bordonaro, K. M., & Clark, M. (2024). *The collaborative IEP: Working together for life-changing special education.* Solution Tree Press.

Boroson, B. (2022). *The general education teacher's guide to autism: Essential answers to key questions.* Solution Tree Press.

Brody, B. (2023, August 28). *How clutter can affect your health.* Accessed at www.webmd.com/balance/ss/slideshow-clutter-affects-health on December 16, 2024.

Brown, P. C., Roediger, H. L., III, & McDaniel, M. A. (2014). *Make it stick: The science of successful learning.* Belknap Press.

Brown, T. E., Reichel, P. C., & Quinlan, D. M. (2009). Executive function impairments in high IQ adults with ADHD. *Journal of Attention Disorders, 13*(2), 161–167. https://doi.org/10.1177/1087054708326113

Carifio, J., & Carey, T. (2015). Further findings on the positive effects of minimum grading. *Journal of Education and Social Policy, 2*(4), 130–136.

CAST. (2024a). Consideration 3.2: Highlight and explore patterns, critical features, big ideas, and relationships. *Universal Design for Learning guidelines version 3.0.* Accessed at https://udlguidelines.cast.org/representation/building-knowledge/patterns-features on December 8, 2023.

CAST. (2024b). Consideration 7.4: Address biases, threats, and distractions. *Universal Design for Learning guidelines version 3.0.* Accessed at https://udlguidelines.cast.org/engagement/interests-identities/biases-threats-distractions on December 7, 2023.

CAST. (2024c). Guideline 1: Design options for perception. *Universal Design for Learning guidelines version 3.0.* Accessed at https://udlguidelines.cast.org/representation/perception on December 16, 2024.

CAST. (2024d). Guideline 6: Design options for strategy development. *Universal Design for Learning guidelines version 3.0*. Accessed at https://udlguidelines.cast.org/action-expression/strategy-development on December 6, 2023.

CAST. (2024e). Guideline 9: Design options for emotional capacity. *Universal Design for Learning guidelines version 3.0*. Accessed at https://udlguidelines.cast.org/engagement/emotional-capacity on September 2, 2024.

Catherine, T. G., Robert, N. G., Mala, K. K., Kanniammal, C., & Arullapan, J. (2019). Assessment of prevalence of attention deficit hyperactivity disorder among schoolchildren in selected schools. *Indian Journal of Psychiatry, 61*(3), 232–237. https://doi.org/10.4103/psychiatry.IndianJPsychiatry_333_17

Center on the Developing Child. (n.d.). *Executive function & self-regulation*. Accessed at https://developingchild.harvard.edu/science/key-concepts/executive-function on November 28, 2023.

Centers for Disease Control and Prevention. (n.d.). *Youth risk behavior survey: Data summary & trends report* [Report]. Author. Accessed at www.cdc.gov/healthyyouth/data/yrbs/pdf/YRBS_Data-Summary-Trends_Report2023_508.pdf on November 23, 2023.

Cepeda, N. J., Pashler, H., Vul, E., Wixted, J. T., & Rohrer, D. (2006). Distributed practice in verbal recall tasks: A review and quantitative synthesis. *Psychological Bulletin, 132*(3), 354–380. https://doi.org/10.1037/0033-2909.132.3.354

Chasteen, S. (n.d.). *Nothing about me without me?* The Center for Disability Rights. Accessed at https://cdrnys.org/blog/disability-dialogue/nothing-about-me-without-me on April 2, 2025.

Chen, Y., Wang, Y., Wang, S., Zhang, M., & Wu, N. (2021). Self-reported sleep and executive function in early primary school children. *Frontiers in Psychology, 12*. https://doi: 10.3389/fpsyg.2021.793000

Clear, J. (n.d.a). *Continuous improvement: How it works and how to master it*. Accessed at https://jamesclear.com/continuous-improvement on October 26, 2024.

Clear, J. (n.d.b). *Lessons on success and deliberate practice from Mozart, Picasso, and Kobe Bryant*. Accessed at https://jamesclear.com/deliberate-practice on May 28, 2024.

Clear, J. (2018). *Atomic habits: Tiny changes, remarkable results—An easy & proven way to build good habits & break bad ones*. Avery.

Cleveland Clinic. (n.d.). *Executive dysfunction*. Accessed at https://my.clevelandclinic.org/health/symptoms/23224-executive-dysfunction on November 20, 2023.

Cleveland Clinic. (2024). *Executive function*. Accessed at https://my.clevelandclinic.org/health/articles/executive-function on May 8, 2025.

Cohen, R. K., Opatosky, D. K., Savage, J. E., Stevens, S. O., & Darrah, E. P. (2021). *The metacognitive student: How to teach academic, social, and emotional intelligence in every content area.* Solution Tree Press.

Connecting Elements. (2016, November 2). *How classroom design affects learning* [Blog post]. Accessed at www.connectingelements.com/OUR-BLOG/how-classroom-design-affects-learning on December 16, 2024.

Costello, S. E., Geiser, E., & Schneider, N. (2021). Nutrients for executive function development and related brain connectivity in school-aged children. *Nutrition Reviews, 79*(12), 1293–1306. https://doi.org/10.1093/nutrit/nuaa134

Cowan, N. (2010). The magical mystery four: How is working memory capacity limited, and why? *Current Directions in Psychological Science, 19*(1), 51–57.

Custer, C. (2019, February 7). *The phone proximity effect: Your phone could be sabotaging your studies.* Accessed at www.dataquest.io/blog/phone-proximity-effect on December 16, 2024.

Dajani, D. R., & Uddin, L. Q. (2015). Demystifying cognitive flexibility: Implications for clinical and developmental neuroscience. *Trends in Neurosciences, 38*(9), 571–578.

Davis, E., DellaRocco, N., Barrett, L., Buka, S., Burke Bryant, E., & Gell, L. (2014, October). *Healthy early childhood development: Supporting the development of executive functions in young children* [Policy brief]. TRI-Lab Swearer Center. Accessed at www.katenuss.com/executive_functions.pdf on December 16, 2024.

Delis, D. C. (2012). *Delis-Rating of Executive Functions* (D-REF) [Measurement instrument]. Pearson.

Diamond, A. (2013). Executive functions. *Annual Review of Psychology, 64,* 135–168. https://doi.org/10.1146/annurev-psych-113011-143750

Dodson, W. (2024, November 1). *Three defining features of ADHD that everyone overlooks.* ADDitude. Accessed at www.additudemag.com/symptoms-of-add-hyperarousal-rejection-sensitivity on October 30, 2024.

Dodson, W. (2025, March 18). *New insights into rejection sensitive dysphoria.* Accessed at www.additudemag.com/rejection-sensitive-dysphoria-adhd-emotional-dysregulation on April 1, 2025.

Duckworth, A. L., Taxer, J. L., Eskreis-Winkler, L., Galla, B. M., & Gross, J. J. (2019). Self-control and academic achievement. *Annual Review of Psychology, 70,* 373–399. https://doi.org/10.1146/annurev-psych-010418-103230

Dweck, C. S. (2016). *Mindset: The new psychology of success* (Updated ed.). Random House.

Edutopia. (2019, June 6). *There's a cell phone in your student's head.* Accessed at www.edutopia.org/video/theres-cell-phone-your-students-head on December 16, 2024.

Eisenberger, N. I., & Lieberman, M. D. (2004). Why rejection hurts: A common neural alarm system for physical and social pain. *Trends in Cognitive Sciences, 8*(7), 294–300. https://doi.org/10.1016/j.tics.2004.05.010

El Wafa, H. E. A., El Latif Ghobashy, S. A., & Hamza, A. M. (2020). A comparative study of executive functions among children with attention deficit and hyperactivity disorder and those with learning disabilities. *Middle East Current Psychiatry, 27*, Article 64. https://doi.org/10.1186/s43045-020-00071-8

Feldman, J. (2019). *Grading for equity: What it is, why it matters, and how it can transform schools and classrooms.* SAGE.

Feller, L., Feller, G., Ballyram, T., Chandran, R., Lemmer, J., & Khammissa, R. A. G. (2020). Interrelations between pain, stress and executive functioning. *British Journal of Pain, 14*(3), 188–194. https://doi.org/10.1177/2049463719889380

Ferguson, H. J., Brunsdon, V. E. A., & Bradford, E. E. F. (2021). The developmental trajectories of executive function from adolescence to old age. *Scientific Reports, 11*, Article 1382. https://doi.org/10.1038/s41598-020-80866-1

Ferster, C. B., & Skinner, B. F. (1957). *Schedules of reinforcement.* Appleton-Century-Crofts.

Flynn, L. (2023, August 15). *Declarative language for developing executive functioning skills in children with ADHD.* Accessed at https://ot4adhd.com/2023/08/15/declarative-language-for-developing-executive-functioning-skills-in-children-with-adhd on December 16, 2024.

Gioia, G. A., Isquith, P. K., Guy, S. C., & Kenworthy, L. (2015). *Behavior Rating Inventory of Executive Function* (BRIEF-2; 2nd ed.) [Measurement instrument]. PAR.

Gladwell, M. (2008). *Outliers: The story of success.* Little, Brown.

Goldstein, S., Naglieri, J. A., Princiotta, D. & Otero, T. M. (n.d.). *Introduction: A history of executive functioning as a theoretical and clinical construct.* Accessed at https://samgoldstein.com/resources/articles/general/a-history-of-executive-functioning-as-a-theoretical-and-clinical-construct.aspx on May 23, 2025.

Gonzalez-Pons, K. (2021, July 29). *How to stop procrastinating if you live with ADHD.* Accessed at https://psychcentral.com/adhd/how-to-stop-adhd-procrastination on December 16, 2024.

Goodman, B., & Shepard, S. (n.d.). *Executive function disorder.* Accessed at www.webmd.com/add-adhd/executive-function on December 16, 2024.

Gravråkmo, S., Olsen, A., Lydersen, S., Ingul, J. M., Henry, L., & Øie, M. G. (2023). Associations between executive functions, intelligence and adaptive behaviour in children and adolescents with mild intellectual disability. *Journal of Intellectual Disabilities, 27*(3), 715–727.

Greene, R. (2010, September 10). *Kids do well if they can Ross Greene #1* [Video file]. YouTube. Accessed at www.youtube.com/watch?v=jvzQQDfAL-Q on December 16, 2024.

Griffin, J. A., & McCardle, P. (Eds.). (2015). *Executive function in preschool-age children: Integrating measurement, neurodevelopment, and translational research.* American Psychological Association.

Hamblet, E. (2023). *Seven steps to college success: A pathway for students with disabilities* (3rd ed.). Rowman & Littlefield.

Hattie, J. (2023). *Visible learning: The sequel: A synthesis of over 2,100 meta-analyses relating to achievement.* Routledge.

Individuals With Disabilities Education Improvement Act of 2004, 20 U.S.C. § 1400 (2004).

Jacob, R., & Parkinson, J. (2015). The potential for school-based interventions that target executive function to improve academic achievement: A review. *Review of Educational Research, 85*(4), 512–552. https://doi.org/10.3102/0034654314561338

Kelly, K. (n.d.). *Types of tests for executive function challenges.* Accessed at www.understood.org/en/articles/tests-for-executive-functioning-issues on September 2, 2024.

Kesty, S. (Host). (2022a, July 18). Empowering conversations around DEI and neurodivergence: Deanna Singh from Uplifting Impact (No. 43) [Audio podcast episode]. In *The executive function podcast.* Accessed at https://podcasts.apple.com/us/podcast/ep-43-empowering-conversations-around-dei-and/id1489096143?i=1000570371446 on May 9, 2025.

Kesty, S. (2022b, December 12). *Three ways to help students learn from their tests.* Edutopia. Accessed at www.edutopia.org/article/3-ways-to-help-students-learn-from-their-tests on December 16, 2024.

Kesty, S., & Ploszay, M. (2023, August 11). *Encouraging teens to develop self-regulation skills.* Edutopia. Accessed at www.edutopia.org/article/guiding-teens-develop-self-regulation-skills on December 16, 2024.

Kesty, S. (2025, April 17). *How to help students avoid procrastinating.* Accessed at www.edutopia.org/article/teaching-students-not-procrasinate on April 20, 2025).

Kircher-Morris, E. (2021). *Teaching twice-exceptional learners in today's classroom.* Free Spirit.

Langreo, L. (2023, December 8). *Digital distractions in class linked to lower academic performance*. Education Week. Accessed at www.edweek.org/leadership/digital-distractions-in-class-linked-to-lower-academic-performance/2023/12 on December 16, 2024.

Learn. (n.d.). In *Merriam-Webster's online dictionary*. Accessed at www.merriam-webster.com/dictionary/learn on November 29, 2023.

Li, Y., Yan, X., Li, Q., Li, Q., Xu, G., Lu, J., et al. (2023). Prevalence and trends in diagnosed ADHD among US children and adolescents, 2017–2022. *JAMA Network Open*, *6*(10), Article e2336872. https://doi.org/10.1001/jamanetworkopen.2023.36872

Lieberman, D. Z., & Long, M. E. (2018). *The molecule of more: How a single molecule in your brain drives love, sex, and creativity—And will determine the fate of the human race*. BenBella Books.

Marzano, R. J. (2017). *The new art and science of teaching*. Solution Tree Press.

Mayo Clinic. (2018, January 6). *Autism spectrum disorder*. Accessed at www.mayoclinic.org/diseases-conditions/autism-spectrum-disorder/symptoms-causes/syc-20352928 on October 20, 2024.

Mills, K. (Host). (2019, March 13). The molecule of more: Dopamine [Audio podcast episode]. In *Speaking of Psychology*. Accessed at https://podcasts.apple.com/am/podcast/the-molecule-of-more-dopamine/id705934263?i=1000431686278 on December 16, 2024.

Moore, C., & Gott, C. (2018). *Coach approach for organizers*. Author.

Morrison, K. (2016, October 1). *Executive function in preschool-age children: Integrating measurement, neurodevelopment, and translational research* [Review]. Accessed at www.nepsy.com/articles/book-reviews/executive-function-in-preschool-age-children-integrating-measurement-neurodevelopment-and-translational-research on December 16, 2024.

Muhammad, A. (2015). *Overcoming the achievement gap trap: Liberating mindsets to effect change*. Solution Tree Press.

Murphy, L. (2010, Winter). The critical importance of declarative language input for children with ASD. *Autism Spectrum Quarterly*. Accessed at https://static1.squarespace.com/static/5a8a1366b0786967f145012e/t/5a8ad07e652deaeaab1297b5/1519046784904/Murphy_ASQ_Declarative.pdf on December 16, 2024.

Murtagh, T. (2023, May 19). *The impact of high cortisol levels on student well-being*. Honor Society. Accessed at www.honorsociety.org/articles/impact-high-cortisol-levels-student-well-being on December 16, 2024.

Naglieri, J., & Goldstein, S. (2017). *Comprehensive Executive Function Inventory* (CEFI) [Measurement instrument]. Multi-Health Systems.

National Center for Education Statistics. (2024, May). *Students with disabilities.* Accessed at https://nces.ed.gov/programs/coe/indicator/cgg/students-with-disabilities on December 5, 2023.

NeuroLaunch. (2024, August 22). *Dopamine and learning: The brain's reward system in education.* Accessed at https://neurolaunch.com/dopamine-and-learning on December 16, 2024.

Panagea, E., Messinis, L., Petri, M. C., Liampas, I., Anyfantis, E., Nasios, G., et al. (2024). Neurocognitive impairment in long COVID: A systematic review. *Archives of Clinical Neuropsychology.* https://doi.org/10.1093/arclin/acae042

Pedersen, T. (2021, October 14). *All about amygdala hijack.* Accessed at https://psychcentral.com/health/amygdala-hijack on December 16, 2024.

Petersen, I. T., Hoyniak, C. P., McQuillan, M. E., Bates, J. E., & Staples, A. D. (2016). Measuring the development of inhibitory control: The challenge of heterotypic continuity. *Developmental Review, 40*, 25–71. https://doi.org/10.1016/j.dr.2016.02.001

Pham, T., & Archibald, L. (2020). *Avoiding working memory overload in students with LDs.* LD at School. Accessed at www.ldatschool.ca/working-memory-overload on April 24, 2025.

Randolph, J. (2020). *The brain health book: Using the power of neuroscience to improve your life.* Norton.

RedRover. (n.d.). *RedRover readers workshop.* Accessed at https://redrover.org/readers/take-the-training on December 16, 2024.

Reflection Sciences. (n.d.). *Minnesota Executive Function Scale* (MEFS) [Measurement instrument]. Accessed at https://reflectionsciences.com/mefs on September 23, 2024.

Rober, M. (2018, April). *The Super Mario effect: Tricking your brain into learning more* [Video]. TED Conferences. Accessed at www.ted.com/talks/mark_rober_the_super_mario_effect_tricking_your_brain_into_learning_more/transcript?subtitle=en on December 16, 2024.

Rollins, K. (2020, January 28). *Memory tricks: ADHDer see, ADHDer do* [Blog post]. Accessed at www.additudemag.com/memory-tricks-adhder-see-adhder-do on December 16, 2024.

Ruhl, C. (2023, October 24). *Cognitive bias: How we are wired to misjudge.* Accessed at www.simplypsychology.org/cognitive-bias.html on December 16, 2024.

Saline, S. (2024, March 29). *Understanding ADHD working memory challenges: Four strategies to improve recall and follow through* [Blog post]. Psychology Today. Accessed at www.psychologytoday.com/us/blog/on-your-way-with-adhd/202402/understanding-adhd-working-memory-challenges on December 16, 2024.

Scarpina, F., & Tagini, S. (2017). The Stroop Color and Word Test. *Frontiers in Psychology, 8.* https://doi.org/10.3389/fpsyg.2017.00557

Schäfer, T., Sedlmeier, P., Städtler, C., & Huron, D. (2013). The psychological functions of music listening. *Frontiers in Psychology, 4.* https://doi:10.3389/fpsyg.2013.00511

Shaw, P., Greenstein, D., Lerch, J., Clasen, L., Lenroot, R., Gogtay, N., et al. (2006). Intellectual ability and cortical development in children and adolescents. *Nature, 440,* 676–679. https://doi.org/10.1038/nature04513

Siegel, D. (2013). *Brainstorm: The power and purpose of the teenage brain.* Tarcher.

Siegel, D. (2014, August 12). How the teen brain transforms relationships. *Greater Good Magazine.* Accessed at https://greatergood.berkeley.edu/article/item/how_the_teen_brain_transforms_relationships on December 17, 2024.

Siegel, D. (2017, April 9). *Dr. Dan Siegel's hand model of the brain* [Video file]. YouTube. Accessed at www.youtube.com/watch?v=f-m2YcdMdFw on September 20, 2024.

Simms, J. A. (2024). *Where learning happens: Leveraging working memory and attention in the classroom.* Marzano Resources.

Singh, D. (2022). *Actions speak louder: A step-by-step guide to becoming an inclusive workplace.* Penguin.

Slade, B. (2024, January 11). *Debunking the myth of linear growth in children with executive function challenges.* Accessed at https://medium.com/illumination/debunking-the-myth-of-linear-growth-in-children-with-executive-function-challenges-e4c90e56cd69 on December 17, 2024.

Soederberg Miller, L. M., Cohen, J. A., & Wingfield, A. (2006). Contextual knowledge reduces demands on working memory during reading. *Memory and Cognition, 34*(6), 1355–1367. https://doi.org/10.3758/bf03193277

Stoelting. (2025). *Barkley deficits in executive functioning—Children and adolescents.* Accessed at https://stoeltingco.com/Psychological-Testing/Barkley-Deficits-in-Executive-Functioning--Children-and-Adolescents-BDEFS-CA~10451 on May 23, 2025.

Tai, X. Y., Chen, C., Manohar, S., & Husain, M. (2022). Impact of sleep duration on executive function and brain structure. *Communications Biology, 5,* Article 201. https://doi.org/10.1007/s11910-023-01309-8

Tabachnick, C. (2024, September 2). *Schools across the U.S. restrict cellphones amid growing behavior, mental health, academic concerns.* CBS News. Accessed at www.cbsnews.com/news/cellphone-bans-in-schools on March 31, 2025.

Terada, Y. (2020, November 19). *The mistake imperative—Why we must get over our fear of student error.* Edutopia. Accessed at www.edutopia.org/article/mistake-imperative-why-we-must-get-over-our-fear-student-error on December 17, 2024.

U. S. Department of Education. (2004). Individuals With Disabilities Education Act. Public Law 108-446. Accessed on www.congress.gov/bill/108th-congress/house-bill/1350/text on April 24, 2025.

Vatterott, C. (2015). *Rethinking grading: Meaningful assessment for standards-based learning*. ASCD.

Voss, P., Thomas, M. E., Cisneros-Franco, J. M., & de Villers-Sidani, É. (2017). Dynamic brains and the changing rules of neuroplasticity: Implications for learning and recovery. *Frontiers in Psychology, 8*. https://doi.org/10.3389/fpsyg.2017.01657

Vygotsky, L. S. (1978). *Mind in society: The development of higher psychological processes*. Harvard University Press.

Weathers, M. (2024). *Executive functions for every classroom, grades 3–12: Creating safe and predictable learning environments*. Corwin.

WebMD Editorial Contributors. (n.d.). *Attention Deficit Hyperactivity Disorder: Causes of ADHD*. Accessed at www.webmd.com/add-adhd/adhd-causes on October 20, 2024.

Wetzel, N., Widmann, A., & Scharf, F. (2021). Distraction of attention by novel sounds in children declines fast. *Scientific Reports, 11*, Article 5308. https://doi.org/10.1038/s41598-021-83528-y

Willingham, D. T. (2009). *Why don't students like school? A cognitive scientist answers questions about how the mind works and what it means for the classroom*. Jossey-Bass.

Willingham, D. T. (2023). *Outsmart your brain: Why learning is hard and how you can make it easy*. Gallery Books.

Zeigler Dendy, C. A., & Hughes, R. (n.d.). *What's the big deal about executive functions?* Learning Disabilities Association of America. Accessed at https://ldaamerica.org/lda_today/whats-the-big-deal-about-executive-functions on November 28, 2024.

Zhang, M., Zhang, Y., & Kong, Y. (2019). Interaction between social pain and physical pain. *Brain Science Advances, 5*(4), 265–273.

Index

Formative Assessment in a Brain-Compatible Classroom
Marcia L. Tate
Marcia L. Tate provides guidance on numerous ways to discern whether your students are truly learning what you need them to know, understand, or be able to do. Gain valuable insights to ensure effective teaching and student retention and comprehension.
BKG244

The Metacognitive Student
Richard K. Cohen, Deanne Kildare Opatosky, James Savage, Susan Olsen Stevens, and **Edward P. Darrah**
What if there was one strategy you could use to support students academically, socially, and emotionally? It exists—and it's simple, straightforward, and practical. Dive deep into structured SELf-questioning and learn how to empower students to develop into strong, healthy, and confident thinkers.
BKF954

Stick the Learning
Eric Saunders
This concise guide bridges brain-based learning theory with everyday instructional practice to maximize teacher effectiveness for visible student achievement. Learn three powerful, doable techniques proven to support long-term retention: spaced repetition, interleaving, and retrieval (SIR).
BKG083

The General Education Teacher's Guide to Autism
Barbara Boroson
In this engaging title, you will find answers to all your questions about students on the autism spectrum in inclusive classrooms. Collect the information and strategies you need to create an effective, welcoming, and supportive environment for these neurodiverse students.
BKG055